The Master Musicians Series

VERDI

Series edited by Sir Jack Westrup

VOLUMES IN THE MASTER MUSICIANS SERIES

Bartók *Lajos Lesznai*
Beethoven *Marion M. Scott*
Bellini *Leslie Orrey*
Berlioz *J. H. Elliot*
Brahms *Peter Latham*
Bruckner *Derek Watson*
Chopin *Arthur Hedley*
Debussey *Edward Lockspeiser*
Delius *Alan Jefferson*
Dvořák *Alec Robertson*
Elgar *Ian Parrott*
Franck *Laurence Davies*
Grieg *John Horton*
Handel *Percy M. Young*
Haydn *Rosemary Hughes*
Liszt *Walter Beckett*
Mahler *Michael Kennedy*
Mendelssohn *Philip Radcliffe*
Monteverdi *Denis Arnold*
Mozart *Eric Blom*
Mussorgsky *M. D. Calvocoressi*

Purcell *Sir Jack Westrup*
Schubert *Arthur Hutchings*
Schumann *Joan Chissell*
Sibelius *Robert Layton*
Smetana *John Clapham*
Stravinsky *Francis Routh*
Tchaikovsky *Edward Garden*
Vaughan Williams *James Day*
Verdi *Dyneley Hussey*
Wagner *Robert L. Jacobs*

IN PREPARATION
Bach *Basil Lam*
Berg *Nicholas Chadwick*
Prokofiev *Rita McAllister*
Rakhmaninov *Geoffrey Norris*
Ravel *Roger Nichols*
Schoenberg *Malcolm MacDonald*
Richard Strauss *Michael Kennedy*
Tallis & Byrd *Michael Howard*

VERDI

by

Dyneley Hussey

*With eight pages of plates
and music examples in the text*

London
J. M. DENT & SONS LTD

IN PIAM MEMORIAM

C. E. H.

1840–1922

PREFACE

WHEN, more months ago than I have the hardihood to number, Mr Blom asked me to contribute a study of Verdi to this series of Master Musicians, I felt a great diffidence in undertaking such a task. Were there not already in existence two up-to-date books by critics possessing exceptional qualifications for the discussion of Verdi's life and music — Mr Toye's ample and elaborate volume, which must remain a standard work on the subject, and Mr Bonavia's shorter monograph in which the sympathy of a compatriot and the knowledge of a practising musician combine with a felicitous literary style to produce a general and radiant illumination of the whole man? What could be added to these? Well, perhaps, something between the two in length, and with a different angle of approach.

As to this last—the angle of approach—I found in practice that this was not easy to attain in the biographical portions of the book. For there is only one set of facts, and those facts are set down contemporaneously by the hands of Verdi and his correspondents. The composer's letter-book, carefully kept throughout the greater part of his working life, must be the ultimate source and authority for the biographer, and the clear and definite terms of Verdi's letters leave little scope for any 'original' interpretation or research. If, therefore, the narrative in this book seems to follow with undue closeness the tracks of my predecessors, that is only because we all had to follow the same path made originally by Verdi himself. All one could do was to make one's own selection from the copious material in the letter-book and, honestly shutting the cribs, make one's own translation.

Apart, however, from the obvious necessity of including Verdi among the Master Musicians, if the series was to lay claim to inclusiveness, there was this additional justification for a new biography, that, since those of Mr Toye and Mr Bonavia were written, two additional volumes of letters and other documents, including the correspondence of Giuseppina Verdi, have been published. It cannot be claimed that this supplement to our sources contains any sensational revelations. Some facts are corrected; many i's are dotted and t's crossed. But there is a great deal of interesting material, not hitherto available to the English reader, upon which I have here been able to draw.

I should have liked to draw more fully upon these 'Carteggi,' and especially upon the long discussions of the abortive *King Lear*, which reached a stage of high elaboration before it was finally dropped. But I had to consider that this volume was to be one of a series for the general reader, who would want all the main facts, and would be more interested in the operas Verdi did write—and especially in those he is likely to hear—than in abandoned projects and forgotten juvenilia. As it is, I have exceeded the span allotted by my patient editor and publishers. I hope, however, to contribute an article on *King Lear* to *Music and Letters* when time and circumstances permit.

Having the general reader in view, I have avoided footnotes as far as possible, because, once annotation had begun, there would have been no end to the references. The student who wishes to verify a statement will have little difficulty in identifying its source with the aid of the dates given in the text and of the excellent indices to the *Copialettere* and *Carteggi Verdiani*.

On the other hand, the general reader may, with some justice, complain that at times I have been too particular. It is fair to warn him, for instance, to skip that part of the chapter on *Aida* in which the shaping of the libretto is discussed. Those pages will, I hope, be of interest to readers who are prepared to go to the trouble of referring to the score.

At the same time, I have not thought it necessary to anglicize the titles of the operas—though there are still people who, misled by the story of the opera, and the analogy of 'treasure trove,' think *Il Trovatore* should be rendered *The Foundling*, and it is tempting to transfer to *La Traviata* the more downright title of Ford's famous tragedy—and I considered it essential not to translate the Italian texts of the musical examples. For the sound of the original language is so intimately bound up with the sound of the music, that to alter the one is to distort the other. This is not to argue that Verdi's operas should not be sung in English, for there are overriding advantages in favour of that. But when it comes to studying the music, it is better to have in mind the vocal sounds that Verdi set.

And now for my gratitude, which is far more than the perfunctory acknowledgment of obligations for the avoidance of actions for the breach of copyright and so on. Nothing could have been more generous than the help and advice given by my aforementioned predecessors in the field. Mr Bonavia, indeed, put at my service a whole library of books, some of which would have been difficult to lay one's hands on. To Mr Philip Hope-Wallace I am in debt for his patient readiness to discuss and criticize many points, whereby ideas as yet in a state of fluidity were precipitated in solid form, and to Mr Derrick Perkins for his assistance, at an abnormally busy time, in the correction of the proofs and of my errant literary style. And if the resultant text is free from slips and inconsistencies, the credit is largely due to the sharp eye and apparent omniscience of Messrs Dent's reader.

I have to thank the City of Milan and the Chancellor of the Royal Academy of Italy for permission to translate and quote lengthy passages from *I Copialettere di Giuseppe Verdi* and *Carteggi Verdiani* respectively. Without their consent to this liberal use of these volumes, this book could not have been written.

The musical examples from *Otello, Falstaff,* and the *Te Deum* have been reproduced by courtesy of Messrs G. Ricordi & Co. of London and Milan, who have also permitted the reproduction of the photographs of Verdi's birthplace, the MS. score and Verdi at Sant' Agata.

The Delfico cartoons are reproduced from *Carteggi Verdiani*.

Boldini's vigorous portrait is included by permission of the Casa di Riposo per Musicisti (the Home for Musicians endowed by Verdi) in Milan.

Finally, which also means most of all, I must thank my long-suffering editor for his unfailing encouragement and help which, including as it does the preparation of the calendar (Appendix A), the personalia (Appendix C) and the index, has really amounted so nearly to collaboration that he ought to have a place of honour, if not of responsibility, on the title-page.

HAMPSTEAD, 14*th April* 1940   D. H.

NOTE TO THE THIRD EDITION

I AM deeply indebted to the literary executor of the late Frank Walker and to his publishers for generously allowing me to make use of new material in his book, *The Man Verdi*. This has enabled me to adjust some details in my portrait of Verdi in this third edition of my book, which appears in the 150th year after the composer's birth. In order not to disturb the pagination, new material too substantial to insert into the original text has been placed in a supplement to which the reader's attention is drawn by footnotes.

CHELTENHAM, *February* 1963.   D. H.

NOTE TO THE FIFTH EDITION

THE text of this edition has been revised by Mr Charles Osborne.

THE PUBLISHERS.

CONTENTS

ILLUSTRATIONS

Between pages 160 and 161

CHAPTER I

CHILDHOOD

THE year 1813 was an *annus mirabilis* in the history of music. Not since 1685 had nature produced two men of genius, equal and opposite, to be the twin glories of German and Italian music in their time—Bach and Handel; Wagner and Verdi! There was this important difference between the pairs, that the earlier composers summed up a musical epoch in a world that was for the moment in a state of political equilibrium; the later ones cut out new paths in a period of rapid growth and violent change. Despite Chartist riots and Reform Bills, Corn Laws and Fenians, Englishmen are apt to regard the nineteenth century as a period of peaceful and stable development; and so, on the whole, for England it was. But in Europe the century saw the gradual assemblage of the German kingdoms and principalities into a new empire and the renascence of political unity and freedom in Italy, neither of which was accomplished without violence and bloodshed. In these movements, Wagner and Verdi each played a part and became in the end (though official Germany failed to recognize Wagner's position until after his death) the Musician Laureate of his newly welded nation.

Politically the Italian peninsula consisted in 1813 of a number of small states with as many petty kings and dukes, whose overlord for the time being was Napoleon. The defeat of the emperor at Leipzig by the armies of Austria and Russia brought a change, and in the following year the victors entered northern Italy and began to turn out the French. As is the way with invading forces, they did not differentiate between the natives and their foreign masters. In the course of their plundering, massacring advance across the plains, they passed through the village of Le Roncole, near Busseto in the duchy of Parma, and murdered such of the inhabitants as had not fled or who had foolishly trusted in the sanctuary of their own church. The incident would have been forgotten, along with many of like brutality, had not one Luigia Verdi had the sense to take her infant son up into the belfry, where the soldiers, finding plenty of easy sport below, did not think to look. So Giuseppe was spared to Italy and the world.

He was born on 10th October 1813, the son of Carlo Verdi, innkeeper and grocer, and his birth, with the names Joseph Fortunin François, duly registered with the French authorities in Busseto. Had he been born a year later, the last of his names might have been registered as Franz; for it was as an Austrian subject that he grew to manhood. Le Roncole was a tiny place in the parched and dusty plain from which a livelihood was to be won only by the hardest toil. Its inn and village shop was a mean building of one story with attics, and the innkeeper, though possibly prominent among its citizens, no more than a peasant. Like Gluck and Haydn, Verdi had the humblest origins. These were exceptions among the great composers, who have mostly come from the lower middle classes, the sons, more often than not, of minor musicians.

Born into a hard world, Giuseppe developed into a serious child. There was little enough to be gay about in Le Roncole, and the dreadful events of 1814 must have been recounted over and over to the boy, too young to have any personal recollection of the terror. 'I had a hard time, as a boy,' he told his French biographer, Camille Bellaigue, in his old age, and this rare breach of his reticence about himself goes some way to explain that reticence. We do not talk readily of the iron that has entered into our souls. He was already shy as a child with that touch of fierceness that is often found in shy natures, when their barriers are broken through. One thing only drew him out: music. He would listen entranced to a strolling player. In church, where he served as an acolyte, the sound of the organ made him forget his duties in the ritual, until the priest called his attention with a nudge that sent him flying down the altar steps. He begged to be allowed to study music.

His father must have been impressed, for he managed to procure for the boy an old spinet, which was repaired by a kindly neighbour. Verdi never parted from this beloved instrument, now in a museum at Milan, and inside it may be seen the record of its renovation: 'These hammers were repaired and re-covered with leather by me, Stefano Cavaletti, and I fitted the pedals which I presented; I also repaired the said hammers gratuitously, seeing the good disposition the young Verdi has for learning to play this instrument, which is sufficient for my complete satisfaction—Anno Domini 1821.' The good Cavaletti thoroughly deserves the little niche in musical history which his careful record has secured.

Such musical education as Verdi received as a child was had from the village organist, and at the age of twelve he was proficient enough to succeed his master. His salary with extras amounted to about £4 a year. There was, however, nothing, apart from his extreme musical sensibility, to mark him out as a genius in these early years. Had he been taught by a man like Leopold Mozart, he might have developed more rapidly. As it was, he showed none of Wolfgang's early creative ability and had to hammer out his technique and style by hard work in the long years to come. His father evidently realized the educational handicap under which Giuseppe suffered at Le Roncole, and sent his son to live with a cobbler at the neighbouring town of Busseto, where there was a Philharmonic Society and a town band, which played in the square on Sundays. There Verdi went to school, returning each Sunday to Le Roncole to play the organ at high mass. One Christmas, starting out before daybreak to perform his duties, he stumbled into the dyke beside the winding road and was only saved from drowning by a woman who happened to be passing.

It was, indeed, a hard boyhood, with little to eat and four miles to walk each way to Le Roncole and back, without sport or relaxation or any of the careless fun that makes men look back on their early years as the happiest time of their lives. Verdi must have been tough to survive it and to live on into the next century. But his health was undoubtedly affected by these early privations, which caused the physical weakness of his later years. Psychologically such an upbringing must have accentuated the natural seriousness of his temperament, making him take hardly a life that had begun with so much severity. His only resource was music—music represented by a village organ and a brass band. It was the band that left its mark upon his development as a composer.

CHAPTER II

A HAPPY INTERLUDE AND A TRAGEDY

THE most important of the citizens of Busseto, at any rate from our point of view, was Antonio Barezzi, a prosperous merchant from whom the innkeeper of Le Roncole bought his supplies of groceries and wine. Barezzi was an enthusiastic music-lover, president of the local Philharmonic Society, which met at his house, and a performer upon a variety of wind instruments, including the flute and the ophicleide or serpent, which, as Mr Penny said, 'was a good old note; a deep rich note.' What more natural than that Barezzi should take an interest in the musical son of his good customer at Le Roncole, who no doubt executed commissions for his father at the warehouse in Busseto? The merchant offered the boy an apprenticeship in his business and took him into his own house to live. It is not clear whether Barezzi perceived at once the boy's genius and regarded the business apprenticeship as a mere cover to his musical education—a means of earning his keep and something to fall back upon, should music fail. But he secured the best training for Giuseppe that Busseto afforded.

The boy responded to all this kindness, opening up like a flower to the sun, so that he soon won the affection of his benefactor and became as one of his own family. He showed his gratitude by hard work, so that soon his Latin master, Canon Seletti, was proposing for him an ecclesiastical career. His music-teacher was Ferdinando Provesi, the organist of the cathedral of Busseto and conductor of the Philharmonic Society. The boy was soon helping his master in preparing the performances of the society, copying parts and assisting at rehearsals. In this way he gained a practical experience of music-making, without which theory is of little use. In Barezzi's house there was a pianoforte at his disposal, on which he also played duets with his employer's daughter, Margherita. We may suppose that, in the intervals of his studies and his music-making, he found time to attend to Barezzi's business. For this part of Verdi's story reads like the moral tale of the Good Apprentice. His life and his fortunes had been changed as if by the wave of a magic wand.

Provesi was just fifty years senior to his thirteen-year-old pupil, and was beginning to feel his years. He seems to have been a competent composer, writing, as usual in the Italy of those days, for the theatre as well as for the church. What is more important from the point of view of teaching than the possession of an extra-ordinary creative talent (which Provesi could not claim), he was also a sensible and agreeable man. So he was able to guide his pupil in the right way, sharpening his interest without cramping his style. The results of his teaching were soon evident, for on one occasion when Verdi deputized for the organist of the Jesuit College chapel his improvisation was sufficiently striking to persuade Seletti to abandon his idea of putting the boy into the church.

In 1829, three years after the beginning of his apprenticeship, Verdi had a further practical opportunity of distinguishing him-self. He conducted, in place of Provesi, a concert of the Phil-harmonic Society, and he was appointed director of the town band. Too much importance must not be attached to these events. Busseto was a small provincial town, and its Philharmonic Society—high-sounding title—was an amateur body of no greater accomplishment than will be found in such conditions to this day. We do not know what they played—apart from some juvenile compositions by Verdi. Francis Toye suggests, on the evidence of Bellaigue and Pougin, 'Porpora and Haydn, whose music was popular in Italy at that time' and 'certainly the brilliant new overtures to *The Barber of Seville* and *Cinderella*' by Rossini. The fact to remember is that at Busseto there was nothing to widen the boy's intellectual or musical outlook. Good musician though he was, Provesi was not a man of wide culture. What he could teach was well, but not well enough. So it must not be imagined that the interest created in this small, provincial town by Verdi's noisy marches and mazurkas for the municipal band, his motets for the cathedral and his orchestral pieces for performance at the Philharmonic Society's concerts would have been aroused in one of the great centres of musical culture like Milan.

There were rivalries and jealousies, too. For in this same year (1829) Verdi's application for the post of organist at the church of Soragna was turned down, despite the strong recommendation of Provesi. Fortunately it soon became evident to Barezzi that Busseto did not afford sufficient scope for the education of genius, and it was decided to send Giuseppe to Milan. Happily there was at Busseto an institution which provided four scholarships of 300 francs tenable for four years by poor children. At Barezzi's instance Carlo Verdi applied for one of these grants in May 1831. The case was considered by the administrators in the following January and Verdi was granted the first available pension, which would not be vacant till November 1833, Barezzi undertaking to provide for the boy in the interval.

So at the age of eighteen Verdi went to Milan, with a view to entering the Conservatorio. On his passport, necessary even for the traveller from one part of Italy to another, he is described as tall, with brown hair, black eyebrows and beard, grey eyes, aquiline nose and small mouth, thin in the face and pale, with pock-marks in his skin. He lodged with a nephew of Canon Seletti, who gave him an introduction, in the Via Santa Marta.

The authorities at the Conservatorio, however, would have none of him. At the interview Verdi was, no doubt, shy as usual, and it may be his provincial awkwardness and want of polish were misinterpreted as ill temper. Nor did his pianoforte playing please the professors. Further, he was much over the age (nine to fourteen), at which he could, according to the rules, be admitted, and there seemed no reason for making an exception for a 'foreigner' from the Duchy of Parma. Verdi was bitterly disappointed, and the sense of injury rankled. Fifty years later, in a letter to a friend, he gave an account of his rejection that is not without

7

rancour, nor entirely in accordance with the facts. For he claimed that he was not told about any rules, although in his application to the Conservatorio he specifically asks that the age-limit should be waived in his favour. This was not a case, it should be mentioned, of failure in a competitive examination for a scholar-ship. Verdi offered himself as a paying pupil and was rejected.

His rejection has often been quoted as a classic instance of the stupidity of academic minds. It is in reality nothing of the kind. Rather it is a revelation of the poverty of Verdi's musical equip-ment at this stage, of the inadequacy of his provincial education. The officials of the Conservatorio were not, all of them at any rate, unsympathetic. They even went so far as to say that, once he had mastered the theory of music, he might go far. The point was that he was not at the moment sufficiently advanced in knowledge to justify their setting aside the age-limit. One of the examiners, Rolla, to whom Provesi had given him a letter of introduction, advised him to study with Lavigna, *maestro al cembalo* at the Teatro alla Scala, Milan's famous opera-house, at which Rolla himself conducted.

Lavigna was a first-rate musician; not a man of genius, but an excellent craftsman, which is what was most wanted for the guidance of the uncouth pupil. Under his instruction Verdi, in his twentieth year, received his full initiation into the mysteries of harmony and counterpoint and fugue. As examples his teacher set before him the works of Palestrina and Marcello, of Bach, Haydn, Mozart and Beethoven.

For two years he studied thus, sending back to his friends at Busseto the fruits of his labours, which were proudly performed by the Philharmonic Society. That he advanced rapidly in his studies is evident from the anecdote which relates how Basily com-plained one day of the poor standard of a batch of candidates, none of whom could work out correctly the fugal exercise set them in the examination. Lavigna asked the director to see what his pupil could do, and Verdi astonished the men who had rejected him two years before by producing a correct solution embellished with double counterpoint, remarking, not without

8

malice, that the subject itself was rather thin. Otherwise it was an uneventful time. Verdi had few friends, except his master, who seems to have been kind to him, entertaining him in the evening when his duties at the opera permitted. There was no money in the young man's purse to pay for much in the way of amusement on his own account.

One incident, however, is of importance. At a rehearsal of Haydn's *The Creation*, which was to be performed by the Milan Philharmonic Society, the conductor failed to turn up, and Verdi was asked to take his place. He was told that all he need do was to play the bass—it was presumably a rehearsal with pianoforte. Verdi was so successful in dealing with this amateur body that he was asked to direct the concert as well. The performance went so well that it was repeated, once before the nobility of Milan and again, 'by command,' at the house of the Austrian governor.

As a result Verdi was commissioned to compose a cantata by Count Renato Borromeo, the president of the society, for the wedding celebrations of a member of his family. More important, he was asked to write an opera for the Filodrammatico theatre. Verdi's first operatic essay was *Rocester*, with a libretto by Piazza. This was completed in 1837 when Verdi offered it to the director of the opera at Parma, who was unwilling to risk money on an unknown composer. Nothing survives of *Rocester* and the first opera to be produced was *Oberto, Conte di San Bonifacio*, also with a text by Piazza, revised by Temistocle Solera, a young poet whom Verdi met in Milan.

Work on this opera, *Oberto, Conte di San Bonifacio*, was, however, interrupted, and it was not performed until 1839. For, in the meantime, Provesi had died at Busseto, and Barezzi urged Verdi to return with a view to the succession to his old master's post. Whatever misgivings Verdi may have felt at abandoning his prospects at Milan, he obediently returned to Barezzi's house. Perhaps he felt obliged to fall in with the wishes of his benefactor. Not improbably the attractions of Margherita, now a girl of twenty, had something to do with his compliance. Over their pianoforte duets friendship quickly ripened into love, and in 1836

Verdi asked her father for permission to marry her, to which he readily consented. The marriage was celebrated on 4th May 1836.

The young composer was not, however, appointed to the organist's post. A more mature candidate, one Giovanni Ferrari, appeared upon the scene with a backing from the ecclesiastical authorities, who thought Verdi too young. In spite of Barezzi's influence, which carried with it the support of the municipality, Ferrari was appointed. The municipal authorities retorted by withdrawing their subsidy towards the organist's salary; the Philharmonic Society removed their music from the cathedral; and the 'fashionable maestrino,' as the ecclesiastics contemptuously called him, was appointed 'Master of Music to the Commune of Busseto' with a salary equal to that formerly contributed to the organist. The feud grew bitter. There were lampoons, brawls in the street and even prosecutions. The Franciscan friars allowed Verdi's music to be played in their church, and the people who took his part deserted the cathedral. He was in demand at neighbouring villages, whither he was escorted in triumph by the town band.

One result of these unedifying events was to alienate the young man from the majority of his fellow citizens in Busseto and the church. This breach with the ecclesiastical authorities widened as Verdi grew older, and he would have nothing to do with the church as an institution. But that this did not mean any relaxation of the standards of conduct inculcated in his early years is amply proved by his whole subsequent life, while the manifest sincerity of his sacred compositions proves that, despite a period of indifference to religion, he retained his faith. He was a better Christian than many a good churchman.

In later years Verdi recounted the story of these years to his friend Giulio Ricordi, who wrote down as well as he could remember them Verdi's *ipsissima verba*. This document is the chief authority for the account of Verdi's early years, and the passages quoted in the following pages are taken from Ricordi's transcript.

Verdi remained at Busseto for three years, during which he composed *Oberto* for Milan, whither he returned in 1839 for its production. Here his difficulties began, for Massini, who had been instrumental in obtaining this opportunity for Verdi, was no longer at the theatre for which the opera was commissioned, and the chance of its being performed seemed at an end.

However, whether Masini [*sic*] had confidence in my talents, or wished to show me some kindness, because after Haydn's *Creation* I had assisted him on several occasions by taking part in or directing the various performances (including *Cenerentola*), without seeming to offer me a reward, he assured me he would leave no stone unturned until my opera was brought out at La Scala. . . .

The result was that the opera was put down for performance in the spring of 1839 for the benefit of the Pio Istituto. Among the interpreters were the four excellent artists, Mme Strepponi, Moriani [tenor], Giorgio Ronconi [baritone] and Marini [bass].

This was, apparently, Verdi's first encounter with Giuseppina Strepponi, who certainly deserves a more prominent place among the company of noble women than is usually given to her. Born in 1815, two years after Verdi, she was the daughter of a music student who became director of music at Monza. She was trained as a singer at the Milan Conservatorio and soon made a name for herself as an artist of exceptional ability at a time when singing still was singing. A contemporary criticism, quoted by Mr Toye, records that her voice was 'clear, sweet and penetrating; her acting adequate and her figure graceful.' She was singularly free from the vices usually associated with *prime donne* and her character was marked not by a selfish vanity, but by a generosity and sense of duty which were exemplified in early years by her devotion to her younger brothers for whose education she paid after her father's death, and which found their fullest scope in her companionship for fifty years with the great artist to whom she sacrificed her own career in order to further his by her loving care and self-effacing wisdom. It is no exaggeration to say that without this remarkable woman Verdi would not have become the Verdi we know. Less familiar to the general public than Cosima Wagner, because she was more retiring by nature and because she was not left to carry on her husband's work, she deserves a place in musical history beside that other Egeria.[1]

Unfortunately the tenor, Moriani, fell ill and the performance had to be abandoned. Verdi 'broke down utterly and was thinking of retiring to Busseto.' But Giuseppina Strepponi and Giorgio Ronconi were sufficiently impressed by the young man's music to press his claims upon Bartolomeo Merelli, the impresario of La Scala, who sent for Verdi:

On my entering his room, he abruptly told me that he had heard my music well spoken of and was willing to produce it during the next season, provided I would make some slight alterations in the compass of the solo parts, as the artists engaged were not the same who were to perform it before. His only condition was that he should share with me the sale of the copyright. This was not asking much for the work of a beginner. And, in fact, even after its favourable reception, Ricordi would give no more than 2,000 Austrian livres [£67] for it.

Though *Oberto* was not extraordinarily successful, yet it was well received by the public and was performed several times; and Merelli even found it convenient to extend the season and give some additional performances of it. The principal singers were Mme Marini, Salvi and Marini. I had been obliged to make several cuts, and had written an entirely new number, the quartet, on a situation suggested by Merelli himself; which proved to be one of the most successful pieces in the whole work.

As a result of this success Merelli offered Verdi a contract to compose three operas at intervals of eight months. Verdi was to receive 4,000 livres for each as well as half the proceeds of the sale of the copyright. The first of these operas was to be *Il Proscritto*, with a text by Rossi; but, before Verdi could set to work on it, Merelli changed his plans and asked for a comic opera. In view of the impresario's generosity in his dealings with him, Verdi could not well refuse, though he seems to have been doubtful of his own ability to direct his talents into a new channel of which he had no experience. He was given several librettos by Romani, all of which had been set by other composers without success. He liked none of them, but chose the one that

[1] See Supplement I, p. 313.

seemed least bad, *Il finto Stanislao*, and changed the title to *Un giorno di regno*.

Misfortune dogged his work. Verdi was then living with his family in 'an unpretentious little house' near the Porta Ticinese:

> As soon as I set to work I had a severe attack of angina that confined me to bed for several days, and just when I began to get better I remembered that quarter-day was only three days off, and that I had to pay fifty crowns. Though, in my financial position, this was not a small sum, my illness had prevented me from taking the necessary steps; and the means of communication with Busseto—the mail left only twice a week—did not allow me time enough to write to my excellent father-in-law, Barezzi, and get the money from him. It vexed me so much to let quarter-day pass without paying the rent, that my wife, seeing my anxieties, took the few valuable trinkets she had, went out, and a little while after came back with the necessary amount. I was deeply touched by this tender affection, and promised myself to buy everything back again in a very short time, which I could have done, thanks to my agreement with Merelli.
>
> But now terrible misfortunes crowded upon me. At the beginning of April my son falls ill, the doctors cannot understand what is the matter, and the dear little creature goes off quickly in his mother's arms. Moreover, a few days after the little girl is taken ill too, and she too dies, and in June my young wife is taken from me by a most violent inflammation of the brain, so that on 19th June I saw the third coffin carried out of my house. In a very little over two months three persons so dear to me had disappeared for ever.

It is extraordinary that these tragic events, which left an indelible mark upon Verdi's character, should not have impressed themselves accurately upon his memory. For this circumstantial account of his triple bereavement within a period of two months can hardly be due to some misunderstanding or fault of memory in Ricordi, though he might, indeed, have made the mistake of placing the son's death before the daughter's. It seems, however, clear that this account, which was accepted by most of Verdi's biographers before Gatti, is inaccurate. The daughter, Virginia, died at Busseto in 1838, a year before the production of *Oberto* on 17th November 1839. Icilio died at Milan in 1839 and

Margherita in 1840.[1] It is, perhaps, of small importance whether these events occurred within a space of two months or three years, but it is at least puzzling that Verdi's recollection of them should have been at fault. At the time he was utterly crushed by these successive blows and a friend at Busseto records that he was reduced to a state of mental aberration. Did he, perhaps, in after years see himself as another Macduff, bereft of his chickens and their dam at one fell swoop? The inaccurate account was published in his lifetime by Folchetto,[2] but was never corrected by Verdi.

However the error arose, there is no question that these successive disasters affected Verdi's whole outlook. Well may they have embittered a mind already turned against the official representatives of religion, so that, like Job, he cursed God. And, in the face of his own bitter experience of the malignity of fate, can it be wondered that he was ready to accept in his librettos any manifestation of the power of destiny, however brutal or far-fetched, that the romantic melodramatists of the nineteenth century chose to invent?

In the midst of these terrible sorrows [continues Verdi] I had to write a comic opera! *Un giorno di regno* proved a failure; the music was, of course, partly to blame, but the interpretation had a considerable share in the fiasco. Harrowed by my domestic misfortunes and embittered by the failure of my opera, I despaired of finding any comfort in my art, and resolved to give up composition.

How bitterly Verdi felt the failure of his opera, or rather the attitude of the public towards it, is evident from a letter written twenty years later to Tito Ricordi after the production of *Simon*

[1] These facts were published in *Carteggi Verdiani* by Alessandro Luzio, Rome, 1935. See also an article by Francis Toye in *Music & Letters*, October 1936.

[2] In the Italian translation of Pougin's *Anecdotes*, which was enlarged with additional material. The proofs were sent to Verdi, who made some important corrections on other matters.

Boccanegra, which failed to please the Milanese public owing to the incompetence of the leading singer. In his own words:

The fiasco of *Boccanegra* at Milan was inevitable. *Boccanegra* without Boccanegra! Behead a man and see if you can recognize him. You marvel at the bad manners of the public. They cause me no surprise. A scandal always pleases them! At the age of twenty-five I had my illusions and believed in their good nature; a year later my eyes were opened and I saw with whom I had to deal. Some people make me smile when, with an air of reproof, they point out what I owe to this or that public. It is true that at the Scala *Nabucco* and *I Lombardi* were enthusiastically received; but then the whole *ensemble* of music, singers, orchestra, chorus and *mise-en-scène* combined to provide such a spectacle as did no dishonour to those who applauded. Only a little more than a year before, this same public maltreated the work of a poor young man, prostrated and heart-broken by a terrible experience. All this they knew, but it did not restrain their discourtesy. From that day to this I have not seen *Un giorno di regno,* and it may be that it is a bad opera, though many no better are tolerated and even applauded. Had the public not applauded, but merely endured my opera in silence, I should have had no words to thank them! . . . I do not mean to blame the public; but I accept their criticisms and jeers only on condition that I do not have to be grateful for their applause.

In this black mood Verdi decided to abandon his career as a composer. He asked Merelli to release him from his engagement, and was scolded 'like a naughty child.' The impresario rightly pointed out that the cold reception of his comic opera—a work written in such tragic circumstances to a libretto which obviously did not arouse any enthusiasm in the composer—was no cause for despondency. Verdi, however, was adamant, and Merelli could only say: 'Now listen to me: I cannot compel you to write; but my confidence in your talent is unshaken. Who knows but some day you may decide to take up your pen again! At all events, if you let me know two months in advance, take my word for it your opera shall be performed.'

Merelli's conduct in this whole business was not only remark-ably perspicacious—for he obviously appreciated that this young man, with one moderately successful opera and one complete failure to his credit, had more than ordinary talent—but also most generous and wise. He perceived that Verdi was too sore at heart to take up more work at once, and that the only thing was to wait until the wounds began to heal. The event proved the sagacity of his kindliness.

It is doubtful whether Verdi, whose whole nature was devoted to music and the theatre, could, in any circumstances, have persisted in the abandonment of his art. But after a suitable lapse of time Merelli broke down his resolution in the gentlest and most tactful way by the simple process of bringing to his notice, without suggesting that he should compose the music, a libretto which he thought would appeal to Verdi. He subtly added, by way of appealing to the young man's good nature, that he was in some difficulty about getting a new opera.

Here is Verdi's own account of the origin of the work which was to be his first masterpiece:

One evening, just at the corner of the Galleria de Cristoforis, I stumbled upon Merelli who was hurrying towards the theatre. It was snowing hard, and he took my arm and invited me to walk with him to his office in La Scala. On the way he never left off talking, telling me he did not know where to turn for a new opera; Nicolai was engaged by him, but had not begun to work because he was dissatisfied with the libretto.

'Only think,' says Merelli, 'here is Solera's libretto! Such a beautiful subject! Take it, just take it and read it over.'

'What on earth shall I do with it? I am in no humour to read librettos.'

'It won't kill you; read it, and then bring it back to me again.' And he gives me the manuscript. It was written on large sheets in big letters, as was the custom in those days. I rolled it up and went away.

While walking home [he had moved to new lodgings near the Corsia de' Servi] I felt an indefinable disquiet, a deep sadness. I got to my room, and throwing the manuscript angrily on the writing-table, I stood for a moment motionless before it. The book, as I threw it down, opened, my eyes fell on the page and I read the line:

'Va, pensiero, sull' ali dorate.'
['Go, thought, on golden wings'.]

I read on, and was touched by the stanzas inasmuch as they were almost a paraphrase of the Bible, the reading of which always delighted me.

I read one page, then another; then determined, as I was, to keep my promise not to write any more, I did violence to my feelings, shut up the book, went to bed. But *Nabucco* was running furiously through my brain, and sleep would not come. I got up and read the libretto again—not once, but two or three times, so that in the morning I had it by heart. Yet my resolution was not shaken, and in the afternoon I went to the theatre to return the manuscript to Merelli.

'Isn't it beautiful?' says he.

'Very beautiful!'

'Well, set it to music.'

So saying, he took the libretto, thrust it into my overcoat pocket, pushed me out of the room and locked the door in my face.

What was I to do? I went home with *Nabucco* in my pocket. One day a verse, the next day another; one time a note, another a phrase . . . little by little the opera was written.

It was the autumn of 1841, and remembering Merelli's promise, I went to him with the news that *Nabucco* was written and that it was ready for performance during the next carnival season.

Merelli declared himself ready to honour his word, but at the same time pointed out that it would be quite impossible to give the opera during the coming season as the repertory was already arranged, and three new operas by unknown composers were already on the list. To give a fourth by a composer who had barely made his début would be risky for everybody, and especially for me. It would, therefore, be safer to postpone my opera until the spring, when, he assured me, good artists would be engaged. I refused; either during the carnival or not at all . . . and I had good reasons, for I knew that I could not find better singers than Strepponi and Ronconi, upon whom I was placing so much reliance.

Merelli, though disposed to give me my way, was not entirely in the wrong from his own point of view as impresario; four new operas in a single season would involve grave risks! But still I had good artistic reasons for opposing him. In the end, after many changes of mind and half-promises, the bills of the Scala were posted . . . but *Nabucco* was not announced.

I was young and hot-blooded! I wrote Merelli a rude letter, in which I let my resentment have full play, of which I repented as soon as

17

it had gone. I feared, too, that as a result the whole business would be ruined.

Merelli sent for me and angrily inquired whether that was the way to write to a friend. 'But you are right,' he continued, 'we will give this *Nabucco*, but I must take into account the heavy expenses of the other operas, and I cannot afford either scenery or costumes for *Nabucco*! We must fit it out as best we can from stock.'

In my anxiety to see the opera given I consented, and a new bill was issued, on which at last appeared: NABUCCO.

The rehearsals began at last late in February and twelve days after the first rehearsal with pianoforte the opera was produced on 9th March, with Signore Strepponi and Bellinzaghi and Signori Ronconi, Miraglia and Derivis in the cast.

With this opera my artistic career may truly be said to have begun; and, in spite of the obstacles I had to overcome, *Nabucco* was born under a favourable star. For everything that might have harmed my work turned to its advantage. I wrote a furious letter to Merelli, which might well have made him send his seconds to a young composer. Yet just the opposite occurred.

The refashioned costumes looked splendid; the old scenery, touched up by the painter Perroni, made an extraordinary impression; in particular, the first scene in the temple produced so great an effect that the audience applauded for ten minutes!

But it does not always do to trust in beneficent stars! My experience has taught me the truth of the proverb: Fidarsi è bene, ma non fidarsi è meglio! [Faith in your luck is good, but lack of faith is better.]

An incident, which I have omitted from this translation of Verdi's own words, deserves mention because it confirms the impression given by this account of his dealings with Merelli: that at the age of twenty-eight Verdi already knew his own mind very clearly, and was not only determined to have his own way but capable of getting it. He disliked a duet in the libretto of *Nabucco* as being too trivial to fit in with the 'Biblical grandeur' of the story, and also because it held up the action. He, therefore, asked Solera for something else to replace it, and when the librettist seemed reluctant to return to a book which he regarded as done with, Verdi locked him in his study and refused to let him go until the required verses were written. Solera was furious, but acquiesced.

Nabucodonosor—which is almost as clumsy and difficult to spell as the English equivalent, Nebuchadnezzar—is now always referred to by the affectionate abbreviation used by Verdi in the foregoing account. The opera must always hold a special place in our affections on account of the romantic circumstances of its composition, and because, as Verdi remarked, with it his artistic career may truly be said to have begun. But the opera has, in spite of its obvious crudities, merits that give it something more than a sentimental and historical value. To Verdi's contemporaries the scenes of Jewry in captivity appealed as an expression of their own unhappiness under alien rule, but the beautiful setting of the chorus, 'Va, pensiero, sull' ali dorate,' remains to this day no less moving because the immediate cause of its inspiration has been removed. It breathes the very spirit of the resigned misery that finds expression in such psalms as 'By the waters of Babylon.'

In addition to this popular appeal to patriotic feelings, which finds a more stirring expression in the magnificent choruses of the first act, *Nabucco* showed at once that a new composer had arisen who could infuse a new vigour and dramatic force into the rather weakly style of Bellini and Donizetti. A modern audience may be struck more by the resemblance of the melodies to those of Verdi's elder contemporaries, but what impressed the Milanese audience in 1842 was the new directness and inspiring forcefulness of expression in this music. And that forcefulness has not even yet lost its power over an audience. Much of the orchestration is, of course, crude and artless, though a performance—it is true in the open-air arena at Verona, where the conditions may have taken the edge off its noisiness—did not seem to justify the witty epigram (quoted by Mr Toye):

> Vraiment, l'affiche est dans le tort,
> En faux on devrait la poursuivre.
> Pourquoi nous annoncer Nabucodonos—or
> Quand c'est Nabucodonos—cuivre?

In fact, the emotional stimulus that went to the making of *Nabucco* was strong enough to give it a permanent musical value that outweighs the weakness of its outworn conventions and the frequent absurdities of the plot. And, apart from its intrinsic merit, *Nabucco* is particularly interesting to the musical historian as showing that already at this early stage Verdi's individuality as an operatic composer was taking shape. Apart from the new vigour of the music which has already been observed, the opera shows an originality in the treatment of the characters that is noteworthy. In particular, it is the part of Abigail, the villainess of the piece, allotted to a mezzo-soprano, who would have been the *seconda donna* of an earlier day, and not the gentle heroine Fenena, who occupies the forefront of the stage. Verdi's creation of these great mezzo-soprano parts is one of his most striking contributions to opera, and Abigail is the first member of an important family that includes Lady Macbeth, Azucena, Ulrica in *Un ballo in maschera*, Eboli in *Don Carlo* and, final apotheosis of the type before it sank back to minor importance in Emilia and Dame Quickly, Amneris in *Aida*. Like Verdi's baritones, among them Macbeth, Rigoletto and Iago, the corresponding masculine types, these women are not lovers. They are actuated by jealousy (Eboli and Amneris) or desire for revenge (Azucena) or ambition (Abigail and Lady Macbeth). For all the splendid melody that Verdi lavished upon his sopranos and tenors, the ill-starred lovers of his melodramatic plots, it is in these mezzo-soprano and baritone parts that he made his most distinctive and original contribution to opera. In this respect *Macbeth*, with its complete subordination of the tenor, is one of his most characteristic works.

There are other intimations in *Nabucco* of the composer's future development, among them the beautiful prayer of Zaccharias, the High Priest, which is the prototype of the Verdian bass aria. It has not, perhaps, the individual melodic style, still less the rhythmical and orchestral resource, that appeared later in Banquo's air or in Fiesco's 'Il lacerato spirito' in *Simon Boccanegra*, but its relationship to these airs is obvious enough in retrospect:

'NABUCCO'
Andante

Zaccaria

Tu sul lab - bro de' veg - gen - ti
ful - mi - na - sti, o som - mo Id - di - o!

'S. BOCCANEGRA'
Andante sostenuto

Fiesco

Il la - ce - ra - to spi - ri - to

ppp   (Timpano)

del mes - to ge - ni - to - re   e - ra ser - ba - to a

stra - zio d'in - fa - mia e di   do -

21

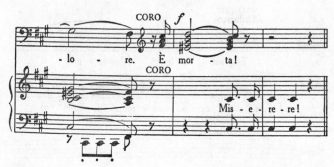

Nebuchadnezzar himself is less clearly defined than the later baritone parts. Although his entry on horseback at the climax of the splendid and turbulent choruses of Act I is finely contrived, he has, indeed, a poor and vacillating part to play. His best music is contained in the scene with Abigail in Act III, a duet which already shows Verdi's skill in handling a conflict of wills and emotions. The wretched king's alternations of mood between impotent fury and supplication are admirably portrayed.

CHAPTER III

EARLY INFLUENCES

AT this point it will be well to pause and consider the musical world into which Verdi was making his entry with *Nabucco*. The first third of the nineteenth century encloses the operatic careers of two important Italian composers. Rossini, born in 1792, made his début in Venice at the age of eighteen and, after two decades of unparalleled success in all the capitals of Europe, retired from the theatre in 1830 to live out the rest of his long life as a wit, a gourmet and, apart from one or two serious excursions into church music, a composer of occasional trifles. Rossini is remembered primarily as a composer of *opera buffa*, but his European reputation was created by *Tancredi*, produced in 1813, and consolidated by such works as *Mosè in Egitto* (1818), *Semiramide* (1823) and *Moïse*) (the French version of *Mosè*, Paris, 1827). The most famous of his serious operas, however, is *William Tell*, the last of his dramatic compositions, which was produced in Paris in 1829.

We are inclined to regard Rossini as the type of old-fashioned operatic composer. But it should not be forgotten that his contemporaries looked upon him as an innovator. To a genera-tion for whom Wagner's *Ring* was still in the womb of time, his orchestration appeared excessive, and he was the first composer, in an age when the *prima donna* was paramount, to curb the extravagances of singers. Compared with that of Mozart and Cimarosa, as set down on paper, his music may seem exceedingly ornate; but that is to leave out of account, as all modern singers do out of a misguided and pedantic regard for the written note, all the ornaments and cadenzas with which the composers ex-pected singers to embellish the plain facts of their vocal melodies. This freedom of the singers to improvise inevitably led to abuse by performers who had more self-conceit than taste, and Rossini set himself to put a check on their vanity by writing down exactly what he wanted them to sing. In his insistence that they should carry out his intentions he set a precedent which Verdi was to follow, while the additional prominence he gave to the orchestra —in which he was following in the steps of his beloved Mozart— provided another example which the younger man did not ignore. We may legitimately suppose that when Verdi came to write the last act of *Rigoletto*, he had not forgotten how Rossini had depicted a storm in the overture to *William Tell*. But that is no more a plagiarism than is Rossini's debt on the same account to Beethoven's 'Pastoral' Symphony.

It is perhaps necessary to remind the modern reader, who has not many opportunities of hearing any but the comic operas of Rossini, that a cleavage of style still persisted between *opera seria* and *opera buffa*. This distinction consisted, as we shall see, not in any real differentiation of the melodies applied to tragic and comic situations, but in the use in tragedy of *recitativo stromentato*—that is, recitative accompanied by the orchestra—and in comedy of *recitativo secco*—that is, accompanied by a harpsichord or pianoforte with or without the lower string instruments. The fully accompanied recitative is obviously a better vehicle for the expression of tragic or heroic sentiments than the quick patter of the *secco*. But the point of importance to us is that the accompanied recitative tends to produce a greater homogeneity of texture in a whole work, so that it is not a long step from recitative and set air to a musical style in which the two become merged indistinguishably in one another. In fact, Mozart had already gone a good part of the way, as a glance at the accompanied recitatives, which are already fully melodic, in *Don Giovanni* and *The Magic Flute* will show. If Rossini, whose admiration for Mozart was as great as it was singular among Italian composers, did not develop the process himself, at least he did not go back upon it.

In another respect, too, Rossini followed the example of Mozart. For although in his operas every one of the singers has an aria in which to express his or her character, an opera like *The*

Barber of Seville represents, no less than Mozart's *Figaro*, the triumph of the ensemble over the soloist. His development of the finale—that concerted piece of music for all the characters in which the dramatic situation of an act is brought to a climax and of which the first finale in *Figaro* is the finest example in existence —is Mozart's most important contribution to the growth of operatic form. It is essentially a symphonic procedure which could only have been so consummately handled by a composer of symphonies, for all that it was based upon a long-standing convention of Italian *opera buffa*. For the finale is a natural development in music of those farcical situations of misunderstanding and cross-purposes which are part of the stock-in-trade of *opera buffa*. Until Rossini's time it finds no place in serious Italian opera, which employs the ensemble of soloists and chorus in comparatively short movements and in a static and contemplative cantata style to round off the action. To contemporary audiences the most familiar examples of the serious finale are the final scenes in *Fidelio* and *The Magic Flute*, which, for all their German characteristics in other respects, conform in this one to the Italian convention. Rossini and his contemporaries, however, broke down this arbitrary division between the serious and comic styles and adapted the dynamic ensemble to the requirements of tragic situations, and, although Rossini had not Mozart's symphonic skill in handling his material, and came to rely too much upon the effective, but in the end too rigid, formula of his famous *crescendo*, this addition to the resources of *opera seria* was of real importance. For it gave the composer a more flexible means of handling his dramatic situations and a greater dynamic scope in the building up of his climaxes. His development of this procedure constitutes one of Verdi's chief claims to greatness as a composer.

The second of the composers who dominated the Italian theatre at this time was Bellini, who was born in 1801 and died, shortly after the production of *I Puritani*, in 1835. His other chief operas are *La Sonnambula*, a comedy, and *Norma*, a tragic grand opera which still survives in the international repertory owing to the superb opportunities it affords to a great dramatic soprano. Bellini's style is lyrical and elegiac, but in *Norma*, at least, it rises to grandeur. In these days, when there are few singers capable of doing justice to his vocal line, it is difficult to assess his music at its true worth, and Bellini was unfortunate in becoming, as the chief exponent of Italian tragic opera, the target of Wagner's most virulent attacks. But now that Wagner's battle is won, we shall do well to forget the dispute and, looking past the obvious weaknesses of Bellini's music, to seek out the merits that Wagner himself had recognized in his earlier years.

Norma is the embodiment in music of the classical vogue of the Napoleonic empire which, be it remembered, had extended to Milan where the opera, based upon a French tragedy, was produced in 1831. The characteristics of this style are, as may be seen in the work of its greatest exponent in painting, Ingres, an insistence upon the beauty of line and a paradoxical combination of austere coldness of presentation with an extreme sensuousness of feeling and a somewhat meretricious taste in ornament. In fact, I can think of no better parallel for the linear beauty of Bellini's melody than the linear beauty of draughtsmanship in Mme Moitessier's portrait at the National Gallery. Indeed the words that came to my lips at first sight of that masterpiece were 'Casta diva!' And if there may seem to be some divergence between the lady's solidity and statuesque pose, and the cavorting *cabaletta* that follows Norma's beautiful *adagio*, there is surely something of a twinkle in her eye.

The *cabaletta* seems strangely at variance with the dramatic situation and with the classical character of the heroine. It belongs to an outworn convention, which however persisted in Verdi's operas until he reached maturity. But at least once he found a situation in which the convention could be employed with complete dramatic propriety, when Violetta puts aside the day-dream of 'Ah! fors' è lui!' and faces with hysterical high spirits the realities of her position in 'Ah! follia.' This first aria in *La Traviata* is nothing more than the traditional *adagio* and *cabaletta* transformed by genius into a masterpiece of characterization.

If many of Bellini's operas are forgotten, the type of melody he created is constantly in our ears, not only when we hear the operas of Verdi, but whenever Chopin is played. The elegiac cantilena in which Chopin excelled is obviously based upon Bellini's melody. For examples we need go no farther than to such familiar things as the trio of the *Marche funèbre*, the Prelude in D flat and almost any nocturne. The Bellinian style of cantilena persisted even in Tchaikovsky (e.g. Lensky's air in *Eugene Onegin*) and Liszt, who however tipped the balance between firmness of line and sensuousness in favour of the latter quality. It is hardly surprising that Verdi also fell under the spell of Bellini's melody. How deep the influence was may be seen from the following quotations, one from an ensemble in *I Puritani*, the other from the most familiar of all Verdi's concerted movements:

But the resemblance between these two pieces goes deeper than the superficial similarity in their melodies. The whole structure of Verdi's piece—its changes of harmony, its manner of reaching the vocal climax and even the handling of the coda—follows closely the example of Bellini. Yet the quartet in *Rigoletto* is not the less a masterpiece nor the less original, for Verdi, besides ranging wider in harmony, gives an individual character and independence to his several parts that were beyond the imagination of Bellini.

The general style of the Bellinian opera is admirably summed up by the nineteenth-century pianist and critic, Edward Dann-reuther:

> Dramatic situations easily understood, and demanding few accessories for their proper presentation, but carefully arranged and graduated for the lyrical utterance of passion; headlong words for rapid recitatives, telling scenas, culminating in some clusters of verses apt for emotional cantilena. All the rest was left to the composer—who again, on his part, knew exactly how to adapt his knowledge and sense of vocal effect to the altogether exceptional gifts and attainments of the great singers for whom he wrote.

That description applies equally to the operas of Gaetano Donizetti, a composer of lesser stature than Rossini and Bellini, but not less popular in his time. Born in 1797, Donizetti wrote sixty-six operas during his working career between 1818 and 1844, an average of more than two works a year. Even these figures do not give a true picture of the composer's extraordinary facility, in which he surpassed even Rossini. For he wrote some of his operas in the space of a few days. That such speed resulted in thin and superficial music turned out according to formula is hardly surprising. What is more surprising is that some of his operas retain their popularity, in spite of the fact that there are few singers nowadays capable of doing justice to his brilliant vocal line. In his melody the Bellinian style is plentifully watered down with the tears of sobbing tenors, as will be seen by comparing the sickliness of 'Una furtiva lagrima' or 'O mio Fernando' with such things as the final duet, 'Ah! crudele,' in Norma. His orchestration is the most elementary imaginable, and if Bellini's must be called 'childish,' there is no word for Donizetti's, which has been likened to 'a big guitar.' His most daring adventure into instrumentation takes him no farther than a feeble obbligato for the flute designed to set off the beauty of the soprano voice. Yet, despite his faults,—or should one say because of them?—

Donizetti is the most characteristic composer of his age. For it is in the music of the second-rate composer, not in the great masters, in the Paisiellos and Cimarosas, not in the Mozarts, that the true character of music at a given period is to be found. So in such things as the 'mad scene' in *Lucia di Lammermoor* and the sextet in the same opera we find the true types of the *adagio* and *cabaletta* and of the vocal ensemble. This was the material of operatic music which Verdi found at hand when he began his career and which he fashioned in his more earnest and less flashy manner to his own purposes. Donizetti retired from the world, mad as his own Lucia, in 1848, having left in *Don Pasquale* at least one masterpiece of *opera buffa*.

The fact is that the Italian style at this period was as ill fitted for the presentation of grand and tragic themes as it was well adapted for comedy. Its swiftness of movement, its mellifluous melody and its entire reliance upon the human voice supported by the simplest and most commonplace harmony produce a ridiculous disproportion between the high-flown sentiments of tragic heroes and the musical language in which they are expressed. Donizetti used exactly the same kind of melody for his Lucia, his Anne Boleyn and his Lucrezia Borgia as he did for the intriguing minxes of *Don Pasquale* and *L'elisir d'amore*. Only Bellini succeeded in transforming tuneful simplicity into something like classic grandeur in *Norma*, and even *Norma* is now rather a monument of music than a living masterpiece like *The Barber of Seville* or *Don Pasquale*. The same may be said of *William Tell*, in which Rossini, with the example of Beethoven's *Fidelio* and Auber's *La Muette de Portici* (not to mention Meyerbeer's *Robert le diable*) before his eyes, created in the atmosphere of the Paris Opéra the first great 'grand romantic opera.'

It will be evident from this account of the operatic history of the day that in 1840 a young Italian composer with a bent towards tragic opera would find in the contemporary music of his most famous countrymen very little that could serve as a useful example in creating a genuinely tragic style. It is hardly surprising, therefore, that, quite apart from the simplicity of his own intellectual equipment, Verdi should have taken many years to mature a style suited to his purpose—a style transcending the naïvety and bathos of the works of his immediate predecessors and purged of the more extravagant vulgarities of grand opera as cultivated in Paris. The slowness of his development is even less surprising when we remember that Wagner, faced with exactly the same problems and endowed with a far greater intellect (which does not necessarily mean a greater creative genius), took as long to solve for Germany the operatic problems for which Verdi found an independent and an Italian solution.

But before we return to strict biography, there is one composer outside Italy who must be considered for a moment. A reference has already been made to Meyerbeer's *Robert le diable*, which was produced in Paris in 1831. After a successful but ephemeral career as a composer of Italian operas in the manner of Rossini's *Tancredi*, Meyerbeer found the proper field for the cultivation of his talent in Paris and his ideal collaborator in Eugène Scribe, the dramatist. With that flair for what a given public wants, so often displayed by artists of Jewish descent, he changed his style, substituting for the classic simplicities of scene and action exemplified in *Norma* an elaborate and extravagantly romantic manner, at once heroic, legendary and allegorical. To this new kind of opera, which we distinguish by the adjective 'grand,' every resource of spectacle and of music contributed. The splendours and the horrors of the Middle Ages as seen through the eyes of nineteenth-century romanticism were the subjects chosen, and the more magnificent, the more macabre they were, the better was the public pleased. To the voices were allotted dramatic recitatives of unheard-of violence, and the melodies, though retaining their Italianate cantilena, made demands upon the singers that were almost superhuman, and are largely beyond their abilities to-day. To all this was added the full power of an orchestral invention that was, if not subtle, at least extraordinarily brilliant. The fact that Berlioz's *Symphonie fantastique* was the exact contemporary of *Robert le diable* indicates which way the wind was blowing at the Paris Opera.

Meyerbeer

That Meyerbeer's grand operas—*Robert le diable, L'Africaine, Les Huguenots, Le Prophète*—are somewhat pretentious needs no underlining, and that they will soon be as extinct as the mastodons they resemble in size and unwieldiness can hardly be doubted. Yet they made a very real contribution to operatic history, quite apart from their development of the orchestral side of opera— a development that was in any case inevitable. For Meyerbeer had a very real sense of dramatic effect, and from him any young composer who had sufficient taste to avoid the imitation of his superficial vulgarity could learn an immense amount. He showed real invention in the handling of tense dramatic situations, and although his manner is an easy target for burlesque—indeed it almost burlesques itself with its extravagant gestures and high-flown heroics—his example, judiciously followed, was of enormous value. The 'cat-like tread' of Verdi's conspiratorial ensembles, directly derived from Meyerbeer, may provoke a smile in Englishmen who cannot forget their Sullivan. Yet one has only to remember the hushed and ominous mutterings of the courtiers as they approach Rigoletto's house or the splendid set-piece finale to the third act of *Otello* to perceive how fruitful in two very different ways Meyerbeer's example could be. And, if Wagner's *Rienzi*, which is certainly inferior to anything Meyerbeer ever wrote, does him no credit as a preceptor, certain passages in *The Flying Dutchman* and *Tannhäuser* are not insignificant feathers in his cap. Although the comparison may seem unduly complimentary to the composer, we may say that, if Bellini is the Ingres of nineteenth-century opera, Meyerbeer has some claim to be regarded as its Delacroix.

The 'Jews' Sabbath,' as Rossini dubbed the vogue of Meyerbeer and Halévy, whose *La Juive* was produced in 1835, had only just begun in Paris at the time we are discussing and had not yet extended its influence abroad. It is not until later, therefore, that we may expect to find its repercussions in the style of Verdi's operas. *Nabucco* was composed on Italian models, among which the influence of Rossini was paramount. It is easy to forget, now that Rossini's tragic operas have all but disappeared from the repertory, that he was, besides a master of comedy, a serious

31

composer, and was so regarded by his contemporaries. The man who could aver to Wagner that 'if Beethoven is a prodigy among men, Bach is a miracle of God' is not to be lightly dismissed as a shallow and cynical wit who retired from the labours of composition so soon as he had accumulated sufficient wealth to assure his ease. His *Otello* may have been killed for ever by Verdi's masterpiece, but it is, within the conventions of its period, which demanded a happy ending, a serious attempt at noble drama, and in his forgotten biblical drama *Mosè in Egitto* is to be found the precedent for Verdi's apocryphal Nebuchadnezzar. The famous prayer in *Mosè*, which was sung at Rossini's funeral, is the model for the choruses in Verdi's early operas.

But it was not as a competent essay in an accepted manner that *Nabucco* won Verdi an immense and immediate popularity. The public perceived the unmistakable tones of a new voice which gave expression to the spirit of revolt that was already beginning to stir in the hearts of the Italian people. This new spirit could best find an outlet in the theatre, which meant the opera, and the people quickly recognized in Verdi their national laureate. It may even be that Verdi consciously identified himself, as Mr Bonavia suggests, with the unknown musician of Mazzini's prophecy, who was to devote his art to the cause of Italy's restoration to independence. The critics might find his music crude and violent, but to the ordinary man there was something vital in it which he missed in the greater accomplishment of Rossini, in Bellini's statuesque sensuousness and melancholy and in the facile fluency of Donizetti. Mr Toye quotes Lualdi's just description of Verdi's music at this period as 'agitator's music,' and adds: 'It is a significant and amusing coincidence that, while Wagner was turning out reams of prose to show that Italian composers of opera had sinned in neglecting the national songs of their country, Verdi was, in fact, writing them.' And it may be added that it is largely owing to the fact that, since the death of Puccini, Italian composers have exchanged their birthright of song for a mess of German orchestration, that Italian opera has ceased to count in the world of contemporary music.

A Tribute to the Past

Verdi himself never lost his admiration for the music of his immediate predecessors. Writing in 1898 to Camille Bellaigue, who had sent him a book that seemed to him too little appreciative of Rossini and Bellini, he says:

About Rossini and Bellini you say many things that are possibly true. But I confess that I cannot but believe *Il barbiere di Siviglia* to be in its wealth of genuine musical ideas, its comic verve and its truth of declamation, the best *opera buffa* in existence. I share your admiration for *Tell*, but how many sublime and exalted passages are to be found in his other operas! Bellini is certainly poor in orchestration and harmony, but rich in feeling and in his own peculiar, individual melancholy! Besides, in his less familiar works, such as *Straniera* and *Pirata*, there are melodies that go on and on and on, such as no one before him had composed. And what truth and power there is in his declamation, for example in the duet between Pollione and Norma! And what exaltation of thought in the introduction to *Norma*! Badly scored it may be, but no one before him had written anything so heavenly.

CHAPTER IV

'I LOMBARDI' AND 'ERNANI'

THE success of *Nabucco* led to an immediate commission from Merelli to compose an *opera d' obbligo* for the following season—one of the new works which the impresario was under contract to produce each year. The subject chosen was the crusades, upon which Solera concocted a libretto entitled *I Lombardi alla prima crociata*. Produced in Milan in February 1843, *I Lombardi* is in the typical romantic style of the period, an affair of violent contrasts and exaggerated passion. It is memorable chiefly for the fact that it brought Verdi for the first time into conflict with the authorities, both in church and state. The Archbishop of Milan, hearing that a baptism was to be represented on the stage and that part of the action was set in Jerusalem, drew the attention of the police to the libretto with a view to its suppression. The police, perhaps already alarmed by the political enthusiasm aroused by *Nabucco*, seem to have found in the crusade preached by the pope an allegory of the proposal, recently put forward, to unite the Italian states under the aegis of the pope.

The collaborators were summoned to appear before Torresani, the chief of police. Verdi characteristically declined to attend the meeting, saying that either the opera should be given as it stood or not at all. As an Italian, Torresani may well have been inclined to give the opera the benefit of the doubt, and Merelli was able to urge that the scenery and costumes were all ready, and that the singers were enthusiastic about the music. Was Torresani prepared to make himself ridiculous by prohibiting a work of genius and go down in history as a man who was afraid of a tune? And what had tunes to do with politics anyhow? If Verdi was obstinate about making cuts or alterations, he was a genius, and geniuses were apt to be wilful. Torresani yielded to Merelli's persuasion, but as a sop to ecclesiastical consciences insisted on one important change: Giselda, praying to the Virgin, must sing, 'Salve Maria,' not 'Ave Maria.'

The fears of the police that the Milanese might read into the opera a political meaning were in the event only too well justified. *I Lombardi* stirred Italian patriotic feeling even more deeply than *Nabucco* with its full-blooded tunes and its romantic glorification of Lombardy's ancient military fame. The chorus 'O Signore dal tetto natio' aroused the kind of fervour that 'Land of our Fathers' creates at a gathering of Welshmen. The success of the opera was, in fact, due rather to its topicality than to its artistic merits. *Nabucco*, for all its crudities, contains some fine music, to whose inspiration the peculiar emotional circumstances of its composition no doubt contributed. *I Lombardi*, produced under normal conditions, is a better measure of Verdi's accomplishment at this date. His command of the orchestra is still undeveloped, and when the scoring it not thin, it takes on a town-band noisiness. The tunes have the merit of directness, so that the audience had no difficulty in carrying them away from the theatre; but they lack the sensitiveness of Bellini's vocal line and the real brilliance of Donizetti. At the same time we find the critics, who were to be echoed fifty years later by George Bernard Shaw, complaining that Verdi's writing was unvocal and ruinous to good singing. One critic, quoted by Francis Toye, wrote that the *prima donna,* 'having nothing to sing, shouts at the top of her voice from beginning to end.' The singer in question evidently did not agree with these strictures, for we are told that when Verdi was, as usual, pessimistic about the prospects of the opera before its production, she proclaimed that either it would be a great success or she would die on the stage.

Merelli treated Verdi with his usual generosity in the matter of payment for this opera, sending the composer a contract with a blank space where the amount of his fee was to be stated. Verdi consulted Giuseppina Strepponi, who was already on such close terms of friendship with the composer that she could act as an intimate and trusted adviser. She suggested that not more than the figure paid for *Norma*, 6,800 francs, should be demanded, and this was inserted in the contract and accepted by Merelli. As this sum was probably greater than had been paid for any other opera in Italy, even to the great Rossini, Verdi, with one previous success to his credit, must be thought singularly fortunate.

The success of *I Lombardi* was not repeated when it was given at Venice in December 1843. Writing to the Countess Giuseppina Appiani, the wife of a Milanese painter and a devoted admirer of Verdi, as she had been of Bellini and Donizetti, he announces '*un gran fiasco*, one of those fiascos that may truly be called classic. They disapproved of or merely tolerated everything, except the *cabaletta* of the "vision." That is the whole truth of it, which I tell you without pleasure and without grief.' However, though the Venetian public was not pleased, the director of the Fenice Theatre commissioned Verdi to compose a new opera, which was produced in March the following year. After toying with the idea of a *King Lear*, a subject which tempted Verdi over a period of many years, and after rejecting or seeing rejected other suggestions, Verdi accepted the director's proposal to turn Victor Hugo's *Hernani* into an opera. Francesco Piave, who combined stage-managing at the Fenice Theatre with the composition of librettos, was to provide the text.

Verdi was delighted with the subject, rather less pleased with his librettist, whom he compared unfavourably with Solera, and frankly doubtful about the police. His fears were well grounded, for Hugo's reputation as a prominent liberal and the stage representation of a plot against a crowned head were sufficient to arouse the suspicions of the authorities. However, these suspicions were once more allayed by a few alterations in the text. Verdi then found himself faced with obstacles of another kind, which were only surmounted by an exercise of his extraordinarily strong will-power. He had to fight the director over the question of a horn player appearing on the stage—'A horn player in the Fenice,' exclaimed the director, 'I never heard of such a thing'— and the *prima donna*, who had taken upon herself to demand of Piave the alteration of the final trio into a solo for herself, over the relative importance of composer and singer.   In the event he won, but at the cost of antagonizing the *prima donna*, who, however, in the light of the opera's subsequent success, confessed herself mistaken.

It is hardly surprising that on the first night *Ernani* did not go too well.   Mme Loewe, still aggrieved, sang out of tune and the tenor, Guasco, was in poor voice, suffering from 'a hoarseness that made one shudder.'   However, Verdi continues in his account of the performance to the Countess Appiani: 'More or less every piece was applauded, except Guasco's cavatina. . . . There were three calls after the first act, one after the second, three after the third and three or four at the end of the opera. That is the true story.'

Ernani has been summed up as showing 'three men in love with one woman, quarrelling about her, and shouting their love, not one behaving in a rational manner; they challenge one another in their hatred and agree only in seeking one another's destruction.' It is hardly to be wondered that Victor Hugo was not best pleased with this highly melodramatic version of his drama, in which all the situations are exaggerated and the details that would make them at all credible are omitted owing to the need for compression.   *Ernani* is the first of many examples among Verdi's operas of the mistake of attempting to turn a stage play into an opera without reorganizing the whole material from the very start.   The same sort of error is made by film producers who use dramas for the screen.   The medium of opera is distinct from that of the spoken drama, and a libretto must be constructed expressly to meet its special needs, not merely adapted as best as may be from a dramatic script.   An opera cannot successfully present all the complexities that go to the making of the kind of romantic melodrama that was in vogue and of which Hugo was the leading exponent.   The music takes too long to unfold the essential situations, leaving the details to be taken for granted and so emphasizing to the point of making them ridiculous all the coincidences and improbabilities of the original plot.   Moreover in opera the characters as presented by the librettist have to be simplified; it is the composer's business to reclothe them with flesh and blood. It proved beyond Verdi's powers at this stage of his development to transform into a semblance of human reality Piave's naïve simplifications of Hugo's already stagy persons and improbable situations. Yet the composer of *Ernani* was hailed by a Venetian critic as possessing 'an abundant and felicitous imagination, equalled only by his good taste,' which is the last quality a modern audience would find in an opera conspicuous for its violence and brutality of expression.

The Italian public, however, took *Ernani* to its heart, once more identifying itself with the outlawed hero, sharing in the stage conspiracy against his oppressor, and substituting for 'Carlo Quinto' in the chorus 'A Carlo Quinto sia gloria ed onor' the name of Pio Nono, when that liberal pope was elected three years later. If the strength of its patriotic appeal won for *Ernani* an immediate success in Italy so great that Verdi's publishers soon had twenty copies of the score out on hire at one time, the finer quality of the music as compared with that of *I Lombardi* has secured it a longer life than any of its predecessors, though in England for many years it was known only by the cavatina, 'Ernani, involami,' to which we used to be treated by sopranos desirous of showing off their *fioriture*.

Indeed, *Ernani* did more than enhance Verdi's popularity at home; it brought him international fame. Within six months of its first performance it was given in Vienna, under the supervision of Donizetti, who was director of the Italian opera, and won the praise of young Hans von Bülow, who recognized Verdi's 'richness of melodic invention and genius for theatrical effect.' In Paris, where Verdi's reputation was long in making headway, there was trouble with Hugo, who insisted on a change of title in order to dissociate the opera from his play. It was the first of Verdi's operas to reach London, where it was given at Her Majesty's Theatre in 1845, the year after its original production. Although, according to Henry Chorley, the critic of *The Athenaeum*, it 'shared the fate of Bellini's and Donizetti's first works in England,' and 'was received with curiosity rather than sympathy,' it remained in the repertory the following year and brought with it as companions *I Lombardi* and *Nabucco*, which was given as *Nino* in order to meet English prejudices about Biblical subjects in the theatre. Chorley, a conservative admirer of the older style of opera, was no lover of Verdi's music, but he acknowledges that *Ernani* struck his ear 'by a certain rude force and grandeur,' and writes of the 'dignity and passion' of the 'great' finale, 'O sommo Carlo,' and the final trio. He records also that the Elvira 'was, in every sense of the word, a stout singer, with a robust voice—a lady not in the least afraid of the violent use to which the latest Italian *maestro* forces his heroines, but able to scream in time,[1] and to shout with breath enough to carry through the most animated movement of those devised by him.' It may have been due to the singer's want of personal attraction, which then, as now, carried great weight with a London audience, that the opera, like the soprano, 'did not enjoy a success such as singers (and operas) far inferior have commanded.'

Chorley was even more critical of *Nabucco*, challenging the appearance in the theatre of 'the personages of Holy Writ,' and expatiating again upon the 'screams' of the soprano in 'Amazonian attire.' *I Lombardi*, on the other hand, 'had the aid of Mme Grisi and Signor Mario,' but even so 'the music betrayed the wear of the lady's voice. . . . The sickly *cavatina* for the tenor, which the barrel-organs made us hate ere "Il balen" was thought of, was given delightfully by Signor Mario; and the rude vigour of certain concerted pieces made itself felt—but the opera did not stand.' *Ernani* was, according to the same critic, doomed by the miserable company of singers. Despite these strictures, the operas remained in the repertory the following year together with two new ones, including *I Masnadieri*, which was composed for London. So they cannot have so completely failed 'to stand' as Chorley suggests.

Within a fortnight of the production of *Ernani* in Venice, Verdi was back in Milan writing to Vincenzio Flauto of the San Carlo Theatre, Naples, stating his terms for the composition

---

[1] *Sic.* Possibly a misprint for 'in tune.'

of a new opera. This letter is the first of the entries in Verdi's letter-book, which contains copies of his correspondence amounting to nearly four hundred documents and covering the remainder of his long life to within ten days of his death on 27th January 1901. These letters, published under the editorship of Gaetano Cesare and Alessandro Luzio as *I copialettere di Giuseppe Verdi*, are among the most remarkable records of a musician's life and methods that we possess, comparable in their interest only with the correspondence of the Mozart family and surpassed in bulk only by the copious writings of Richard Wagner.[1] This first letter is very typical of Verdi in its decisive and business-like statement of his terms:

1. The management shall pay me 550 (five hundred and fifty) gold napoleons of 20 francs payable in three equal instalments: the first on my arrival in Naples; the second after the first orchestral rehearsal; and the third immediately on the day after the first performance.

2. The management shall deliver to Milan the libretto of Signor Cammarano by the end of the present year 1844.

And so on, defining his and the management's obligations with all the precision of a legal contract. Verdi was no 'bohemian' artist, careless of his rewards and thinking only of his art. He was a shrewd and scrupulous business man, capable of driving a hard bargain and insisting on his rights. He had in matters of finance a peasant's thriftiness, and the very fact that he found time and energy in his busy life for the laborious task of copying out all his business correspondence, as well as many letters of a more personal nature, proves the orderliness of his mind. But it must not be deduced that, because Verdi was shrewd, he was also mean. There is ample proof of his generosity, usually exercised quietly and even anonymously. He combined with acumen in affairs the warmth of a great heart.

[1] These letters, which are the chief source of Verdi's biography, have been supplemented by four further volumes, also edited by Alessandro Luzio, containing the correspondence of Giuseppina Verdi and a vast quantity of invaluable letters from, among others, Boito, the librettist of *Otello* and *Falstaff*.

At this moment of triumph Verdi was overwhelmed with commissions. The second entry in the letter-book shows him declining, with courteous regrets, an offer to compose an opera for Padua. During the next few months he had under consideration three separate librettos, and it was for Rome, not for Naples, that his next opera, *I due Foscari*, was composed. The libretto, based upon Byron's tragedy, was by Piave, who once more exercised his powers of compression to produce an effect of violent and improbable coincidence. The choice of this subject, gloomy even among Verdi's gloomiest, is difficult to account for, unless the name of Byron, the Liberator of Greece, was regarded, along with the patriotic *pietas* of the senior Foscaro, who like the first Brutus sacrifices his son to his political loyalty, as sufficient to secure the success of the piece with the Roman public. If so, there was a miscalculation; for the opera did not please, and, although its failure was due in part to the unpopularity aroused by the raising of the prices of admission, it cannot be said that its failure was undeserved.

The chief interest of the music lies in the fact that here for the first time Verdi definitely attached characteristic themes to the chief persons of the drama. These themes are not, and they never became in Verdi's practice, *Leitmotive* developed symphonically in the manner of Wagner. They are just melodies which serve to characterize the persons or the action, and to remind the listener, when he recognizes them on their reappearance, of what has gone before. This simple expedient is capable of producing a powerful dramatic effect when the themes themselves have beauty and distinction, as they have in *La forza del destino* and *Aida*, in *Otello* and *Falstaff*. But Verdi had not yet reached the stage when he could create melodies with sufficient individuality to characterize the actors in the drama. However, although *I due Foscari* failed with the public, it was this opera which moved Donizetti to proclaim its composer as a man of genius.

Within three months of the first performance of *I due Foscari* Verdi's next opera was ready for production at the Scala, where it was given in February 1845. This time the patriot chosen was

Joan of Arc, italianized as *Giovanna d'Arco* and provided with the indispensable love interest, Carlo, King of France (tenor), being the object of her affection. The libretto by Solera is after—a long way after—Schiller's *The Maid of Orleans*, and its conventional treatment of a subject which has evoked poetry and respect even from Bernard Shaw, the irreverent arch-jester of the English theatre, makes it difficult to take the piece seriously as a drama. More-over, even if the libretto had been less superficial, the opera was composed in so short a space that there would have been no time for Verdi to work out a considered and original musical conception of the Maid. What he did was to write a con-ventional opera, with more than a touch of 'grand'-ness after the manner of *William Tell,* which had an ephemeral success and soon disappeared from the stage, despite the fact that among those who sang the title-part were such great artists as Stolz and Patti.

The projected opera for Naples, *Alzira*, was now taken up and, after some postponements, produced at the San Carlo Theatre in August 1845. The delay was due, in the first place, to the com-poser's illness, which made work impossible for a time. Verdi suffered a good deal during the coming years from digestive troubles, probably due to nervous exhaustion. This was evidently the weak spot in an iron constitution, and one extremely difficult to protect, for in these cases the functional cause of the illness sets up a nervous irritation which in turn aggravates the symptoms. Flauto, with whom Verdi made the business arrangements for the production, was unsympathetic and made light of his illness, suggesting that the air of Naples, doses of wormwood and the *eccitabilità di Vesuvio* would soon put him right. The sick man was irritated by his silly suggestions and retorted hotly:

I am extremely sorry to learn that in your opinion my illness is no great matter and that tincture of wormwood will do me good. As for the excitability of Vesuvius, I assure you that that is not what I need to get all my functions working again; but I benefit from quiet and rest.

To his librettist, Cammarano, he wrote complaining bitterly

that 'artists are apparently not allowed to be ill' and asking him
to impress upon Flauto the real gravity of his condition, of which
a doctor's certificate had failed to persuade him, and to assure him
that the composer would conscientiously fulfil his contract as soon
as his condition improved. Verdi was obviously hurt by the
implied reflection on his good faith, which was always one of
his conspicuous virtues.

After the first performance of *Alzira*, Verdi was able to record
a success 'as great as that of *Ernani*,' a statement which gives the
lie to the suggestion that the opera did not go well until the
second act. Verdi was not, however, blind to its faults, for a
few months later, when *Alzira* was given without success in
Rome, he confesses that it has irremediable faults, redeemed
by the overture and the last finale, while in later years he dismissed it as a 'really dreadful' work. Mr Toye bluntly writes
it down as the worst of Verdi's operas, and with that we
may leave this version of Voltaire's drama of 'noble savages,'
to whose lack of inspiration the composer's ill-health no doubt
contributed.

Attila, produced in Venice during the carnival of 1846, had
a greater success, not on account of its dramatic or musical
superiority, but because it contained, besides other patriotic sentiments which echoed the aspiration of a resurgent nation, the line
'Avrai tu l' universo, resti l' Italia a me' ('Take the whole universe, but leave Italy to me'). A more parochial patriotism was
aroused by the presentation of the founding of Venice, 'mother of
great men and brave.' The libretto of this opera was originally
entrusted to Piave, who was given minute instructions by the
composer as to how he was to treat the play by Zachariah Werner
upon which it was based. Piave, however, handed the task over
to Solera in exchange for a libretto commissioned for another composer. Solera was less pliable than his colleague, whom Verdi
addressed in terms of affectionate contempt, calling him, among
other zoological names, 'a dirty cat of a poet,' 'a crocodile,' and 'a
rat,' all of which was apparently taken in good part by Piave.
Solera was also lazy and far away in Barcelona. So there were

delays increased by a recurrence of Verdi's illness, which forced him to take to his bed in January (1846), so that he missed the first Venetian performance of *Giovanna d' Arco*, which, in spite of a new air for Loewe (the soprano who had been refused one in *Ernani*), was coldly received by the public.

The subject of *Attila* greatly appealed to Verdi, and he had had it in mind for two years before its production. He even wrote to the sculptor Luccardi in Rome, asking for a description of the figure of Attila in the 'tapestries or frescoes' by Raphael in the Vatican. Apart, however, from its obvious patriotic appeal and the crude force, bred of sincerity, of the music, *Attila* shows no very real advance upon the previous operas, while Solera's handling of the plot, as apart from his fiery expression of popular sentiments, is undistinguished and often unintelligible. After the first performance Verdi wrote to the Countess Maffei: 'The applause and calls were too much for a poor invalid. Perhaps it was not all understood and will be this evening. My friends will have it that this is the best of my operas; the public questions that; I say that it is not inferior to the others; time will decide.'

The composer was evidently still in a low state, but it is clear that the success of *Attila* was not overwhelming at first, but grew with each performance.

During the rehearsals of *Attila* Verdi entered into a contract with Lumley to write an opera for London. The arrangements were made through Francesco Lucca, a Milanese publisher, whose appetite was no doubt whetted by the profits, said to amount to 30,000 Austrian lire, which *Ernani* had brought to Ricordi. Verdi's illness, however, prevented the fulfilment of his contract. In January he was on a diet of boiled milk and water and in March he sent Lucca certificates from two doctors attesting to the danger to the composer's health which the journey to London would involve. In vain Lumley, like Flauto, urged that a change of climate would do him good and, since he could not offer him 'the excitability of Vesuvius,' protested that England had 'un air moins excitant que celui de l'Italie.' In May Lumley was able to record the successful production of *I Lombardi* in London before the queen dowager and other members of the royal family, and again begged Verdi 'to come as soon as possible and try the good remedy I propose.' Verdi replied politely, but firmly, that there was no possibility of a visit to London at the moment, and retired to Recoaro to drink the waters.

Note: Since this book first appeared, a number of Verdi's early operas, which had long seemed past resuscitation, have been performed in Great Britain in response to the revived interest in early nineteenth-century opera. These have included the notable production of *Nabucco* by the Welsh National Opera, and performances at the St Pancras Festival, in Liverpool and elsewhere of, among others, *Giovanna d'Arco, I Masnadieri, La Battaglia di Legnano, Attila, Stiffelio* and *Alzina. Alzina* has also been produced, with some success, at the Rome Opera House.

CHAPTER V

GROWING MATURITY

THE assumption of the role of mouthpiece to the patriotic senti/
ments of his countrymen had brought Verdi a swift success and
enormous popularity. But it may be questioned whether it did
not delay and even permanently injure the development of his
musical genius. It is impossible for a composer with a popular
audience in view to indulge in experiments. He must use the
vulgar tongue, which in music means writing in accepted forms
and without resort to fine shades and subtle ingenuity. The music
of a Mozart, aristocratic, sensitive, *spirituel*, would be far above
the heads of such an audience, and, if *Figaro* can be said to have
any political implications—and they were surely not in the fore/
front of the composer's consideration when he wrote it—those
implications are a warning, carried over from Beaumarchais's
tendentious comedy, to its aristocratic audience, not a summons
to revolt. Verdi who, like the majority of Italians, never rated
Mozart at his true worth, was at this period a democratic com/
poser—indeed, though not in the bad meaning the word has
acquired, a demagogue, a leader of the people. And to lead the
people it is usually necessary to indulge in a little tub/thumping.

It must not, however, be supposed that it is an easy thing to
write popular music. Composers of good 'light' music with
sufficient virtue to outlast the day of its creation are no more
numerous than the masters whom we rightly call 'great' because
they concerned themselves with the noblest themes conceived by
the human mind. Modern aesthetic theory is contemptuous of
the idea that the quality of a work of art has any relation to the
quality of its subject. That is regarded as an outworn Victorian
superstition. But while it is true that a good cause does not neces/
sarily make good art, the conjunction of the good cause and good

46

art does make a great masterpiece. A Madonna may be but a tawdry image, a hymn of freedom mere doggerel, and a symphony no more than a dull piece of musical carpentry. But in the hands of a Raphael, a Milton or a Beethoven, these things are transformed into the highest manifestations of the human mind. We have every right to claim that *Fidelio* is a greater work than, say, *The Mikado*, which has fewer faults and is certainly, in the eyes of the majority, better entertainment. But it is also certain that it is no more 'easy' to write a *Mikado* than a *Fidelio*; else it would have been done a hundred times, since nothing could be more profitable to a composer. So we must beware of underrating Verdi's music simply because it was frankly popular in appeal and was written, if not with the extraordinary facility of a Rossini or a Donizetti, with ease and fluency. At the same time it cannot be claimed that he achieved in these early operas anything that can, by ultimate standards, be called true greatness. He did not aim at that. He was a craftsman turning out work to order within a given time-limit and without an eye to the judgments of posterity. That was the basis upon which every operatic composer, including Gluck and Mozart, had worked, and it was not until the middle of the nineteenth century that the idea of self-dedication to an artistic ideal arose, partly as a result of the doctrines of Richard Wagner and partly owing to the more leisurely methods of composition imposed by the growing complexity of music itself. It is only in our own time—for Wagner, despite the claim made on his behalf that his was 'the music of the future,' was primarily writing for his contemporaries—that composers have deliberately appealed to the verdict of posterity from the adverse judgment of to-day.

Verdi's political preoccupation may well have retarded his musical development, making him complacent with easy successes due to the non-musical elements in his operas. But the experience gained in the composition of so many operas to order in a short space of time must nevertheless have contributed not only to his facility in writing, but to the development of that sense of theatrical effectiveness which was to be the conspicuous quality of his

47

mature work. Journalism, which is what these early operas amount to, is no bad exercise for a young writer, provided he can resist the temptation of the second-rate and the second-hand. Verdi may not always have avoided clichés and meretricious effects; but in the end he rose triumphantly above them, creating an original and individual style, which, for all its frankly popular character, bears the stamp of true greatness.

In his next opera he almost achieved that greatness, and it has been argued that, but for his experience of operatic journalism, he might have risen higher. It is doubtful, however, whether at the age of thirty-four his genius had sufficiently developed for him to do justice to so magnificent a tragedy as Shakespeare's *Macbeth*. But, apart from any question of the composer's own qualifications for the task, the contemporary view of Shakespeare, especially in a foreign country, must be taken into account. Even in England he was regarded rather as a romantic dramatist than as a great poet, and this view of him, accentuated in countries where his actual language, now regarded as his most precious quality, could even less be appreciated at its true worth, inevitably militated against the transformation of one of his greatest tragedies into an opera that would accord entirely with modern taste. Even if we cannot see eye to eye with Verdi in his attitude towards the poet, his enthusiasm for Shakespeare is in itself sufficiently remarkable. It was of long standing and he had, as has been mentioned, already considered the possibility of writing an opera on the far more difficult subject of *King Lear*.

The choice of *Macbeth* was, in the event, accidentally determined by the fact that a good tenor was not available at Florence, where the opera was produced in the spring of 1847, and that the tenor could be given a subsidiary part. The libretto—or rather its versification—was entrusted to Piave; for Verdi himself provided the complaisant poet with a complete version in prose in order to ensure that his ideas about the treatment of the subject should be strictly carried out. He adhered closely to the action of Shakespeare's play, and, although some of the minor characters, including Macduff and Malcolm, are reduced to the merest shadows of their real selves, all the more important features of the tragedy are retained.

In one vital respect Shakespeare's scheme is modified. In the tragedy Macbeth is the protagonist, for all that he is dominated by his wife. We are shown a man of potentially noble character and a great soldier, as well as a man in whom ambition leads to crime, remorse and neurotic weakness. In the opera, owing to the compression of the first scenes, Macbeth's nobility is not defined at all and his hesitations in the face of temptation are barely touched upon. As a character he is reduced to the stature of a conventional melodramatic villain. We shall see, when we come to consider *Simon Boccanegra*, that Verdi was curiously blind to the need for creating a character completely in the round, with all the mingled qualities, good and bad, of a real human being. It was not until he came to write *Otello* that, with Boito's help, he created a genuinely convincing tragic hero comparable with his Shakespearian prototype.

In his opera it is Lady Macbeth who occupies the centre of the stage, and even here Verdi misses the opportunity of her tremendous invocation:

> Come, you spirits
> That tend on mortal thoughts! unsex me here,
> And fill me from the crown to the toe top full
> Of direst cruelty . . .

which, one would have thought, should have inspired him to something more impressive than Lady Macbeth's first aria. If he failed here, he does not seem to have attempted to make any effect of the fight between Macbeth and Macduff. Here was an opportunity, if ever there was, for one of those grand tenor-baritone duets that are among the special glories of his later operas. Yet in this scene the two characters are given no more than one sentence apiece to sing, and the whole thing is over in a few bars. Perhaps Verdi felt that he could not entrust an important move-ment to the second-rate tenor cast for Macduff.

Apart, however, from the initial failure, Lady Macbeth's

character is finely drawn. Her aria, 'La luce langue,' with its tremulous accompaniment, is a sensitive expression of dawning doubt in Lady Macbeth's mind, and although the succeeding *allegro vivo*, in which doubt is dismissed and she exults in her newly acquired royalty, smacks too much of the jumpy conventional *cabaletta*, the melody has a bold vigour that makes it very effective in the theatre. Her *brindisi*, or drinking-song, in which she toasts the guests at the banquet, again looks on paper no more than the trumpery kind of music that so often serves for social occasions in the early operas of Verdi. Yet in the hands of a good singer it can make a tremendous effect. The ludicrous melody then takes on the nervous energy of a factitious gaiety assumed for the occasion. It is the exact expression of a neurotic temperament unsure of itself. And when, after Macbeth has been unmanned by the first appearance of Banquo's ghost, Lady Macbeth repeats her song, lifting her cup to the absent guest, the detached notes and elaborate *fioriture* take on a new meaning and become the faltering accents of a soul shaken to the core. It may be that Verdi did not himself realize the tremendous effect of this piece, that he was not conscious of writing anything but a conventional drinking-song. I can find no reference to it in his letters revealing his intention to create this vivid dramatic effect. But the effect remains and the experience of it must make one chary of dismissing as trivial any passage in Verdi's operas until one has seen them on the stage.

If the *brindisi* was, perhaps, in the nature of a fluke, there can be no question of the genuine mastery of the *gran scena del sonnambulismo*, which must be numbered among the finest individual pieces in all Verdi's operas. This sleep-walking scene is set exactly as Shakespeare wrote it, with the doctor and gentlewoman in attendance, whose hearing of it adds so much to the horror and pathos of its effect upon the audience. Here, at any rate, the composer rises to the level of the poet and gives the full equivalent in music of the spoken word. Verdi has not attempted to relate this scene musically to the previous scene after Duncan's murder— a wonderfully effective duet carried through in undertones—as he would almost certainly have done in his later years. A chromatic *ostinato* in the bass with a quick *staccato* figure above it to depict Lady Macbeth's rubbing of her hands serves to create the mood and define the action. Out of her muttered phrases a fine melody grows until the end is reached with the hurried repetitions of 'andiam' ('to bed') followed by a lovely slow cadenza that with *un fil di voce* touches D flat above the treble stave and thins out to nothing.

If Macbeth is, by comparison with his lady, too flatly drawn, he is not without his moments of greatness. The 'dagger speech' is set to expressive music and the horror-stricken panic of Macbeth, in contrast to his wife's nervous attempt to pretend that nothing is amiss, is admirably portrayed. It cannot be said, however, that any of his airs rise to the same poetic heights as the Shakespearian soliloquies whose place they take, and his best music is contained in the duets with Lady Macbeth and in the scene of the apparitions, which is imaginatively handled. It is impossible to accord the same praise to the Witches' music. Verdi had already shown his incapacity for handling the fantastic or the supernatural in the angel and demon choruses of *Giovanna d' Arco*. The *Macbeth* Witches show no advance in this direction. At their best they use the idiom of liturgical responses in church:

At their worst they are no more than the conventional bogy women of the nineteenth-century theatre. The chorus of murderers lying in wait for Banquo is no better. Its presentation of the 'cat-like tread' provokes a smile at its artlessness. It is a relic, surviving in *Rigoletto* and even in the music of Tom and Sam in *Un ballo in maschera*, of an operatic style that is outworn because it was never, either dramatically or musically, very convincing, and was made for ever ridiculous by Sullivan's parody in *The Pirates of Penzance*. The other choral movements are on a different plane altogether. That which ends the first act after the discovery of Duncan's murder is a splendid piece of music, static in feeling, but wholly admirable as a musical summing-up of the dramatic situation. The banquet-scene chorus is more dynamic and brings the second act to an effective climax. But best of all is the reflective chorus of Scottish exiles at the opening of the last act, which portrays their home-sickness in a most poignant way and shows an enormous advance in subtlety upon the straight-forward Bellinian manner of the famous 'Va pensiero' in *Nabucco*.

Of the minor characters Banquo alone has any individuality. His aria, 'Come dal ciel precipita,' is in the direct line of bass arias that runs through Verdi's operas from Zaccharia's Prayer in *Nabucco* to such things as 'Il lacerato spirito' in *Simon Boccanegra*. Yet it has a pathetic character of its own which admirably fits the situation of the doomed man. Malcolm is but a shadow of his Shakespearian prototype and Macduff's air, a charming enough melody, is a poor substitute for

> What! all my pretty chickens and their dam
> At one fell swoop?

Verdi himself was intensely enthusiastic about *Macbeth* and, as a result, more than usually exacting about the details of its performance. He dictated exactly how Banquo's ghost should appear and was very angry when the singer of the part apparently proposed that a super could take his place in this scene. Verdi pointed out that the ghost must resemble Banquo in face and form, and asked whether operatic artists were not paid to act as well as sing. The ghost, he insists, must appear from underground, clad in ashen veils so fine as to be barely visible, and with his hair matted about his wounds. These ideas, he assured the impresario, came from London, 'where this tragedy has been performed continuously for two hundred years and more.'

When the opera was in rehearsal for performance at the San Carlo Theatre, Naples, in 1848, Verdi appended to a letter to Cammarano about the libretto of *Luisa Miller* the following interesting postscript, which proves how close *Macbeth* was to his heart and how advanced were his ideas of dramatic propriety in opera:

I understand that you are rehearsing *Macbeth*, and as this opera interests me more than any other, I ask you to allow me to say a few words about it. Mme Tadolini is, I believe, to sing Lady Macbeth, and I am astonished that she should have undertaken this part. You know how highly I think of Mme Tadolini, and she knows it too; but in all our interests I think it necessary to remark that she has too great qualities for this part! This may seem an absurdity! Mme Tadolini has a beautiful face and looks good, and I would have Lady Macbeth ugly and wicked. Mme Tadolini sings to perfection, and I would not have Lady Macbeth sing at all. Mme Tadolini has a wonderful voice, clear, liquid and powerful, and Lady Macbeth's voice should be hard, stifled and dark. Mme Tadolini's voice is the voice of an angel, and Lady Macbeth's should be the voice of a devil. Please bring these comments to the notice of the directors, of Maestro Mercadante, who will understand my ideas better than any one, and of Mme Tadolini herself, and do what you think for the best.

Note that the two most important scenes in the opera are the duet between Lady Macbeth and her husband, and the sleep-walking scene. If these fail, the opera falls to the gound, and these scenes must not be sung:

> Here is need of declamation
> In a veiled and gloomy tone;
> Else the whole effect is gone,
> Note, the strings must have their mutes on.

The scene is very dimly lit. In the third act the apparitions should appear (as I saw it done in London) at an opening in the scenery with a thin, ashen veil in front of them. The kings must not be lay-figures, but men of flesh and blood, and the floor over which they pass should have a slant up and down, so that they appear to rise and descend again.

The scene must be very dark, especially when the cauldron vanishes, and only lighted where the kings pass by. The band under the stage should be strengthened for a large theatre like the San Carlo, but mind that there are no trumpets or trombones. The sound must seem to come from afar off in a muffled tone, so the band should consist of bass clarinets, bassoons and contra-bassoons, nothing else.

He was also more than usually careful about the details of the orchestration, and when the opera was given in Paris in 1865, he complained about the substitution of key trumpets for valve trumpets in the fugue describing the battle of Dunsinane, which, he declared, detracted from the effect of dissonance representing the din of battle.

For the Paris production Verdi revised the opera—in itself a proof of the high regard he had for the work, since his revisions are extensive and important. It is in this new version that the opera is given nowadays, and the hearer must beware of attri-buting to the thirty-three-year-old Verdi excellences that are in fact the product of another eighteen years' experience. Some of the finest things in the opera are additions to or radical revisions of the original score and the rest was to a large extent touched up, both in the voice parts and the orchestration. One can only deplore that Verdi did not wholly rewrite the opera, for so he might have added a third Shakespearian masterpiece to *Otello* and *Falstaff*. As it stands, *Macbeth* is too uneven to be placed in that august class.

In Florence, whither Verdi went in order to supervise the pro-duction of *Macbeth* early in 1847, the composer was introduced by Alessandro Manzoni to a cultured society, which included Giuseppe Giusti, a poet who touched up Piave's verses, Gilbert Duprez, a sculptor, and Andrea Maffei, whom Verdi already knew, and who was at work upon an operatic version of Schiller's *Die Räuber*. Duprez showed him the sights of Florence, of which the sculpture of Michelangelo made the greatest impression on the composer. It is easy to imagine the appeal made upon a man of Verdi's virile temperament by the masculine power of those figures hewn in the white heat of excitement from the solid marble. In the theatre Verdi adopted a more than ever dictatorial attitude, and the rehearsals of *Macbeth* did not run too smoothly. But the opera pleased the public and Verdi's belief in its merits was justified. It is worth remarking that he dedicated it to his father-in-law, Antonio Barezzi, as though he considered that this was the first of his works worthy to repay the debt he owed to the man who had made his career as a musician possible. 'For a long time,' he wrote to Barezzi, 'I have had it in mind to dedicate a work to you, who have been to me a father, a benefactor and a friend. . . . Here, then, is *Macbeth*, which I love above all my other works and for that reason deem it most worthy to be presented to you.'

On his return to Milan the projected visit to London was revived. But first a promised opera for Naples had to be postponed by agreement with Flauto. An arrangement was finally reached in December (1846), by which Verdi was to produce a new opera for performance at Her Majesty's Theatre during the following summer. As usual he made stipulations about the cast, which was to include Jenny Lind. After considering Byron's *Corsair* as a possible subject, the composer decided to use Maffei's libretto based upon Schiller's *Die Räuber*, which in its Italian dress became *I Masnadieri*. The first performance took place on 22nd July before an audience which, according to Muzio, included Queen Victoria, the Prince Consort and the Prince of Wales, and, among other celebrities, the Duke of Wellington.

Verdi arrived in London to supervise the production on 7th June, after a journey which he describes in a letter to Clarina Maffei as 'most uncomfortable, but not without its diversions.' He stopped two days in Paris on the way and went to the Opéra, where the singers were 'vile,' the chorus 'second-rate' and the orchestra '(*pace* all our lions) little better than mediocre.' 'What I liked most about Paris,' he continues, 'is the free life one can lead there. Of London I can tell you little because yesterday was Sunday and there was not a soul to be seen. I find all this smoke and smell of coal very disagreeable; it is like living on a steamboat.' In later letters he continues to grumble at the climate, 'which takes away all desire to work,' but expresses his admiration for the city, its fine buildings, clean lodgings and its enormous wealth. 'If only,' he sighs, 'it had the Neapolitan sky, I think it would be unnecessary to long for Paradise!' And again: 'Oh! if I could stay here a couple of years, I could bring away a sack of these *santissime lire*! But it is useless to entertain such lovely ideas, for I could never stand the climate.' He found the Londoners keen theatre-goers and Jenny Lind all the rage.

A week before the first performance he tells Clarina Maffei that he has had two orchestral rehearsals and 'were I in Italy I could give you a considered opinion of the opera, but as it is I understand nothing. Blame the climate!' However on the day after the performance Emmanuele Muzio, already Verdi's pupil and most faithful friend, who travelled to England with him as his secretary, was able to tell Antonio Barezzi that it had been a triumphant success:

From the prelude to the last finale there was nothing but clapping, shouts, recalls and repetitions. The master himself conducted the orchestra, seated on a high stool, stick in hand. When he appeared in the orchestra there was applause lasting a quarter of an hour. . . . The boxes were filled with gentlemen in evening dress and the pit cram full of people as it has never been before. . . . The performance was good, the orchestra marvellous . . . and the singers did well, in spite of much nervousness. . . . The master is well pleased; the management is so delighted that they have made an offer through me for as many years as he likes at the rate of 60,000 francs an opera; and that is the best proof of the success or otherwise of the opera. The press, *The Times*, the *Morning Post*, the *Morning Chronichle* [*sic*], etc., speak well enough of the music and also of the libretto.

The *Morning Post* was, indeed, enthusiastic, as also was the *Illustrated London News*, and Davison of *The Times*, who had criticized Verdi's previous operas severely, saw the composer's point of view. 'It must be remembered,' he said, 'that Verdi writes more for the ensemble than for bringing forward any single personage and hence there are not those opportunities for individual display which are to be found in the works of earlier composers.'

Verdi himself took a more balanced view of his success than

did his enthusiastic young admirer. To Emilia Morosini he wrote: '*I Masnadieri*, without having caused a furore, was well received, and I shall return to London next year to write another opera if Lucca, the publisher, accepts the 10,000 francs I have offered him for the cancellation of my contract.'

I Masnadieri was, in fact, a conventional melodrama with a poor libretto, for all that it was written by Maffei, a poet of greater distinction than the average librettist, and was derived from one of Schiller's dramas. It is hardly surprising that the composer, preoccupied by his first essay in Shakespearian tragedy and prob-ably exhausted by the effort, should have produced only a conven-tional score, or that the opera should have all but disappeared, along with so many of Verdi's early works, from the current repertory.

However, the opera was successful enough to bring from Lumley, hard hit by the defection of the conductor, Costa, who had joined the company at Covent Garden, the tempting offer mentioned by Muzio. Verdi, however, felt that he could not bind himself to the prospect of remaining in London each season and of confining himself to the production of only one opera a year. It appears from the letter quoted above that he was at least willing to give the plan a trial. But Lucca proved a stumb-ling-block. He refused the 10,000 francs for the cancellation of his contract. In the event Lumley withdrew his offer, possibly, as Mr Bonavia suggests, under pressure from Lucca, or possibly because on reflection he considered Verdi's terms too high.

Verdi was furious with the stupidity of the publisher, who got his pound of flesh in the shape of *Il Corsaro*, which was produced at Trieste in October 1848. Hurriedly written without en-thusiasm, the opera, to which alone of Verdi's compositions the term 'hack-work' may justly be applied, failed and quickly disappeared. Lucca would have done better to accept Verdi's offer instead of losing his money and antagonizing the composer for ever into the bargain. There may well have been a touch or irony in the lack of restrictions placed upon Lucca in regard to *Il Corsaro*, with which he was 'at liberty to do what he pleased

both in Italy and in all other countries, whether by the publication of the opera with all possible reductions for all manner of
instruments, or by its production on hire in any theatre.' He had
already determined not to provide 'this most exacting and in-
delicate Lucca' with a work of any importance and he took no
personal interest in its future career.

CHAPTER VI

A HOME AND A DOMESTIC OPERA

AT the end of his letter of 30th July 1847 to Emilia Morosini,
Verdi wrote of his intention to return to Milan 'presto, presto.'
Three days later he was in Paris, where he remained, except for
one brief visit to Italy, for nearly two years. The 'free life' of
the French capital had attracted him on his previous visit, as
we have seen. But there was another attraction. Giuseppina
Strepponi had retired from the stage and settled in Paris as a
teacher of singing. It is impossible to discover precisely when
Verdi's friendship with Giuseppina ripened to love, but it seems
clear that within the next year they were living together, and in
January 1849 Verdi, writing from Rome, gives her address in
the rue de la Victoire, five minutes' walk north of the boulevard
des Italiens, to the directors of the Opéra for the delivery of a letter.

Soon after his arrival in Paris, MM. Duponchel and Roqueplan, the newly appointed directors, approached Verdi with a
proposal to produce *I Lombardi* in a revised French version. As
he comments amusedly, he was confronted with 'two directors,
two poets [Royer and Vaëz] and two music-publishers [Léon
and Marie Escudier]—they always come in couples.' The opera
was renamed *Jérusalem*, and the additions included the long ballet
without which no French opera was considered complete. Great
pains were taken to secure the success of the opera, of which the
production was 'absolutely stupendous,' not, as Verdi records,
'because it is my work, but because it is the first opera given under
the new direction, and they have every reason to let the public
realize that their object is to raise the Opéra out of its decadent
condition.' *Jérusalem*, produced in November 1847, was successful enough, and its success had, from Verdi's point of view,
the disadvantage of bringing him into the public eye and ending
the quiet and simple life he desired to lead.

The year 1848 was a troubled one for Europe. In February Louis-Philippe lost his throne, and the French Republic was re-established. In Germany there were abortive risings, for his participation in which Richard Wagner became an exile. In Vienna, too, there were riots, and the Italian patriots took advantage of the preoccupation of their foreign masters; Milan rose in revolt on 18th March and at Venice a republic was proclaimed a few days later. Verdi, who watched events in Paris with an amused detachment—'I have to buy twenty papers a day (not to read them, please understand) in order to avoid the importunities of the newsboys'—was deeply stirred by events in his own country. He returned to Milan in April, only to find the bright hopes of the patriots destroyed by want of co-ordination, mutual jealousies and general muddle. Sadly disillusioned, he retired to Paris at the end of May.

During this brief visit to Italy Verdi agreed to compose an opera for the Argentina Theatre in Rome, a contract with the San Carlo Theatre at Naples having lapsed owing to the political disturbances. The subject of the opera, *La battaglia di Legnano,* was topical and patriotic—the defeat of Frederick Barbarossa by the Lombard League at Legnano. Cammarano's libretto was, in fact, only concerned nominally with the Emperor Frederick; its real subject was the Italy of 1848. The weak spot in the opera, from the modern point of view, is the intrigue on the usual 'eternal triangle' theme introduced in order to give 'human interest' to a patriotic melodrama. Verdi's music is more concerned with broad dramatic strokes than with the delineation of character, and the patriotic outbursts glow with the fervour of genuine emotion. As a whole the opera shows an advance upon anything Verdi had done in the past both in its breadth of outline and its elaboration of orchestral and choral writing. It was produced in January 1849 amid scenes of tremendous enthusiasm, and the last act had to be repeated. After a brief career, which included performances at Florence and Ancona—where, Verdi characteristically complained, 'the value of the royalties was enormously reduced by payment in paper money'—the opera was suppressed when the Austrian censorship was re-established after the abortive revolutions had collapsed. It was revived in 1861 at Milan under the title of *L' assedio di Haarlem* with the emperor reduced to the rank of a Spanish duke and the Italian patriots turned into Dutchmen. In this guise it failed to repeat its success, the occasion of which had passed by.

During the composition of *La battaglia di Legnano* Verdi continued to take an active part in Italian politics. He added his signature to a manifesto drawn up by Guerrieri, a member of the provisional Government of Lombardy, and other leading Italians in Paris, appealing to the French Government to intervene on behalf of a nascent sister-republic. Verdi was not sure in his own mind that intervention by a foreign Government in the affairs of another people was a wise course. To Clarina Maffei, who asked for news of French reactions to the Italian situation, he replied that those who were not actively opposed to Italian unity were indifferent. He thought armed intervention unlikely and Franco-British diplomatic action dangerous, 'ignominious for France and disastrous to ourselves.' For the probability was that, while Austria might under pressure from France yield Lombardy, she would retain Venice. Such a prospect, added to the possibility that the Lombardy plain would be sacked and pillaged before the evacuation, afforded no pleasure to Verdi. He saw little cause for hope from French or British support. There was more to be hoped for from Austria herself—from an Austria disrupted and crumbling. Then Italy might seize her opportunity and secure her freedom. As to France herself, she was approaching an abyss.

Although Verdi begged his correspondent to attach no importance to his forecast, 'for I understand nothing of politics,' it proved singularly accurate in the event. In October the French Government, replying to an interpellation in the Assembly, professed itself unable and unwilling to make a pronouncement on Italian unity. 'What a fine republic!' exclaimed Verdi. In 1859, as Verdi foretold, Austria evacuated Lombardy, but, with French approval, held the Venetian province, and it was only when, as the result of her defeat by Germany in 1866, her grip upon Italy relaxed, that a united kingdom was possible, and then only at the sacrifice to France of Savoy and the Maritime Alps. In the meantime the idealists squabbled among themselves and the Austrian rule was re-established, though with less security than before.

Besides *La battaglia di Legnano*, Verdi made, in response to a request from Mazzini, another musical contribution to the cause, a setting of a poem by Mameli, 'Suona la tromba.' The clarion call to action was, however, sounded too late and Verdi's song never attained the popularity of its companion piece by Novaro, 'Fratelli d' Italia,' which had appeared some months earlier, when hopes were still high.

During his two months' visit to Milan in the spring of 1848 Verdi took a step that was of great importance for his future. He acquired a small property near Busseto, called Villa Sant' Agata, making himself responsible for a mortgage of 12,000 francs due from the previous owner to a money-lender at Soragna. The property consisted of a house, in which he installed his father and mother as caretakers for the time being, farm-lands and vineyards with a river running through them. In this unpretentious retreat in an unprepossessing landscape Verdi found the quiet he longed for during the remainder of his long life. For the time being, however, he remained in Paris, whence he sent instructions about the repairs and decoration of his house, and to Ricordi about payments to be made to his father on account of expenses. In acknowledging one of these payments Carlo Verdi exclaims: 'Heaven made me a father, the adventurous and happy father of a son who does honour to me and to his country.' We know very little about Verdi's relations with his family, and this is one of the glimpses we have of their simple affection and pride.

During 1849 Verdi was occupied with the composition of *Luisa Miller*, which was produced at Naples at the end of the year. The libretto is based upon Schiller's play, *Kabale und Liebe*, and is in an entirely new vein, closer to the *bourgeois* themes of German romantic opera, as typified in *Der Freischütz*, than to the aristocratic political melodramas with which Verdi had hitherto concerned himself. The action takes place in a Tyrolese village and its heroine is the daughter of a retired soldier. Such a theme calls obviously for a less grandiose treatment than the courts and council chambers of kings and the patriotic struggles of whole nations. The result is a more intimate style of music that fore-shadows for the first time the tenderness and pathos of *La Traviata*.

Luisa Miller is the subject of an interesting series of letters between Verdi and his librettist, Cammarano, in the course of which the composer suggests that the character of the villainous Wurm should be given a certain touch of comedy, which would add to the terrible effect of his scene with Luisa in Act II. Already Verdi was breaking away from the conventional operatic charac-terization and attempting to substitute for mere types of good or evil human beings of flesh and blood. It may be that a modern audience may find Wurm, like some even of Verdi's later villains, comic in a way that he did not intend, but here is the first step towards the creation of an individual character that was to be finally achieved, with the help of Shakespeare and Boito, in Iago.

In one of his letters to Verdi Cammarano makes some generaliza-tions about the relations of drama to music in opera which show that other minds than Wagner's were working in the direction of a more complete unification of these elements:

Were I not afraid of being written down as Utopian, I would venture to say that to reach the highest possible perfection in opera one single mind ought to be responsible for both words and music. From this concept it clearly follows, I think, that where two authors are concerned, their collaboration must be close and friendly. Poetry must be neither the slave of music nor its tyrant.

Since the context makes it clear that it is in no way a protest against any dictation from Verdi, who always treated Cammarano with respect, this declaration is remarkable, coming from a professional librettist who is too often regarded as a mere hack.

As usual Verdi hated the idea of going to Naples, where he had been annoyed by the gossip that flew about during his previous visit, not to mention the importunities of well-meaning enthu-siasts. At first he refused categorically to attend the production of

Luisa Miller, telling the impresario that he was much mistaken if he imagined that his own presence would contribute to the success of the opera. He added firmly that, in spite of his long sojourn in Paris ('where one is supposed to acquire a certain polish') he was more of a 'bear' than ever, and declined to pay court to the wealthy or curry favour with journalists. However, in the end he went, though his visit had to be postponed owing to an outbreak of cholera which necessitated the imposition of quarantine regulations. True to his word, he snubbed an impertinent critic, who had prepared alternative notices of the opera with a view to extracting a bribe for the publication of the more favourable: 'Print what you please!'[1]

Then there was the tiresome Capecelatro, a musical amateur, who, in addition to the other vices of the species, was said to be possessed of the Evil Eye. Verdi's friends were so concerned that he should not be approached by this menacing bore that they formed a bodyguard to keep watch over him. Their precautions were successful until the interval before the last act, when the dreadful bearer of ill-omen managed to greet the composer. It was too late, however, to mar the success of the opera, which became a favourite in Italy although it has never won much popularity elsewhere. Such comedies must have been tiresome to the chief actor in them, and Verdi hurried back to Busseto, whence he wrote to de Sanctis at the end of the month:

I hear from Naples that there are schemes afoot to make a failure of

---

[1] That Verdi was not always lacking in cordiality towards journalists is shown by the following account of an interview given to a French journalist at Milan in 1845:

'I found him anything but the cold and reserved person he had been represented to be, absorbed in his art and taking no personal interest in anything else. He received me with the utmost friendliness and with an ease and grace truly French.

'In person Verdi is extremely handsome, with chestnut hair and blue eyes that have an expression at once soft and vivacious. When he speaks his face lights up and an incessant mobility of expression reflects the variety of his moods. . . . His tastes are the most simple in the world.'

Luisa Miller and that one of the artists at the Opera is for political reasons a party to the plot. I am not inclined to believe this, but it may be true; however it is of no importance. What fools ! ! ! Do they imagine that their dirty intrigues can prevent an opera, if it is good, going the round of the musical world?

Verdi himself seems to have had no very high opinion of the work, for only two years later he wrote to Escudier to the effect that *Ernani* and *Luisa Miller* had better be left to sleep, though he adds: 'Do not attach any importance to this remark, for once they are written, I allow my operas to take the road as God or the impresarios will.' Subsequent critics, however, have seen in *Luisa Miller* a turning-point in Verdi's musical development, the beginning of his 'second period,' which, because this opera is quite unknown outside Italy, is generally supposed to begin with *Rigoletto*. Verdi was already considering Victor Hugo's *Le Roi s'amuse* (from which *Rigoletto* is adapted) as a possible subject for his next opera while he was still engaged upon *Luisa Miller*. The first reference to the project is contained in a letter to Flauto, in which Verdi suggests that Cammarano should have a look at Hugo's play, 'a beautiful drama with astonishing situations,' with a view to future use. Verdi was rarely off with the old opera before he was on with the new.

In the meantime, however, his thoughts returned to *King Lear*, and in February 1850 he sent Cammarano a complete synopsis of the proposed adaptation, prefaced with the following comments:

King Lear appears at first sight so vast and complicated that it seems impossible to make an opera out of it. However, on closer examination, though the difficulties are no doubt great, they are not insuperable. You understand that there is no need to turn *King Lear* into a drama in the hitherto accepted form; it should be treated in an entirely new and spacious manner, without regard for the conventions. The parts can be reduced to five principals: Lear, Cordelia, the Fool, Edmund and Edgar; two secondary feminine roles—Regan and Goneril (though the latter may have to be a second *prima donna*); two basses (as in *Luisa*)— Kent and Gloucester; and the rest subsidiary parts.

Do you think the pretext upon which Cordelia is disinherited too childish for the present day? Some scenes must come out altogether, for instance the blinding of Gloucester. . . . The scenes can be reduced to eight or nine, and you may observe that in *Lombardi* there were eleven, which presented no difficulty in production.

There was obviously no danger—and compatriots of the poet might well shudder at the thought—that Verdi would have turned the most sublime of Shakespeare's tragedies into a conventional melodrama. The very fact that a project so dear to him and to which he was to return again and again, was in the end abandoned, is proof of his strong artistic conscience. He must have felt at heart that he was not equal to the task he had set himself, and, when he had reached the point in his development as a composer at which, possibly with the help of Boito, the thing might have been feasible, other subjects were in the forefront of his mind and the first impulse to creation had lost its force. It is interesting to note that in reply to a suggestion made at this time by Giulio Carcano, a poet and painter who had translated Shakespeare into Italian, that he should set *Hamlet* to music, Verdi wrote that, if *King Lear* is difficult, *Hamlet* is far more so.

It is a steep descent from these lofty heights to *Stiffelio*, which was the next opera actually to be completed. It was originally intended for production at Naples, but Verdi's dissatisfaction with the San Carlo authorities led him to transfer it to Trieste, where it was performed in the autumn of 1850. There were difficulties with the censorship over a scene in the last act, wherein the hero, a German pastor (tenor), preaches in church. In spite of the resulting omissions, the opera achieved a certain measure of success and a contemporary critic, quoted by Mr Toye, wrote admiringly of its 'sweet and tender melodies' and added that it achieved 'the most moving dramatic effects without having recourse to bands on the stage, choruses or superhuman demands upon vocal chords or lungs.' *Stiffelio* soon disappeared from the repertory, although it was revived at Rimini seven years later with a new libretto by the patient Piave under the title of *Aroldo*. In recent years it has again been performed.

CHAPTER VII

THREE MASTERPIECES

WHENEVER *Rigoletto* is performed, someone is sure to talk of 'early Verdi.' Actually it is the seventeenth of his twenty-eight operas and the first fruit of his maturity as a composer. With it Verdi transformed himself at one stroke from a popular composer of Italian operas into an artist whose genius overleapt the frontiers of nationality. Popular he remained, and *Rigoletto* was the foundation of his popularity outside Italy. Indeed its popularity has served to obscure the fact that it is the first complete example of a style whose development is the basis of Verdi's claim to be a great innovator as well as a great melodist. It was not only for august Shakespearian tragedy that he reserved 'an entirely new and spacious style without regard for the conventions.' The same principle was applied to Hugo's melodrama, difficult though it is for us, more than eighty years later, fully to appreciate the originality of his procedure which has now in its turn become 'conventional.'

Rigoletto was nearly strangled at birth. The Austrian censorship, which saw profanity in a parson's sermon on the stage, scented blasphemy in 'La Maledizione' ('The Curse') which was the original title proposed for the work. And political susceptibilities were even more seriously offended by the presentation of a reigning sovereign as a good-for-nothing libertine whose court jester dares to upbraid him for seducing his daughter. Those who were responsible for the safety of royalty so soon after the dangerous convulsions of 1848 naturally frowned upon anything that set the ruling caste in a bad light, and even an unsuccessful attempt at assassination was considered highly undesirable as putting ideas into hotheads. In addition objection was raised to Gilda's body being brought on in a sack and to the fact that the protagonist was a hunchback—though what these purely artistic questions had to do with the censorship it is difficult to see. The directors of the Fenice Theatre in Venice consequently received a communication from the Austrian military governor, who expressed his surprise that 'the poet Piave and the celebrated Maestro Verdi should have chosen no better field for their talents than the revolting immorality and obscene triviality of the libretto entitled *La Maledizione.*' An absolute ban was put upon its performance, with the added request that no more should be heard of the matter.

Faced with this veto, the management of the Fenice suggested that Verdi should write another opera. This Verdi refused absolutely to consider. Assured by Piave that the libretto had been approved, he had already composed a great part of the music and was working very hard to complete it by the agreed date. As a gesture of goodwill, however, he would agree to substitute *Stiffelio*, which would be a novelty in Venice, and would write a new last act to satisfy the objections raised against the original one.

In spite, however, of the peremptory tone of the governor's veto, discussions went on behind the scenes to discover some accommodation with the authorities. Verdi had a friend at court in Martello, the very secretary who had signed the governor's decree, a musical amateur who regretted having to deprive him-self and the world of a new opera by Verdi. He arranged a meeting with Piave, who was very willing to compromise, even to the point of reducing his libretto to nonsense. Verdi charac-teristically would take no part in these negotiations, and when the proposed modifications were submitted to him, his criticisms were scathing. He was willing to substitute a duke or prince for the French king of Hugo's play, adding: 'If the names are to be altered, the locality must be altered too.' But when it came to turning the libertine Francis I into a blameless nonentity, he put his foot down. The anger of the courtiers against Triboletto (the original form in which Rigoletto's name appears), he argued, would not make sense. The old man's [i.e. Monterone in the opera] curse, so terrible and sublime in the original, would become ridiculous because the motive for his curse has no importance, and because he no longer has any reason for speaking so hotly to the king. Without this curse what range, what meaning can the drama have? The duke is a nonentity: the duke must be a complete libertine; otherwise there is no justification for Triboletto's anxiety for his daughter. . . . And how comes the duke to be at the tavern without an invitation or appointment?

The objection to Gilda's body being sewn in a sack and to Rigoletto's deformity moved Verdi to almost speechless bewilderment. What had the sack to do with the police? Were they afraid of the effect? And why should not Rigoletto be a hunchback? The idea of a deformed and ridiculous jester moved by a great passion and a noble love seemed to Verdi a splendid theme and was in fact the very thing that attracted him in *Le Roi s'amuse*. He would not dogmatize about the effect before the event, but how could the police know any better than he?

Verdi's obstinacy in the end won the day. King Francis became an anonymous Duke of Mantua and had to surrender the latchkey to Gilda's room — another cause of offence. But the essentials remained and *Rigoletto* has, in spite of all the difficulties through which it passed, the most satisfactory of all the librettos Verdi set before his collaboration with Boito. The action is straightforward and intelligible, and though Rigoletto's transformation from the heartlessly brutal jester of the first scene into the loving father of the second is rather too sudden to be wholly convincing, the characters are consistently drawn and their motives are always intelligible. Well might Piave cry: 'Alleluia' and 'Te Deum laudamus' when he was able to announce to Verdi that 'our *Rigoletto* has come through safe and sound, with no bones broken or amputations.'

It may seem odd that *Rigoletto*, to many the very archetype of old-fashioned opera, could possibly be regarded as an example of originality in design. The contemporary revolution in German opera associated with the name of Wagner—*Lohengrin* was first performed the year before *Rigoletto*—has been so voluminously discussed that musical historians have been inclined to overlook the less radical but hardly less remarkable change wrought by

Verdi in Italian operatic conventions. The conservative critics of his day, men like Chorley and Davison—admirers of Bellini's gentle melancholy and the sparkling polish of Rossini—hardly saw past the new vigour of Verdi's melody, which they wrote down as crude vulgarity. They missed the fundamental symptoms of his originality as an operatic composer; and his admirers missed it no less in their enthusiasm for the obvious attractions of that same melodic vigour.

Verdi himself was quite conscious of what he was doing—there is no question here of an intuitive genius working better than it knew—and gave the clue to the direction in which his mind was working. In reply to a request from the husband of Teresa Borsi, the *prima donna* who sang Gilda in Rome, that she should be provided with a new aria in which to show off her powers as a singer to advantage, he wrote:

If you were convinced my talent is so limited that I can do no better than I have done in *Rigoletto*, you would not have asked for an aria for this opera. Wretched talent! you may say. I agree; but there it is. If *Rigoletto* can stand on its feet as it is, a new number would be superfluous. And where is it to be placed? Verses and notes can be written, but they would make no effect without the right time and place. . . . As to the *cavatina* in the first act ['Caro nome'], I do not understand where its 'agility' comes in. Perhaps you have not understood the tempo, which should be an *allegretto molto lento*. At a moderate pace and sung throughout quietly (*sotto voce*), it should not be difficult. But to revert to our first question, let me add that my idea was that *Rigoletto* should be one long series of duets without airs and without finales, because that is how I felt it. If any one retorts: 'But one might do this or that or the other' and so on, I reply: 'That may be all very well, but I did not know how to make a better job of it.'

It is clear that Verdi was preoccupied with problems of operatic construction which had not troubled the heads of men like Donizetti and Rossini, who had been content to pour their material into the accepted moulds. It resulted that from *Rigoletto* onwards—since we may fairly take *Rigoletto* as the first completely successful product of this preoccupation with form—Verdi's operas have a greater musical consistency and a greater individual character than any that had preceded them in Italy. It could hardly be claimed that *Norma* or *Lucia di Lammermoor* or even *Il barbiere di Siviglia* have a musical character of their own which differentiates them respectively from *I Puritani, Lucrezia Borgia* and *Cenerentola*. The first-named operas may be considered superior or inferior as works of art to the others, according to individual judgment, but it is impossible to say that any one of these pairs of operas has an individual style which would make it possible to be sure that a movement from one of them could not, on purely musical grounds, belong to the other. But it is possible to say that there is no more excuse for confusing an excerpt from *Rigoletto* with one from the more heroic *Il Trovatore* than there would be for mistaking a passage from Mozart's G minor Symphony for one out of the 'Jupiter.' Such qualities as are common to Verdi's different operas are no more than the idiosyncrasies of manner that mark as his own the music of any composer of genuine talent, not to say genius, throughout his career. This individual ap-proach to each new subject must be borne in mind when we come to consider the magnificent series of operas, all of them from the box-office point of view at least partial failures, which come between *La Traviata* and *Aida*.

The existence of 'Pari siamo,' 'La donna è mobile,' and 'Caro nome' itself, which we have become accustomed to hearing as concert excerpts, may seem to contradict Verdi's argument. Yet if these pieces are examined with a fresh eye, instead of being taken for granted as the familiar war-horses of operatic singers, it will be seen that, so far from being conven-tional arias holding up the action in order to display the singers' virtuosity, they are rooted in the very substance of the dramatic action. The effect of 'La donna è mobile' is made not by its rather facile melodic charm, but by its context. The contrast of its airy gaiety with the sombre setting of Sparafucile's tavern produces a powerful sense of tragic irony that is carried to the extreme limit when Rigoletto hears the careless strain as he drags away the supposed body of the duke. No painter has ever placed a 'high light' with a greater assurance and accuracy of touch than Verdi commands here.

At the very rise of the curtain, after the brief but highly effective prelude, there is a striking instance of the new malleability which Verdi was introducing into the rigid conventions of opera. The duke's 'Questa o quella' is not a set aria, but the end of a conversation and the beginning of a ballet. In the short dialogue with the Contessa di Ceprano that follows it one may see a reflection—inferior to 'Là ci darem' it must be confessed—of the seductive manner of Mozart's Don Giovanni. An unusual influence this, for Verdi seems to have had no great affection for Mozart's music, though he was not blind to his greatness. It is, perhaps, unfortunate that he was unable to learn more from Mozart's example, for the music of the court ball, played behind the scene by a military band, is not only extremely banal but is lacking in precisely that aristocratic elegance of which Mozart was the master. Verdi never managed in such scenes as this—though the ball in *Un ballo in maschera* shows a great advance upon *Rigoletto*—to rise above the homely standards of a provincial 'hop.'

There are other weak patches in *Rigoletto*. The duet for Gilda and the duke, which begins so tenderly, peters out in a conventional *vivacissimo* as they say farewell. Even poorer is the duke's air, 'Parmi veder le lagrime,' which opens Act II, perhaps because here Verdi has lapsed for once into the old style of aria. The recitative which introduces it is, on the other hand, an example of the composer's new-found mastery in wedding words and music, of which the finest in this opera is the scene for Rigoletto and Sparafucile in Act I. Here as elsewhere in the recitatives there is a perfect fusion of musical and dramatic ideas expressed in a harmonically supple and characteristic *arioso*. The Sparafucile scene must be bracketed with the familiar quartet in the third act as one of the most imaginative strokes in the opera. They are, besides, of a technical originality that makes them models of their kind.

Another facet of this new expressiveness is evident in the duets for Rigoletto and Gilda. That in the second act is full of an exquisite tenderness that gushes up in lovely melody at Gilda's inquiry about her mother:

and reaches a climax in Rigoletto's charge to the duenna: 'Ah! veglia, o donna':

How finely dramatic is the breaking-off of this exquisite theme by the sound of the duke's footsteps outside! The duet in the second act is no less admirable from its piteous opening with Gilda's confession to the pathos of Rigoletto's 'Solo per me l'infamia.' And, although the final section ('Si vendetta'), after Monterone's brief and somewhat arbitrary appearance, is not musically on the same high level, its effect when capably sung is so exciting that its actual quality is easily overlooked. The feeling of excitement is achieved not only by the vigorous impulse of the rhythm, but by a harmonic device which recurs again and again in Verdi's duets for soprano (or tenor) and baritone. Owing to the difference in compass of the two voices, it is necessary to transpose the melody stated by the one voice, if it is to be trans-ferred note for note to the other and still lie within the most effective part of that voice. But this harmonic step-up, usually of a third or a fourth, necessitated by practical considerations, produces a most dramatic effect, especially when the change is made without modulation. Examples of this very simple device are innumerable and it will suffice to mention the Radamès-Amneris duet (tenor and mezzo-soprano) in the last act of *Aida*.

It is of such elementary processes as these that Verdi's music for the most part consists, and it is just because the processes are elementary, compared (say) with the complex symphonic structure of a Wagnerian score, that the quality of his genius is apt to be overlooked. There is no need at this time of day to adjudicate upon the relative order of merit in which Wagner and Verdi should be placed. Indeed there is no basis for such a judgment, since there is no real common denominator in their work. Verdi was a true Latin in the clarity, simplicity and directness of his methods, Wagner as truly Teutonic in his elaboration of texture and his philosophical ideas. Their faults reflect this dissimilarity as clearly. Verdi lapsed into banality out of a naïve trust in his peasant intuition and in the dramatic and musical conventions of his time; Wagner out of a sensual delight in richness of sound for its own sake and a natural verbosity which sometimes led him into an empty magniloquence. And, for all that on the face of it Wagner appears to be the more original musician and the more profound thinker of the two, it is a mistake to dismiss as shallow and uninventive the mind that created the third act of *Rigoletto*.

This last act as a whole is, in many respects, the most perfect Verdi wrote. There are obviously 'greater' things—the last act of *Otello*, where a finer tragic situation is handled with consummate mastery, and that Nile scene in *Aida* which never fails to ravish the senses with its poetic evocation of all the scents and sounds of a moonlit night—but the perfection of the musical structure of this act must be evident to any one who does not go to the opera merely to hear how the tenor will sing 'La donna è mobile,' and to drown with 'bis, bis' the lovely passage that joins it to the succeeding dialogue. Not less important is the wonderful creation of atmosphere. Herein lies the true originality of the act.

Rossini had, it is true, depicted in *William Tell* a storm and the quiet breaking of dawn with great mastery, and Verdi owes something to his example, even as Rossini was indebted to Beethoven's 'Pastoral' Symphony for certain details of procedure in the art of landscape-painting in music. But to state a precedent is not to diminish the stature of the artist who, following it, makes the old procedure his own by right of imagination. There is a river in Macedon, and there is moreover also a river at Monmouth; there is a flash of lightning in *William Tell* and a flash of lightning in *Rigoletto*, and there are piccolos in both.

Let it suffice for us, then, that in the last act of *Rigoletto* the sordid rendezvous and the dark stormy night are delineated with unmistakable sureness in music that is all the more powerful for its economy of means. By the creation of this atmosphere, whose gloom is deepened by the contrast of the duke's frivolous love-making, a sense of impending doom is established that lifts the scene out of its squalid setting on to a plane of poetic tragedy. Although we are taken to the very brink of the *verismo* which was a generation later to reduce Italian opera to the level of a sixpenny shocker, there is no falling into the abyss.

Incidentally Verdi has never, I think, been given full credit for his originality in handling the storm music. For although in certain details, especially in the way the ominous quiet before the bursting of the storm is depicted, he follows the examples of Beethoven's 'Pastoral' Symphony and Rossini's *William Tell* overture, Verdi's procedure is strikingly novel, especially in his use of a wordless chorus 'off' to suggest the moaning of the wind. It is usual to regard Debussy and Delius as the inventors of this kind of choral colour-effect. But here was Verdi instinctively hitting upon this very device as the best means of producing the effect he wanted.

The minor characters in *Rigoletto* are drawn with unusual care, if we except the somewhat colourless courtiers—and even among them the Countess of Ceprano in her few sentences comes vividly to life. Sparafucile is a magnificent creation, a sort of tragic Pistol not without a touch of comedy in his ruffianly swagger.

Monterone, though dramatically reduced to a couple of brief appearances, is given music of such impressiveness that he creates an effect out of all proportion to the amount he has to sing. And Maddalena, the mezzo-soprano, takes her place as a distinct personality alongside the more fully developed characters of Gilda, Rigoletto and Sparafucile. Like Antonio in the first finale of *Figaro*, she has a place only in the ensemble, but she is none the less skilfully drawn. There was difficulty in finding a singer to take the part at the first performance, because it contains no aria in which to win a personal success with the audience. The name of Mme Casaloni, who undertook it, deserves to be recorded *honoris causa*.

Verdi's troubles with the censorship did not end with the Venetian production of *Rigoletto*. When the opera was given in Rome during the autumn of the same year (1851), it was so mutilated that the composer wrote indignantly to his friend Luccardi, the sculptor:

These impresarios do not yet grasp the fact that if operas cannot be given integrally according to the composer's conception, it is better not to give them at all. They do not see that the transposition of an air, a scene and so forth always accounts for the failure of an opera. . . . What would you say if they put a black mask on the nose of one of your beautiful statues?

At one time it was customary, at least at Covent Garden, to omit the extremely fine duet for Gilda and Rigoletto at the end of the opera—whether because the *prime donne* thought it beneath their dignity to sing in a sack, or because the Rigolettos found dragging their too, too solid flesh across the stage too much of a strain, one cannot tell. It was Maria Ivogün, who did not suffer either from such vanity or from the physical disadvantage, who first reintroduced the London public to this number in 1924,[1] besides proving that 'Caro nome,' if simply sung, is not an exhibition of virtuosity but a very subtle and tender exposition of Gilda's character.

[1] Bernard Shaw mentions a performance of it in the nineties.

Already in April 1851 Verdi was in correspondence with Cammarano about his next project:

I have received your scenario, and you, who are a man of talent and character above the ordinary, will not take it ill if I, meanest of wretches, take the liberty of saying that if this subject cannot be handled in our opera with all the novelty and bizarrerie of the Spanish play [Gutiérrez's *El Trovador*] we had better give it up.

After a detailed criticism of Cammarano's scheme and a full sketch of his own ideas, he reverts to his misgivings about the suitability of the subject and suggests the substitution of something 'simple, pathetic and, as it were, ready-made.' Verdi had good cause to be doubtful about the possibility of transforming Gutiérrez's drama into a satisfactory opera. *El Trovador* is a vast historical melodrama in which, against the background of one of the innumerable Spanish civil wars, a complex series of plots and sub-plots is enacted. To reduce this mass of material to the limits manageable in opera meant leaving out the political back-ground, which alone makes the actions of the main characters intelligible, and compressing what remained into a series of violently dramatic scenes, in which coincidence is more evident than causation.

Aristotle, it will be remembered, had a great deal to say about probabilities and possibilities in tragedy and strongly recom-mended the dramatist to choose possible probabilities rather than possible improbabilities. He would no doubt have condemned the libretto of *Il Trovatore* as being too full of the latter. It is necessary to emphasize this, because there is a common notion that the action of this opera belongs to the category of improbable and inexplicable impossibilities. There is nothing inherently impossible in the story and the difficulty audiences find in under-standing it is due simply to the over-compression of an exceed-ingly complicated plot. Verdi and Cammarano, knowing the whole original drama, were no doubt quite clear in their own minds what was happening, and did not realize that for others not so informed the summing-up in a couple of sentences of an important motive or turning-point in the drama is insufficient to establish a proper connection between cause and effect. It was an error into which Verdi fell time and again—in *Simon Boccanegra* and in *La forza del destino*, to name two masterpieces which have been crippled by it. It is the one blind spot in Verdi's eye for theatrical effect.

Il Trovatore suffers from the added disadvantage that, owing to its popularity, the absurdities of its plot became an easy butt for satirists. The subject of the changeling child provided an easy mark for the humours of Gilbert and Sullivan in *H.M.S. Pinafore* and *The Gondoliers*. Yet it was *Il Trovatore* that moved Alfred Noyes to write one of his best poems, even as *Rigoletto* had caused Rossini to exclaim: 'In this music I at last recognize Verdi's genius.'

Even Chorley, who thought it 'a dismal opera,' admitted that in *Il Trovatore* Verdi's 'best qualities are combined and indica- tions scattered throughout earlier productions present themselves in the form of their most complete fulfilment.' He is even en- thusiastic about the 'Miserere,' 'though the leading phrase might never have been found, had there not been an apparition scene in *Semiramide* in which Signor Rossini had shown how terror might be told in rhythm,' while di Luna's 'Il balen' moves him to say that never before had Verdi been so happy in tenderness, in beauty, in melody. It is all the more strange that, though Chorley calls attention to the Spanish gipsy colour suggested in the chorus that opens Act II 'before the Italian anvils begin,' he finds Azucena's music monotonous, inexpressive and, again, dismal. His only qualification of this extraordinary judgment is a word of praise for her *cantabile* in the last scene ('Ai nostri monti'), which as sung by Pauline Viardot was 'among the most beautiful and pathetic things heard on any stage.'

Yet it is the character of Azucena that gives *Il Trovature* its real distinction. The heroic Manrico was to be surpassed in Radamès and Othello; the no less heroic Leonora in her later namesake in *La forza del destino*. The Conte di Luna is the most colourless of Verdi's important baritone parts; he is neither wholly a villain like Macbeth or Iago, nor a 'sympathetic' victim of misfortune like Rigoletto or Amonasro, but something of both, and the inconsistency nullifies his character. But Azucena is a unique creation. It was her character that attracted Verdi to *El Trovador*, and in a letter to Cammarano already quoted he points out the importance of preserving 'the force and originality of this strange and novel character,' torn between love of mother and love of son. During the composition of the opera Luigia Verdi died, and it is not unreasonable to see in the passionate tenderness of the duets for Azucena and Manrico an expression of Verdi's love for his mother.

Before the libretto was finished Cammarano fell ill and died. Cesare de Sanctis, one of Verdi's Neapolitan friends, arranged for the book to be completed by Leone Emmanuele Bardare, a young friend of Cammarano's, who was 'beside himself with joy' at the prospect of working for Verdi. De Sanctis also called Verdi's attention to the desperate circumstances in which Cammarano's widow and family found themselves—an appeal which met with an immediate response from Verdi, who was as generous to any one in misfortune as he was 'close' in his dealings with publishers and operatic impresarios. He sent the widow the full fee that had been agreed upon with an additional 100 ducats.

In spite of the delays caused by Cammarano's death and the distraction of his own bereavement, followed, as it was, by the serious illness of his father, the composition of *Il Trovatore* was completed by December 1852. A month later Verdi was able to write to Clarina Maffei from Rome, where the opera was produced on 19th January 1853, announcing yet another popular success. 'Some people,' he added despondently, 'say the opera is too sad and there are too many deaths. But in life all is death!'

Verdi was worn out with work and worry. Yet his urge to create did not leave him for a moment. Already on 1st January he had written to de Sanctis, expressing his desire for 'subjects that are *new, grand, beautiful, varied, bold* . . . and bold to the extreme limit, *novel in form* and at the same time suitable for music.' From this same letter it appears that he had already in hand a project that was bold enough, though its boldness was of a very different nature from that of *Il Trovatore* with its grand gestures and big sweeping melodies:

> For Venice [he writes] I am setting *La Dame aux camélias*, which I shall probably call *La Traviata*. It is a contemporary subject. Another might have avoided it on account of the costumes, the period and a thousand other foolish scruples, but I am delighted with the idea. Every one groaned when I proposed putting a hunchback on the stage. Well, I enjoyed writing *Rigoletto*.

It is important to remember that *La Traviata*, which has for a twentieth-century audience all the charm of a period piece, was designed as a picture of contemporary life. This was boldness and novelty indeed! For a *prima donna* to appear on the stage in the same style of dress that she might wear outside the theatre was quite unheard of. In consequence the opera was at first produced in the settings and costumes of around the year 1700, regardless of their absurdity in a piece whose whole action is conditioned by the social morality of the eighteen-fifties. And then there was the character of Violetta herself. No longer is the heroine's frailty a matter of innocence, nor are her misfortunes due to villainy or a cruel fate. She is, shocking to relate, a courtesan. And, by way of adding absurdity to scandal, she dies of consumption in the last act. Chorley who, to his credit, did not boggle at the 'immorality,' could not stomach the phthisis: 'It might have been seen that, whatever was the temptation of the spoken drama, *La Dame aux camélias* was a story untenable for music. Consumption for one who is to sing! A ballet with a lame *Sylphide* would be as rational.'

It is necessary to recount these outworn objections because, unless their existence is realized, we cannot appreciate to the full the extent of Verdi's courage in composing this work. He was flouting all the conventions, and only a man of genius can afford to do that.

The public's first reaction to *La Traviata*, which was produced at the Fenice Theatre, Venice, in March 1853, seemed to show that even Verdi could not afford to go so far. He announced the initial failure laconically to Emmanuele Muzio: '*La Traviata*, last night, was a fiasco. Is the fault mine or the singers? . . . Time will show.' And to Ricordi: 'I am sorry to give you bad news, but I cannot hide the truth. *La Traviata* has been a failure. Let us not inquire into the causes. That is the fact. Good-bye, good-bye.'

The first act, which Chorley grudgingly praised as 'the solitary act of gay music from the composer's pen,' seems to have pleased the public. But 'Di Provenza il mar,' badly sung, started a hostile demonstration, which developed into loud ridicule during the last act, where the figure of Mme Salvini-Donatelli, as double-barrelled as her name, seemed all too much at variance with the symptoms of Violetta's fatal disease. The piece was laughed off the stage.

Time, however, proved that the confidence we may read between the lines of Verdi's brief announcements was fully justified. *La Traviata* remains, both with musicians and with the general public, one of the most popular of all operas. This reversal of the original verdict is hardly surprising. Apart from the excessive number of letters, whose purport is not always too clear, written and received during the course of the opera, Piave's libretto is an excellent adaptation of Dumas's play, which itself is an effective and, once its basis upon contemporary social morality is understood, convincing drama. The music, besides affording singers splendid opportunities that have unfortunately too often been abused, and apart from its extraordinary wealth of melodic invention, has a subtlety and an intimate charm that had hitherto only been hinted at in *Luisa Miller*.

It is not easy to put a finger upon the way in which the new atmosphere of gentle and tender melancholy is created in *La Traviata*. But a comparison of the duet between Manrico and Azucena ('Ai nostri monti') in *Il Trovatore* with that between Alfredo and Violetta ('Parigi, o cara') will make the difference of the musical style between the two works evident. Both duets express the same nostalgia for lost scenes and past happiness in the presence of death, and the musical themes are closely related. Yet the one has a broad, heroic effect that is completely absent from the other, which expresses a *maladif* pathos.

The strong upward melody with which Manrico answers his mother is a typical example of *Trovatore* style.

An even more instructive comparison may be made between 'Parigi, o cara' and Manrico's first entry:

It will be seen that the first three notes are an inversion of those in the *Traviata* duet. Yet the continuation of the melody coupled with the higher *tessitura* of the voice gives to the troubadour's song a bold and soaring quality that makes the resemblance of the rhythm and intervals imperceptible except on paper. This bold type of melody is to be found in the famous 'Miserere,' whose dramatic effect never fails despite its hackneyed familiarity, and no less in the music of Leonora:

83

The heroic manner certainly involved, in *Il Trovatore*, a certain monotony of rhythm which is the counterpart of the opera's lack of subtlety. In this respect *La Traviata* shows a great advance even upon *Rigoletto*. The rhythms are more varied and are handled with far more suppleness than Verdi had hitherto displayed. The figure, played by the clarinets, which runs through the card-playing scene in Act II, scene ii is a good example of this new mastery, as well as of the new delicacy in instrumentation that is evident throughout the opera:

The orchestration of *La Traviata*, no less than the style of its melodies, truly reflects the nature of the drama. The opening of the prelude, with its pathetic melody given to divided violins—itself a remarkably novel effect at least in Italian opera, which gives the passage for a bar or two a deceptive resemblance to the *Lohengrin* prelude [1]—at once establishes the mood of intimate tragedy.

The 'party' music of the first act is far superior to anything Verdi had previously written in this vein, and the dovetailing of the

[1] *Lohengrin* was produced at Weimar in 1850. Verdi did not hear a performance of it until 1871, when it was given at Bologna, and there is no reason to suppose that he was acquainted with the score at the time he was engaged upon *La Traviata*.

conversational passages into the background and the gradual definition of the principal characters, who appear at first to be no more than members of a crowd, are typical both of a new technical mastery and of a psychological insight into character not hitherto displayed. It is perhaps natural that, given this subject, the melodies should remind one more closely of Bellini than anything in *Rigoletto* or *Il Trovatore*. In this scene 'Un dì felice' provides an obvious instance. But how much more flexible and natural is the handling of the material, which never gives the impression of a rigid form, than anything achieved by Bellini! And when he comes to Violetta's soliloquy what brilliant use Verdi makes of the old *andante* and *cabaletta* form of aria, which proves a perfect vehicle for the heroine's change of mood! The coloratura itself reflects equally the hectic desperation to which she gives way and the brilliance of the diamonds which here at any rate the *prima donna* may appropriately wear.

Before we leave the first act it will be worth while to glance a little more closely at the duet. For beneath its deceptive simplicity lies a depth of psychological understanding that gives us the measure of Verdi's ability as a dramatic composer. The contrast between the tender melody given to Alfredo and the cynical brilliance of Violetta's reply is obvious enough, but not on that account less admirable as a piece of character drawing. But there is more to this passage than a contrast of character and temperament; it is a coherent musical composition. Anybody might have devised the mere contrast between a gentle melody and a series of *fioriture*. Verdi did more than that. Alfredo's tune, so smooth at first, develops passion as he confesses his love, and its rhythm dissolves at the end into triplets without, however, losing its essential character of tender passion. It is those triplets that Violetta takes up, breaking up the *legato* line with hectic pauses and making an entirely different rhythmical use of them. So the one musical theme develops into the other with a complete naturalness and inevitability that is as convincing as the arrival of the second subject as the true complement to the first in a great classical symphony:

The first scene of the second act takes us into another world, both social and musical. Indeed it is one of the problems of Violetta's part that she must command a wide variety of qualities —technical bravura for the brilliant music of the first act, a lyrical sweetness of voice and an exceptional *legato* for the second and third, and a great dramatic power for the *scène à faire* in the second scene of Act II. It is questionable whether Verdi ever surpassed the delicacy and tact of his handling of the duet between Violetta and her lover's father. What might be—and indeed is in an inferior performance—an absurd and ludicrous scene, becomes one of the most moving things in opera. It is unfortunate that both the opening of this act and the final scene between Germont and Alfredo are upon a more conventional level of tunefulness and sometimes lapse, especially in the finale, into triteness. 'Di Provenza il mar' in particular has been criticized for its banal melody and tiresome repetitiveness. But, although as a tune it is inferior to 'Il balen,' with which it is comparable, it is a perfect expression of nostalgic sentiment, and I confess to a sneaking affection for its naïve gentility. Verdi himself was of the opinion in 1855 that it was the best cantabile for baritone he had written.

After his success with the first part of the second act it is hardly surprising that Verdi should have been able to make a splendid effect in the highly dramatic scene at Flora's party. The music here becomes more vigorous and Alfredo's denunciation of Violetta aptly expresses his scorn without becoming crude. And, although Germont's appearance in this scene (the only regrettable invention of Piave's in this libretto) is dramatically unexplained and improbable, his music is excellent, while Violetta's appeal to Alfredo in the final ensemble is extraordinarily moving. Nevertheless this scene contains the weakest music in the opera. Apart from the card-playing scene already mentioned, the earlier part of it is conventional, while the ballet music is poor in quality and not to be compared with the waltz that runs through the first act. The final ensemble, too, is more rigid and lacking in definite characterization than the comparable movements in *Rigoletto*.

Verdi himself felt that the second act was not wholly satisfactory, and for the production of the opera in Paris he rearranged the first scene in order to make Alfredo's discovery of Violetta's departure come at the end as a dramatic climax. To Cesare de Sanctis, who criticized this act, however, Verdi gave a categorical negative:

You find the second act weaker than the rest! You are wrong. It is better than the first act. The third is the best of all, and so it should be. If, however, you saw it produced with two suitable artists, the duet in the second act [Violetta-Germont], which seems to you too long, would not fail to produce a tremendous effect, and you would agree that it is equal to any other duet I have written in idea, and superior in form and feeling.

87

If we may suspect that Verdi, relying upon what is certainly the finest thing in the act, has overlooked the passages that are open to criticism, we need not disagree with his pronouncement about Act III, which, in its very different way, ranks with the last act of *Rigoletto* as something perfectly done. In it the lyrical poetic feeling peculiar to the opera as a whole achieves its finest expression. The very opening of the act, which reveals the sick Violetta asleep while the extraordinarily beautiful and tender prelude is being played, at once creates an intimately tragic effect without parallel. The use of the spoken voice for the reading of Germont's letter—a convention he had employed in Lady Macbeth's first scene—makes a most poignant effect. Did Verdi, perhaps, remember Leonora's spoken 'Nothing, my Florestan' at the dramatic climax of *Fidelio*, which moves us by its very contrast with the singing voice more powerfully even than the joyful up-rush of the 'Namenlose Freude' duet? Verdi even dares to repeat this effect without losing its dramatic force at the emotional climax of the opera, when the dying Violetta speaks her lover's name. Even the street music heard through the window heightens the tension for all its lack of distinction, or perhaps one should say by reason of the contrast between its banal merriment and the pathos of Violetta's end. Verdi had, whether by intention or accident, produced a similar effect with the town-band music that accompanies Duncan's arrival at Macbeth's castle, which creates a curiously eerie sense of impending tragedy.

A few months after its initial failure *La Traviata* was performed again in Venice at the San Benedetto Theatre, thanks to the good offices of Antonio Gallo, whose faith in the merit of the opera deserves recording. For this performance Verdi made a few changes, but, as he assured de Sanctis at the time, these were only minor alterations in the voice parts—'not a piece was changed in position, added or left out, nor a musical idea altered'—and they do not explain why the fiasco at the Fenice became the furore at the San Benedetto.

CHAPTER VIII

A PARISIAN OPERA

DURING the composition of the three operas discussed in the last chapter Verdi was living at Busseto, at first in the Palazzo Orlandi while the alterations to Sant' Agata were being completed. It seems that he did not move into his own house until after the production of *Rigoletto* in the spring of 1851. The letters of this period show that, in addition to the exasperating struggle with the censorship over the libretto of *Rigoletto* and the anxieties caused by the illness of his parents, Verdi had other worries to preoccupy his mind. During 1850 there was a long correspondence with Ricordi about his royalties. The publisher complained that times were bad and suggested a reduction of the percentages payable under Verdi's various contracts. In support of this proposal he argued that *La battaglia di Legnano* had been a comparative failure after its initial success in Rome, and that owing to the excessive cost of producing the operas, due to the royalties payable, piracy was being encouraged.

There was no international agreement about copyright at this time, and the only protection a composer had was the careful restriction of the circulation of the full score. But any skilled musician could produce some sort of score from the pianoforte reduction, however far it might be from the composer's notion, and Ricordi cites the instance of a hack at Seville who was doing a thriving trade with his unauthorized instrumentations of operas. It will be remembered that many years later Sullivan suffered from the same piratical practice in the United States, where the rights of foreign authors and composers in their own works were wholly unrecognized.[1]

[1] In England the composer's position was hardly more satisfactory. By a decision of the House of Lords of 1st August 1855, which ended a lengthy litigation about the rights in Bellini's *La Sonnambula*, it was established that subjects of states which had not entered into a reciprocal

Verdi, after caustically expressing his surprise that 'a poor composer should have to provide a living for a rich publisher,' agreed to a reduction, and despite the superficial acrimoniousness of the letters he remained on genuinely friendly terms with the Ricordis, father and son. In 1851 he objected vigorously to the performance of *Stiffelio* at the Scala Theatre, where the poor standard of the productions aroused his disgust, and threatened to sue for damages if certain alterations to the opera were made. But in a separate postscript he made it clear that this threat was only made for communication to the management in Milan.

A more distressing worry arose from a quarter that touched Verdi most closely. He had persuaded Giuseppina Strepponi to leave Paris and join him at Busseto, and the liaison which had aroused no comment in the French capital provoked a great deal of comment in a provincial town. Verdi paid no attention to ill-natured gossip, and we may suppose that the very existence of such talk only strengthened his and Giuseppina's objections to regularizing the union in the eyes of the church and the law. It is not altogether clear upon what grounds these objections were based. On Verdi's side they may have arisen from his natural independence of spirit and a sentimental or superstitious dread of tempting fate a second time by putting Giuseppina in Margherita Barezzi's place. On her side, Giuseppina seems to have felt that she was not worthy of Verdi. Like most opera-singers of the day she had a past; she had been Moriani's mistress and had borne him two children. Verdi's relationship with her was one of an

---

copyright agreement with Great Britain had no protection for their compositions, unless the author were present at the first performance in England and the contract with the British agent signed before two witnesses. Verdi, as a subject of the Duchy of Parma, was by this decision in danger of losing the English copyright in his works. His remedy, he wrote to Ricordi, was to adopt British, French or Pied-montese nationality. But characteristically he preferred to remain what he was, 'a peasant of Roncole,' and as such to move his Government, which had nothing to lose in this purely artistic and literary question, to enter into a copyright convention with Great Britain.

ideal friendship as well as of physical union. They were happy together and, perhaps, they did not care greatly what the world in general thought about a matter which was no concern of any one but themselves.

When, however, he received from Antonio Barezzi, his first patron, the father of Margherita and the dearest of his elder friends, a letter rebuking him for causing a scandal, he was hurt to the quick. Barezzi's letter, which has significantly not been preserved, reached Verdi in Paris, where he spent part of the winter of 1851-2. Verdi replied with characteristic vigour, but with less than characteristic frankness, as follows:

PARIS, 21st January 1852.

MY DEAREST FATHER-IN-LAW,

After so long an interval I hardly expected to receive so cold a letter from you, containing, unless I misread them, some remarks that I deeply resent. Were this letter not signed *Antonio Barezzi*, that is by my bene-factor, I should reply with great vigour or not at all. As, however, it bears a name that I must always respect, I shall try to persuade you that your rebukes are undeserved. . . .

I do not believe that you would have written of your own accord a letter that was bound to distress me, but you live in a place where people take a wicked pleasure in meddling in the affairs of others and disapprove of everything that does not conform to their own ideas. I never mix myself up with other people's business, unless I am asked, and I therefore object to others meddling with mine. That is how tittle-tattle, whisperings and head-shakings arise. I expect the same liberty of action in my own home that I should enjoy in less civilized places. Judge for yourself, severely if you will, but coldly and dis-passionately: What harm is there in my living in retirement, in my preferring not to pay visits to any one who happens to have a title, in my taking no part in the festivities and rejoicings of other people? If I choose to manage my property because it amuses me and gives me an occupation, what harm, I repeat, is there in that? And who is a penny the worse for it? . . .

So much for my opinions, actions and wishes in all that concerns what may be called my public life. But as we are on the road to making revelations, I have no objection to lifting the curtain that veils the mysteries enclosed within four walls, and speaking of my private life. I have nothing to hide. In my house lives a lady, free and independent, and possessed of a fortune that places her beyond the reach of need, who shares my love of seclusion. Neither I nor she need render account of our actions to any man. Nor does any one know what our relations are to one another, how we manage our affairs, what bonds exist between us, or whether I have any legal claims upon her or she upon me. Who can say whether she is my wife or not, and, if she is, what private motives may lead us to avoid publishing the fact? Who knows whether that is a good or a bad thing? It may be good, and, even if it is bad, who has the right to pronounce our ostracism? This much I will say: in my house she has the right to be treated with even greater respect than is due to myself, and no one is allowed to forget it. Finally she deserves the same considerateness that she displays in her own char-acter and in her conduct towards others.

This long and rambling letter is only designed to establish my claim to that liberty of action to which every man has a right. My nature rebels against submitting to the prejudices of other people. I trust that you, in all fairness and of your goodness of heart, will not listen to or be influenced by the gossip of a town that—I must say it!—once thought me unworthy to be its organist, and now whispers lies about my doings and behaviour. I will not put up with it, and I am not the man to shirk a decision, if it becomes necessary. The world is wide, and the loss of twenty or thirty thousand francs will not prevent my finding a home elsewhere. There should be nothing in this letter to offend you, but should anything I have written displease, I beg you to believe on my honour that that is not my intention. I have always thought and still think of you with pride and gratitude as my benefactor.

Two things will be obvious from this letter. Verdi was genuinely grieved by Barezzi's references to the scandal and desperately anxious not to offend his oldest friend. In the second place, his conscience was not as clear as he pretends. When a man says he has nothing to hide, it usually means that he is con-cealing something, especially if, after a promise of frank revelation couched in metaphors about 'lifting veils,' he reveals nothing at all. But, though Verdi's threats sound a little hollow and he protests too much about his rights, it must be allowed that the special nature of his relationship with Barezzi, which indeed was the justification of the elder man's interfering in the matter, placed Verdi in a difficult position. He could tell other people to mind their own business, but he could not explain to his father-in-law, whose regard for the conventions prevented him from perceiving them for himself, the motives that, if my suggestion is correct, made Verdi and Giuseppina unwilling to marry.

It is certainly difficult, on any other reading of the situation, to understand why they should not have gone through a form of marriage, to which there was no impediment of any kind. For the usual explanation, that Verdi was 'too honest' to go through a ceremony in which he did not believe, is not very convincing. Nor does it really do him the credit that is generally supposed, since it meant placing Giuseppina in a position that must have been cruelly unhappy to a Catholic. We do not know what in the end made them give way, but it is permissible to suppose that they came to realize that a compromise with the social conventions was really necessary. To his intimates Verdi had already been referring to Giuseppina as 'my wife' for several years before on 29th August 1859 they were married 'quietly,' as the saying is, in the church of St Martin at Collonges, a village near Annecy in Savoy, at this date still within the kingdom of Piedmont—a long way from Busseto!

Verdi's presence in Paris at the time of the correspondence with Barezzi was due to the revival of the offer from the Opéra. The contract signed in 1848 for an opera with a libretto by Scribe had lapsed, owing apparently to the failure of the French poet to produce his book. Early in 1852 a new contract was signed with Roqueplan, under which Verdi undertook to set for the Opéra 'a poem in five acts or in four acts by Mr Scribe alone or by Mr Scribe and a collaborator,' the book to be ready by the end of the year at the latest. Eighteen months later Verdi was still without news of the libretto. He protested to Roqueplan that he must have a definite decision, in default of which he would cancel the agreement. The libretto was eventually sent to him on the last day of 1853. It was entitled *Les Vêpres siciliennes*.

While he was awaiting Scribe's libretto, Verdi's mind reverted once more to the adaptation of *King Lear*. Now that Cammarano was dead, he turned to Antonio Somma, a Venetian poet and lawyer, as a possible collaborator. Somma, who had written a number of tragedies that had won him a considerable reputation, had suggested that he should provide Verdi with a libretto. Verdi's reply, dated 22nd April 1853, which is not included in the letter-book and has been printed complete only in the *Daily Telegraph*, is of sufficient interest to justify its full reproduction here:

DEAR SOMMA,

I am very sorry that I have not before this answered your welcome letter, but an infinity of trifling matters to which I have been obliged to attend and, in addition, the necessary consideration of the subjects you suggested have been the cause of the delay. Nothing indeed would please me better than to unite mine with your great name, but as to setting to music to the best of my ability the beautiful poetry which certainly you would not fail to create, allow me to give you some of my opinions for what they are worth.

Long experience has confirmed me in the ideas which I have always held as to theatrical effects, although in my earlier works I may not have had the courage to put them into practice. (For example, ten years ago I should not have dared to write *Rigoletto*.) I find that the fault of our opera is excessive monotony, so much so that to-day I should refuse to write in the manner of *Nabucco, Foscari,* etc., which present many most interesting points, but without *variety*. There is only one motive—elevated, if you like, but always the same.

To make my meaning clearer, Tasso's poetry is perhaps the better, but I prefer a thousand times that of Ariosto. For the same reason I prefer Shakespeare to all other dramatists, not excepting the Greeks. It seems to me that as to effect the best subject which I have up to the present set to music (I do not in the least mean to speak of its literary or poetic merit) is *Rigoletto*, which has very powerful situations, variety, spirit, pathos. All the incidents arise from the light libertine character of the duke: from this come Rigoletto's apprehensions, Gilda's passion, and so on, and so on, which give many excellent dramatic points, among others the scene of the quartet which, as to its effect, will always be one of the best of which our theatre can boast.

Many have treated *Ruy Blas*, leaving out the part of Don Cesare. Now, should I ever write music for this subject, what would please me most would be the contrast produced by that most original character. You already understand how I think and feel, and as I know that I am speaking to a man of true and frank character, I allow myself to tell you that in the subjects you propose, although they are highly dramatic, I do not find all that variety which my mad brain desires. You will say that in *Sordello* one can put a feast, a supper, even a tournament; nevertheless, the characters would still have a heavy serious tone.

As for the rest, do not be in any hurry. Should my engagements compel me to write for a coming season, I should force myself to write the music for a tolerable libretto, hoping on a future occasion to have the good fortune to clothe with notes a work of yours, which in the eyes of the literary world would have all the importance of a great event. When poor Cammarano was alive I suggested *King Lear* to him. Give it a glance if it is not troubling you— I will do the same, as it is some time since I read it—and give me your opinion.

Forgive this rambling gossip, and believe me,

Your admirer and most sincere friend,

G. VERDI.

The correspondence with Somma continued over a space of two years, Verdi criticizing in detail the poet's work and Somma diligently refashioning it to the composer's requirements. Verdi even paid Somma an advance of 2,000 Austrian lire for the libretto before he left Busseto for Paris in October 1853. The libretto was in the end virtually finished, and Ricordi proposed at various times that the opera should be produced at Genoa, at Naples and at Milan. But nothing came of it and, although Verdi returned to it again and again later in life, *Lear* remained an unrealized dream. There can be no doubt that some of the music was written, but this has disappeared, presumably with all the other sketches which, in accordance with Verdi's wishes, were destroyed after his death. All that remain of his most ambitious project are the elaborate scenarios and sketches of the text preserved in the letter-book and the *Carteggi Verdiani*, which afford an interesting study of Verdi's procedure as an operatic composer.

The work on *Lear* was interrupted by the visit to Paris for the composition and production of *I Vespri siciliani*, to give the opera the Italian title by which it is now generally known. Apart from the delay in the delivery of the libretto, which did not reach him until he had been in Paris for nearly three months, Verdi found himself faced with a multitude of difficulties, major and minor, that fully account for the fact that *I Vespri siciliani* shows a distinct retrogression from the standards set in the operas that preceded it.

In the first place Scribe, besides being dilatory in producing his book at all, ignored all Verdi's requests for alterations and modifications in the text. The popular and prolific playwright was, unlike Verdi's more complaisant Italian librettists, too grand or too lazy to make those compromises that are the basis of a successful collaboration. Even his choice of subject was a tactless one to offer an Italian composer for production in France. For the plot showed the French garrison of Sicily massacred in a popular uprising and the Sicilian leader is drawn in an unfavourable light.

The more I think of it [wrote Verdi to Louis Crosnier] the less I like it. It will wound the French because they are slaughtered. It will wound the Italians because M. Scribe has altered the historical character of Procida [the Sicilian leader] and has made of him, according to his favourite device, a common conspirator with the inevitable dagger in his hand. There are, God knows, in the history of every people good deeds and villainies, and we are no worse than the rest. Anyway I am before all else an Italian, and I will not be a party to an insult to my country.

Crosnier had succeeded Roqueplan as director of the Opéra in November 1854 on account of a scandal, which also affected the production of Verdi's opera. Early in October Cruvelli, the *prima donna* cast for the leading part, suddenly and inexplicably disappeared from Paris. Her departure was timed for the evening on which she was due to sing Valentine in *Les Huguenots*, her most popular part. There was a resounding scandal, which even found an echo in London, where a burlesque called *Where's Cruvelli?* was promptly staged. There were rumours of an elopement with a Baron Vigier, whom she did subsequently marry. Roqueplan was suspected by the authorities of complicity in Cruvelli's disappearance and, as they were dissatisfied with the financial position created by his management, the opportunity was taken to get rid of him.

Verdi's rehearsals were held up, and the management proposed that, as *I Vespri siciliani* could not be given without Cruvelli, he should write a new opera in three acts or produce a French version of one of his other works. This proposition Verdi flatly declined to consider and, with many complaints about the loss and inconvenience to which he had been put, talked of packing his bags.

In the midst of this disturbance the composer received from Genoa the most flattering proposal imaginable. A new opera house was under construction there and the management asked Verdi's permission to call it by his name and also his consent to compose an opera for it. Verdi expressed himself as deeply flattered but declined the honour, 'owing to one of those strange whims that perhaps occur only to my mind.' He was willing to provide an opera and Ricordi suggested *Lear*.

Just when all seemed settled, the temperamental Cruvelli reappeared as suddenly as she had vanished, calmly explained that the note announcing her intention to absent herself from the Opéra awhile must have miscarried, and took her place in the performance of *Les Huguenots* on 7th November. Verdi had to drop *Lear* again and attend to the rehearsals of *I Vespri*. The Genoese decided to name their theatre after Paganini, their fellow-citizen.

Things still refused to go well at the Opéra, and Verdi expressed his dissatisfaction in forcibly sarcastic terms:

It is distressing and humiliating to me that M. Scribe has not taken the trouble to improve the fifth act, which every one finds lacking in interest. I am not ignorant that M. Scribe has a thousand other things to do, which are nearer to his heart than my opera. But, had I suspected in him this complete indifference, I should have stayed at home, where, truth to tell, I was contented enough!

I had hoped that M. Scribe would find a way of ending the drama with one of those moving passages that bring tears to the eye, and whose effect rarely misses the mark. The situation in my opinion lends itself to such treatment. . . .

I had hoped that M. Scribe would have the goodness to appear now and again at the rehearsals to alter unsuitable words and lines that are awkward to sing; and to see whether anything needed touching up and so on.

In addition Verdi complained that three of the acts had exactly the same sequence of the same kind of numbers. Nor was this the sum of his grievances:

I must add [he continues] a word about the rehearsals in the foyer. I hear remarks bandied about which are, if not deeply wounding, at least out of place. I am not accustomed to such treatment and will not tolerate it. It is possible that So-and-so considers my music below the high standards of the Opéra, and that another thinks his part unworthy of his talents. It is also possible that I, on my part, find the performance and the style of singing very different from what I should like! Finally, unless I am much mistaken, we do not see eye to eye about the manner of feeling and interpreting the music, and without perfect agreement on that point *success is impossible.*

In the face of all these disagreements and petty obstacles, it is rather surprising that Verdi did not throw in his hand. But he seems to have been fascinated by the glamour of the Opéra, at that time, as he put it himself, 'the first theatre in the world' of which Paris was the artistic capital. Many other composers had felt its irresistible attraction. Meyerbeer and Rossini had gravitated to Paris and settled there for good. Wagner was yet to come —and singe his wings. There were even rumours that Verdi was proposing to follow Rossini's example and make it his permanent home. But on that score he set Clarina Maffei's mind at rest:

Take root here? Impossible! Why should I, indeed? What scope should I have? For glory? There is none here that I know of. For money? I can make as much, perhaps more, in Italy. Even if I wished to stay, it is impossible. I love my own solitude and the Italian sky too well. . . . Besides I am not a millionaire and I do not intend to spend the few thousand francs I earn on publicity, a *claque* and suchlike dirty things. That seems to be necessary for success. The other day Dumas wrote in his paper apropos of Meyerbeer's new opera: 'What a pity Rossini did not produce his operas in 1854! But then Rossini had not the German wit to set a success simmering six months in advance on the stoves of the newspapers and so prepare for an explosion of intelligent appreciation on the night.' It is very true. I was at the first performance of his *Étoile du Nord* and understood little or nothing of it, but the good public here understood it all and thought it beautiful, sublime, divine! And this same public has not yet, after twenty-five to thirty years, appreciated *William Tell*, and so it is crippled and mutilated, reduced from five to three acts and miserably staged! And this in the first theatre in the world.

In spite of these caustic references to Meyerbeer, it was precisely Meyerbeer whom Verdi seems to have chosen for his model in composing *I Vespri*. No doubt he wished to give the Parisians the kind of thing they seemed to like. And Scribe, for his part, at least took trouble to provide Verdi with the kind of situations that had established the success of his early operas. There was plenty of patriotism—Procida's 'O to Palermo,' one of the two arias in the opera familiar to English audiences as concert pieces, is one example—and such a deal of battle, murder and sudden death that Wagner dubbed the work 'a night of carnage.' But Scribe could not give to his characters and situations that genuineness which marks even the most conventional of the earlier Italian librettos, because he did not feel the situations. The result was a stiff and pretentious piece, redeemed now and then by some splendid music. The duet with its great sweeping melody between Arrigo and Monforte at the end of the first act, for example, is a fine example of the heroic tenor-baritone duet that was henceforth to be one of the great features in Verdi's operas. Verdi groaned at the length of the work—'an opera at the Opéra is enough to stun a bull. Five hours of music. . . . Hauf!' But it would be unjust to say that his heart was not in his work. He took the trouble to ask de Sanctis for details of the popular festivals at Palermo, inquired whether the tarantella was always in the minor key and in 6–8 time, and requested him to find a genuine Sicilian folksong—'not something written by one of your composers.' As a whole, however, *I Vespri* must be judged an uninspired essay in 'grand' opera. The best that can be said of it is that the experience of writing it was valuable when he returned to this grandiose style in some of his later works, of which *Aida* is the supreme example.

I Vespri siciliani was produced on 13th June 1855, the various difficulties having been successfully surmounted. Verdi seems to have given way before Scribe's intransigence, for the opera as published contains all the features to which Verdi had objected. It was a great success with the public and the critics. The *Journal des Débats*, of which Berlioz was the chief music critic, though he seems not to have been responsible for this particular notice, praised Verdi for breaking with the formal conventions of opera and for the novel colour of his orchestration. But the popularity of the opera did not survive the Great Exhibition, during which it was produced, and in Italy, where the scene was changed to Portugal in order to avoid hurting Italian susceptibilities, it had no great success. Oddly enough in London, where it was given in 1859, Davison of *The Times*, who had called *Rigoletto* a 'feeble' opera, judged the composer of *Il Trovatore* to be inferior to Rossini, Auber and Meyerbeer, and written of the 'foul and hideous horrors' of *La Traviata*, pronounced *I Vespri* to be among Verdi's finest works.

Verdi did not leave Paris for some months after the production of his opera. He was detained by a dispute with the Théâtre Italien where under his very nose Calzado, a rich Spaniard who managed the theatre, was proposing to stage unauthorized and pirated versions of *Il Trovatore, Rigoletto* and *La Traviata*. Verdi, who had been annoyed by the production of *Luisa Miller* in a mutilated form and 'with wretched resources' at this theatre, was furious. He snubbed Calzado, who impertinently wrote to inquire whether there was any truth in the rumour that he objected to these performances, with the reply that he was not accustomed to answer such questions from gentlemen to whom he had not been introduced. He threatened an injunction, which had the desired effect. By the end of the year the angry bear had become almost lamblike, and we find him writing to thank Calzado for falling in with his wishes, and acquiescing (with the proviso that he would have prevented it if he could!) in the performance of *Ernani*, although, with one more growl, he is afraid it will be badly done.

How deep was Verdi's exasperation is evident from his correspondence with Ricordi at this time. He was highly indignant to find that Ricordi claimed the French rights in his operas, and complained that the publisher relied too much on commas and full stops, while the plain fact was that he had made out of *Il Trovatore* four times as much as the unhappy composer. Ricordi pointed out at great length and with much patience what his rights were according to the contracts, remarking that Verdi could produce his operas in Chinese at Pekin, if he chose, but it would be illegal, and suggesting that Verdi was being prejudiced by certain persons whom he likened to 'not two-faced, but four-faced Januses'—a phrase that particularly wounded the honest Verdi's susceptibilities. For honest he certainly was. The cause of his discontent was a feeling that he had been done out of his rights by a cleverer man than himself. Ricordi was not guilty of any sharp practice, but he had certainly made a good bargain, and Verdi's annoyance was due to the discovery that he, on his part, might have made a better one.

CHAPTER IX

'SIMON BOCCANEGRA'

VERDI returned to Busseto early in 1856 and occupied himself with the revision of *Stiffelio*, which was to be produced under the title of *Aroldo* at the opening of a new opera house at Rimini during the summer of 1857. Piave was summoned to join the composer and bring such literary material as he might require. 'You know there are not many books here,' he explains, 'only a modest library.' In the new version the nineteenth-century German pastor became an English crusader living in 'Kenth,' a transformation to which Verdi agreed against his better judgment. We may imagine, however, that he did not greatly care what happened to this tiresome piece.

He was much more interested in yet another proposal to produce *King Lear*, this time at Naples. The project lapsed only because Verdi could not get the singers he required. The soprano at the San Carlo Theatre was in his opinion unsuitable for Cordelia. He wanted Mme Piccolomini, who had established the success of *La Traviata* by her performance as Violetta, despite the scandalized protests of men like Chorley against her lack of 'maidenly reticence and delicacy.' He wanted, as well he might, a 'great' baritone for the part of Lear and, at this stage, a first-rate contralto to play the Fool. But it was not to be. He flatly refused to proceed unless his views about the casting of the opera were accepted. 'I am not in the habit of allowing any artist to be *imposed* on me,' he wrote to Naples, 'not though Malibran herself should return from the grave.'

In the midst of these preoccupations Verdi had to return to Paris in order to deal with a new dispute with Calzado, who was threatening litigation over the French translation of *Il Trovatore*. He remained in Paris until the end of the year, and had the satisfaction of seeing *La Traviata* make a resounding success, with Piccolomini in the part of Violetta.

On the abandonment of *Lear* Verdi considered various other subjects, among them *Ruy Blas* and Scribe's *Gustave III*, which was eventually to become *Un ballo in maschera*. Unfortunately for Verdi Scribe's drama centred upon the murder of King Gustavus of Sweden at a court ball, which did not commend the project to the authorities. Before the objections of the censorship to regicide could be overcome, Verdi turned his attention to another drama which, though it involved the poisoning of a Genoese doge, presented him as so magnanimous a figure that there was no offence in it. Besides, the victim was an Italian and a plebeian with republican ideas, and it all happened a very long time ago.

The new opera, *Simon Boccanegra*, was produced at the Fenice Theatre, Venice, on 12th March 1857. Like *La Traviata* it was a complete failure, and unlike *La Traviata* it has never won the position in the popular favour that is due to it on musical grounds. Verdi himself had a special affection for the opera, and in 1881 he revised it with the help of Arrigo Boito for the Scala Theatre. This revision was much more radical than that to which *Macbeth* was subjected. The orchestration was largely rewritten; Piave's original libretto was overhauled and new scenes were added in an attempt to clarify the obscurities of the intrigue and to give more interest to a work that even the composer felt was too monotonous and chilly. It was in this form that the work was revived in Germany and Italy in the 1930's. But even now its success has been a *succès d'estime* with musicians and connoisseurs; the general public seems to have remained indifferent. At Florence, where the opera was given for the first time during the May Festival of 1938, the audience received it politely, but without enthusiasm.

The reason is not far to seek. *Simon Boccanegra* is hampered by a story that is not only gloomy and so obscure as to be quite unintelligible without a close study of the libretto, but is marred by a cardinal fault in its presentation. Simon is by definition a *condottiere,* the Italian equivalent of Sir Francis Drake, who freed Genoa from the pirates and, in the face of the opposition of the patrician families, was elected its ruler by the popular vote. Yet this man of action is never, except in the scene in the council chamber added by Boito, seen in action. In the prologue, which happens some twenty-five years before the first act, we are shown not a man of action, like Otello at his first entry, but a distraught lover who is only persuaded to stand for election because success means gaining possession of Maria Fiesco, daughter of the leader of the nobles, whom he has seduced and who has been shut up by her outraged father. Maria, however, is dead, and his election as doge comes to him as Dead-Sea fruit.

In the main action that follows (after an interval of twenty-five years) Simon remains, except in the one scene already mentioned, the more or less passive victim of intrigues and repeated futile attempts at revolution, the second of which happens off stage and so contributes nothing effective to the drama. He responds to every attempt upon him with a consistent clemency that rivals even that of Mozart's Titus. Magnanimity may be an admirable quality in a ruler, but it makes a poor denouement to dramatic situations. In the end Simon dies of a slow poison taken in the middle of the second act. It is hardly surprising that Boito, who undertook the revision with reluctance, could do little beyond clearing up some of the obscurer points in Piave's libretto. But it is odd that Verdi, who felt the need for some contrast in the prevailing gloom, should not have done more to lighten its sombreness. Even the festivities that celebrate the suppression of the second insurrection are singularly bleak and the lovely lyrical scene between Maria Boccanegra, the doge's illegitimate daughter, and Gabriele Adorno, her lover, who, needless to say, belongs to the opposing political party, is the only ray of light in the general darkness.

Beside the failure to present Simon as a man of resolution in action and the gloominess of the libretto, the complexities of the story are of minor importance, though they certainly contribute to the failure of the opera to make its proper effect. *Simon Boccanegra* is based on a play by Gutiérrez, the author of *El Trovador*, who seems to have had a mania for lost babies and mistaken identities. The result is a plot that may be described as a hybrid, a real *lusus naturae* between *Othello* (without the jealousy motive) and *The Gondoliers*. Two of the main characters appear under assumed names, which adds to the confusion of an already tangled tale, though Maria's disguise as Amalia Grimaldi certainly provides a most moving recognition scene, when the doge discovers in her his long-lost child. But this beautiful duet, which should have ended with a curtain, is followed by a scene that seems once more to indicate that blind spot in Verdi's eye for theatrical effect.

Simon had come to tell the supposed Amalia that she must marry Paolo, the villain of the piece. After the recognition Amalia departs on a high B flat.

Enter Paolo.

Simon. Renounce all hope [of marrying Amalia].
Paolo. I cannot.
Simon. I wish it!   [*Exit.*

That is all! Then Paolo, to music reminiscent of the conspirators in *Rigoletto*, plots with a friend the abduction of Amalia and the curtain falls. The little scene is necessary to the action, but both musically and dramatically it produces in performance a quite ludicrous effect of anticlimax after what has gone before. As we have noted in discussing *Macbeth*, Verdi sometimes attempted to embody an important dramatic idea in a couple of phrases, but unless those phrases are more telling than they are in the present instance, they are apt to go for nothing. The immediate establishment of Amonasro's identity at the first mention of his name in the messenger's scene in *Aida*, Act I, is a contrary example of how effective such a swift stroke can be.

For the music of *Boccanegra* generally, however, there can be nothing but the highest praise. The score as we have it represents Verdi at the full maturity of his powers. With the exception of the final chorus of the first act, acclaiming Simon's election, there is hardly a page of it that is not first-rate. As a whole the score produces an effect of sombre magnificence, like some richly woven tapestry in which there is a preponderance of dark and oppressive colour. In the midst stands the radiant figure of Amalia Grimaldi (alias Maria Boccanegra), a remarkable and individual creation, youthful, charming and delightfully human. Nowhere else in Verdi's operas do we find any similar character outside *Otello* and *Falstaff*. She is neither so tragic as Desdemona nor so light-hearted as Nannetta Ford—how could she be? But she shares with them the bloom of youth and innocence. Gilda might be thought of as a close relation. But Gilda's music is of a different type, less aristocratic and less subtle. Indeed the distance that Verdi's genius had travelled since the composition of *Rigoletto* may be measured by the difference between Gilda's music and Amalia's. But we must beware of attributing the creation of Amalia as we know her to the Verdi of 1857; she belongs to the period between *Aida* and *Otello* twenty years later. Something of her individuality and charm must nevertheless have appeared in the earlier version, and the next operas Verdi wrote provide sufficient evidence that there had been an advance in his powers and a change in his attitude to opera.

This change may be summed up as a move away from the lyrical style of his earlier works towards a more heroic type of opera. *Il Trovatore* had already given some indication of the direction in which he was moving. But both that opera and *I Vespri siciliani* depend much more upon the stimulation of the senses by passionate or graceful melodies than upon the more carefully planned and less intuitive handling of the material that is evident in *Boccanegra* and its immediate successors.

We must beware of the easy division of Verdi's works into 'periods.' Nothing, in one sense, could be planned with greater judiciousness than *Rigoletto*, and in the even earlier *Macbeth* there is much evidence of that kind of intellectual grasp which becomes more and more marked from *Boccanegra* onwards until it finds its ultimate expression in the supreme masterpieces of the composer's old age, where all his knowledge, experience and intuition are marvellously fused together.

But, if we are to see intellect at work in *Boccanegra*, how comes it that such a muddled libretto could have been for one moment considered as possible? The paradox may be explained by Verdi's deficient education and want of literary sensibility. Knowledge of a kind he had acquired, but, as Mr Bonavia has well put it, not the art to use knowledge.

Verdi [he continues] had the knowledge, not the education. Had he had the advantage of a literary training he could never have accepted the librettos of *Trovatore* or *Boccanegra*. In *Trovatore* we see the effects of romanticism on a mind powerful and responsive but untrained, and therefore apt to err in judging the values of facts and words. His is the romanticism of the masses, ever ready to listen to a tale of adventure, awed by the supernatural, by mystery, by the glamour of valour and power. . . .

This limitation in Verdi's intellectual equipment accounts for his readiness to accept and indeed to suggest librettos that have served only to cripple some of his finest music. It was not until he found, in Boito, a poet who could supply his own deficiencies that Verdi's genius was able to put out its full strength.

The very simplicity that hampered Verdi in this way certainly proved of vital importance to the success of such works as *Rigoletto* and *Il Trovatore*, since it enabled him to give to them that directness of utterance and that power which come only from a blind and passionate sincerity. But those qualities were the very ones that had to be sacrificed in a more intellectual approach. It came about, therefore, that Verdi could no longer blind his audience by the sheer beauty of melody and the obvious power of soaring voices, whose very sound produces a thrilling dramatic effect, to the defects in his plots that he was himself unable to perceive.

Part and parcel of this new development in Verdi's style was an enlargement of the limited and conventional range of his harmony. The simple harmonic texture of his earlier operas, in which the accompaniment often consists of little more than arpeggios of the common chord (e.g. Leonora's 'D'amor sull' ali rosee' in *Trovatore*) and relies for harmonic interest on a frequent recourse to the diminished seventh—that 'rock and refuge of us all who can hardly write four bars without a dozen such chords,' as Verdi confessed—is certainly lit up by frequent flashes of happy ingenuity. But such resources were inadequate to his purpose in works like *Boccanegra* and *Un ballo in maschera*. In these and many of the later operas there remain threadbare patches, where he has fallen back upon the simpler harmonic language of his earlier style, and they sound all the more perfunctory in contrast with the greater suppleness and resource of their context. The final chorus of the prologue to *Boccanegra* is a striking example of this kind of lapse.

With this enlargement of his harmonic range went also a gradual improvement in the variety and sensitiveness of his orchestration. The crude and simple instrumentation that often justifies the criticism of 'brutality' made against it, gives place to a wonderfully rich and delicate sense of orchestral colour and propriety. Once more the occasional lapses into the old vulgarity stand out the more plainly by contrast.

It is necessary only to compare Leonora's air, to which reference has just been made, with Amalia's 'Come in questa ora bruna.' Between the two airs as musical compositions there is a most astonishing difference of quality, quite apart from the relative merits of the melodies and the diversity of the characters portrayed. Oddly enough the skeleton of the accompaniment is much the same, a downward arpeggio of the notes of the common chord. But how much more luscious are the sextolets that accompany Amalia than the simple triplets of Leonora's air! How much wider the sweep and flow of the phrases! How much subtler the rhythm!

bru - na   sor - ri - don

simile

ghia - stri e il ma - re!

Leonora

D'a - mor sul - l'a - li ro - se - e

van - ne so - spir___ do - len - te.

It is impossible to indicate here the orchestral colouring, a shimmering texture of wind and harp supported by the strings, beside which the *Trovatore* excerpt, for all the real pathos of the falling figure for the violins, is like a child's exercise. Nor is it possible to show within the space of a few bars the variety of rhythm and harmony through which Amalia's air passes before it resumes the even surge of its opening, in which Verdi has caught up in the notes of the common chord all the freshness of the lucid air at sunrise and the sparkle of the first rays upon the gentle waters of the Gulf of Genoa.

It would not be putting it too high to say that no other air of Verdi's surpasses this in radiant sweetness, excepting Nannetta's fairy song in the third act of *Falstaff*. It was obviously a difficult piece for which to find a sequel, and the little *aubade*, sung off stage to a harp accompaniment by Gabriele, who thus makes his first entry like Manrico in *Il Trovatore*, gives the measure of Verdi's development between the first and second versions of *Boccanegra*. Yet even in this song, which harks back to the style of the serenade in *Don Pasquale*, there is a subtlety and charm both in melody and rhythm that differentiates it from Manrico's direct and heroic phrases and lifts it far above the commonplaces, pretty though they are, of Donizetti. The old conventional vein appears, too, in the subsequent love duet, but again with a new sensitiveness in the writing that is an advance upon comparable passages in *La Traviata*. It is again the sea and the Genoese landscape—'How lovely is the blue sea and the shimmering water,' sings Amalia, 'and Genoa there towering above its foaming bride,' a metaphor the Venetian audience would understand—that evoke the finest music. Indeed throughout the opera we are made unusually conscious of its setting by the sea. This atmosphere pervades the recognition scene, in which the newer Verdi reasserts himself, and the monologue of the dying Boccanegra in which he apostrophizes the sea that brought him fame and power. It would be something more than mere supposition to suggest that the opera is an expression of Verdi's affection for Genoa, which he loved to visit above all other towns, and that this personal and, if you will, sentimental association gave the work its peculiar place in his affections. Such considerations may not wholly redeem weaknesses in a work of art, but they give to it a special claim upon the attention and regard of those who love and honour its creator.

But *Boccanegra* revolves around the figure of the doge. It is, among Verdi's works, the baritone's opera *par excellence*, even as *La Traviata* is the soprano's and *Il Trovatore* the tenor's. Even *Rigoletto* with its duet-scheme of construction does not thrust the protagonist so much to the fore. And the doge is not, on the whole, a satisfactory creation. He is not drawn fully in the round owing to the failure of the librettist to display him as a man of action anywhere outside the council scene of the revised version, where for a moment he comes magnificently to life as a powerful and dominating personality. For the rest his brooding sadness and rather perfunctory nobility of gesture produce an effect at once monotonous and unconvincing, which all Verdi's superb skill in handling the dramatic scenes of the prologue and the sombre splendours of the final act cannot wholly redeem. This, far more even than the very real difficulty that the spectator who has not spent some hours studying the libretto finds in identifying characters under assumed names, or rather in perceiving which of them at any given point of the action is aware of the real identity of the others and what are the motives of their actions— it is this that has prevented the opera from gaining the popularity it deserves on its merits as music, and has deprived us of the opportunity of hearing, except on rare occasions, one of Verdi's finest scores. Even the belated production of the opera at Covent Garden in 1965 failed to establish it in the repertory there, despite the excellence of Tito Gobbi's performance in the title-part.

CHAPTER X

TRAGICAL—HISTORICAL

FROM this point onwards the tempo of Verdi's output slows down and the gaps between one opera and the next progressively widen. *Rigoletto, Il Trovatore* and *La Traviata* were produced within a space of two years. The same period elapsed between *Boccanegra* and *Un ballo in maschera*, after which three years passed before *La forza del destino* was produced, and another five before *Don Carlo*. This slowing down was due, in part, to the greater amount of thought that had to be given to these later operas, and to their more elaborate texture, which enormously increased the mere physical labour of writing them. Gone were the palmy days of Donizetti and Rossini, when a composer could turn out two or three operas a year, his only need being the ability to think of enough good tunes which could be quickly supplied with a simple tonic-and-dominant accompaniment and joined together by a conventional recitative.

But during these years Verdi was also increasingly preoccupied with activities outside music. He became more and more engrossed in the management of his estate, and his solicitude for all the details of his crops and for the welfare of his employees is displayed in the numerous questions on the subjects contained in his letters when he was away from home. He had not always cared for such things, and years later Giuseppina revealed to Clarina Maffei that it was she who persuaded Verdi to leave Paris and settle at Busseto. She relates in this letter, with rueful amusement, how she began to lay out a garden, which was to be 'Peppina's garden,' but soon it became *his* garden and Peppina was restricted to a few square feet. These were evidently the happiest years of Verdi's life. Antonio Barezzi had become reconciled to Peppina's presence in the house, even before the surreptitious marriage of 1859.

But if his home was happy, his country was far from being so. After the unsuccessful revolt of 1848 discontent in Italy smouldered on, fanned by the plots Mazzini engineered from London and given a focus in the brave romantic figure of Garibaldi. But it was the conservative Cavour, aided by good fortune, who achieved by statesmanlike astuteness what the idealist republican and the inspiring soldier alone could hardly have accomplished. After the revolutionary outbreaks of 1848 the monarchical system re-established its authority over Europe. In France the Second Republic was succeeded by the Second Empire, and Cavour perceived that the greatest hope for Italy lay in unity under his own sovereign, Vittorio Emanuele. The King of Piedmont had won the trust and affection of all but the doctrinaire republicans among the Italian patriots, by his firm refusal to abolish the constitution that had been granted his people, at the bidding of the Austrians, after the disaster of Novara. He might be a boor without manners, but he was a man of his word, and the Italians expressed their gratitude by nicknaming him 'Rè galant-uomo.'

Cavour, born at Turin in 1810, was able to further the Italian cause in his newspaper, *Risorgimento*, which played an important part in securing the granting of the constitution by Vittorio Emanuele's predecessor, Carlo Alberto. He soon took a prominent part in politics and by 1852 was Prime Minister. His foreign policy aimed at securing an alliance with France and England, which would strengthen him against Austria, and to this end, in the face of the opposition of colleagues endowed with less foresight than himself, he dispatched a Piedmontese force to join the allies in the Crimea. So it came about that, when peace was made with Russia, Piedmont was represented at the council table among the Great Powers. Cavour secured from Napoleon III a defensive alliance and from England benevolent support. But he could not attack Austria, since the French were engaged to assist Piedmont only if she were attacked.

For the next few years Cavour set about arming his country, both as a necessary precaution and in the hope that his action would provoke an attack from Austria which would bring in France. A bomb intended for the Emperor Napoleon nearly shattered all his careful schemes. It was thrown on the evening of 14th January 1858, as the imperial party were driving to the Opéra, by Orsini, a close associate of Mazzini. However, whether because he was moved by Orsini's appeal to him before execution to deliver Italy, or because he was frightened into thinking that a contented country would be less likely to produce assassins, the emperor did not rescind the treaty with Piedmont. On the contrary he entered into a secret agreement with Cavour to drive the Austrians out of Italy in return for the cession to France of Savoy. But Austria must be provoked to attack in order that public opinion in Europe should be on the side of France and Piedmont.

At last, in the spring of 1859, the Austrians made the move Cavour hoped for. The English Government had given signs of hostility to Italian ambitions and the Emperor of the French, always unstable in his enthusiasms, had cooled off. The Austrians took the opportunity to send an ultimatum to Piedmont, in ignorance of the fact that a few hours before Cavour, under pressure from France and England, had agreed to disband his army. An ultimatum from the enemy to disarm within three days was a different matter and Cavour saw that his hopes, which had seemed but a moment before destroyed by the action of his allies, were approaching fulfilment.

It was a miserable little war. The Austrians were beaten rather by their own bad generalship than by the superiority of their enemies. After a few weeks Napoleon, to the amazement and disgust of his allies, broke off hostilities and made his peace with the Emperor Francis Joseph at Villafranca. This was not an act of treachery so much as of expediency. The Prussians had been mobilizing on the Rhine and, moreover, Napoleon began to be alarmed by the realization that if Piedmont absorbed Venetia and Tuscany, a united Italy would soon be established.

By the terms of the peace only Lombardy was freed from the Austrian rule. Venice remained a part of the empire and

Tuscany and the other states were returned to their former masters to be formed into a confederation, in which Austria was to have a voice, with the pope at its head.

Cavour was a bitterly disappointed man. He called the 'gentleman king,' who wisely refused to fight on alone, a mountebank, resigned his office and retired to his estate. His failure was only partial. Certain states, including Parma, were allowed to decide by a plebiscite whether they wished to join Piedmont. Victor Emmanuel's kingdom was enlarged by the accession of Lombardy and the plebiscites went in his favour. Thus was formed a sufficient nucleus of union to ensure the freedom of Italy at the next opportunity. The defeat of Austria by Prussia in 1866 provided that opportunity. Venice was restored to Italy and Garibaldi drove King 'Bomba' out of Sicily and Naples. Only Rome remained outside the newly united kingdom and Rome, too, was ripe to fall into the basket four years later when the disaster of Sedan had loosened France's support of the pope.

In all these happenings Verdi took an intense interest and at times an active part. His sense of what was practical made him an ardent admirer of Cavour, and so far had he moved from his earlier republicanism that, when Napoleon III came to Piedmont's assistance, he was willing to write a cantata in his honour for performance at Milan. The emperor's defection naturally prevented the completion of this project.

When the duchy of Parma opted for union with Piedmont, Verdi was one of the delegates chosen to convey the homage of his new subjects to Victor Emmanuel at Turin. The composer had, indeed, become in a peculiar way the focus of Italian aspirations at this time, through the coincidence that the letters of his name were the initials of Vittorio Emanuele Re D' Italia, so that to shout 'Evviva Verdi!' was a simple way of wishing the Austrians over the Brenner without open offence.

Verdi took the opportunity provided by his mission to Turin to pay a visit to Cavour in his retirement. The meeting was arranged by the English minister, Sir James Hudson, whose sympathy with the Italians made him almost more royalist than the king and caused some embarrassment to his Government at home. Cavour was delighted by the compliment paid him by the composer of 'Di quella pira,' which he had sung to express his elation at the news of Austria's invasion of Piedmont. From this time Verdi corresponded on political matters with the states/man, whom he hailed as the 'Prometheus of our nation,' until Cavour's death in 1861.

Verdi's work as a composer was immediately affected by the political unrest of the time. For the objections of the Neapolitan censorship to the libretto of his new opera based on Scribe's *Gustave III* were reinforced by Orsini's attempt on Napoleon's life. Was not the assassination of a reigning sovereign at a masked ball, it was argued, a deliberate incitement to anarchists to throw bombs at emperors on their way to the opera? The censors evidently wished to strangle this opera at birth, so ludicrous were the changes upon which they insisted.

The recent publication in Luzio's *Carteggi Verdiani* of the correspondence with Somma, the librettist entrusted with the task of turning Scribe's drama into an opera book, together with Verdi's detailed comments upon the libretto as revised by the censor, reveal the full extent of the censor's stupidity and lack of humour. *Una vendetta in domino*, the title originally proposed, was changed into *Adelia degli Adimari* which, as Verdi remarked, is meaningless. The period and scene were moved from seventeenth/century Sweden to Florence in 1385, the characters becoming leaders of the Guelph and Ghibelline factions. Even the names of the persons were needlessly altered, Amelia becoming Adelia, and the page, Oscar, who was in the event to be one of Verdi's most brilliant musical creations, became Arpini (or, by some strange association of ideas, Orsini), a young knight. Verdi's annotations upon these proposals are scathing. The whole character of the drama would be falsified by its transfer from the north to Italy and backwards in time over three centuries, when habits of thought were utterly different. Besides, the situations in the drama were often altered beyond recognition, and, in particular, the omission of the maskers at the ball would destroy the whole effect of this important scene. Verdi sums up with the statistical facts:

> The *Vendetta in domino* consists of 884 verses, of which 297 are altered in *Adelia*, besides many additions and a great many omissions. Moreover what remains of my work in the drama as revised?
>
> The title? No.
>
> The poet? No. [Somma's name was omitted from the title-page.]
>
> The period? No.
>
> The place? No.
>
> The characters? No.
>
> The situations? No.
>
> The drawing of lots? No.
>
> The festival ball? No.

Had Verdi already been reading Falstaff's speech about honour, that he cast his exasperation in this form?

The upshot was that Naples did not have the privilege of seeing the first performance of the new opera, which was given in Rome on 17th February 1859. But not before other changes had been made in the libretto. Somma was permitted to retain the eighteenth century as his period and northerners as his characters, but at the price of transporting them to Boston, where Gustavus became the English colonial governor, and the Count Ankar-ström his creole (!) secretary. The Counts Horn and Warting lost their titles and assumed the homely names of Tom and Samuel, while the fortune-teller, Ulrica, became a black practitioner of the black arts. To make the matter more ridiculous the governor of Boston, about 1715, was dressed in puritan fashion, and to this day the opera is usually given in Van Dyck costumes, the scene being sometimes transferred to an Italian court—a procedure to which Verdi would have strongly objected.

These modifications were possibly accepted by the composer out of sheer weariness. But at least they did not interfere with the main principles of his dramatic scheme. Indeed, there is not the slightest reason that one can see why nowadays the original Swedish scene and names of the characters should not be restored. Indeed, this has been done in more than one production in recent years; the restoration removes at one stroke several incongruities in the opera as a picture of English colonial administration and enormously heightens its dramatic effect by the association of the action with the well-known historical figure of King Gustavus.

Wherever set, *Un ballo in maschera*, as it was ultimately called, is a magnificent work. Musically it marks an enormous advance upon its predecessors—*Simon Boccanegra* being left out of account—both in its grandeur as a whole and in the subtle light and shade of its characterization. Compare Richard, Earl of Warwick (as the Gustavus of the original became), with the duke in *Rigoletto*. His music often has the same sort of airy elegance, but there is far more character and consequently much more charm in 'È scherzo od è follia' than in 'La donna è mobile.' That the earl, unlike the duke, is not a mere pursuer of women is, of course, a part of the story, but a composer with less sense of character might easily have reduced him to the level of the duke. When he assumes a plebeian disguise in order to test Ulrica's prophetic powers, his music takes on a popular air, which is cast off when his identity is revealed:

He is in fact drawn in the round, not presented as a flat surface with only one aspect.

This greater range is everywhere apparent. Renato, the wronged husband, is an interesting figure throughout, and his great aria, 'Eri tu che macchiavi quell' anima,' remains unsurpassed even in Verdi's later operas as an expression of tragic suffering. The *cantabile* melody of its second strain ('O dolcezze perdute') contains all the heart-ache of disillusionment. Amelia, too, is more complete in her humanity than Verdi's previous heroines. She has at once a more heroic nature than the girlish Gilda or the pathetic Violetta, and more subtlety than the Leonora of *Il Trovatore*. The sombre horror of her midnight visit to the gibbet is depicted with imaginative power that makes Micaela's fears in the smuggler's cave in *Carmen* seem trivial, and in the succeeding duet with her lover Verdi was able for the first time to give complete and convincing expression to passion, because he had already created two credible and adult characters to take part in it.

Not only the principal figures in the drama are characterized with this new mastery. Even the conspirators, despite their ridiculous names and their 'cat-like tread' music, come to life because, as Mr Toye remarks, they have learnt to laugh. They have, in fact, become human beings, a description one could hardly apply to the murderers in *Macbeth*. This new contrast of humour to lighten a gloomy tale—of which, we have seen, Verdi felt the need in *Boccanegra*—is heightened by the delightful figure of the page Oscar. Here is a type entirely new to Italian tragic

119

opera, a genuinely comic creation. The character exists in
Scribe's drama, and there is operatic precedent for him in Meyerbeer and Auber, but is it too much to suppose that we owe
Oscar as he is to the example of the fools who lighten the darkness
of Shakespeare's tragedies? The mocking impertinence of 'Saper
vorreste' serves precisely the same dramatic purpose as Osric's
scene just before the catastrophe in *Hamlet*.

It has been said that Ulrica, the fortune-teller, derives from
Azucena and the witches in *Macbeth*. But she, too, is humorously
observed. We are never quite sure how seriously she is to be
taken, and even her gloomy incantations are lightened by the
comic incident of Silvano, the sailor, who finds the earl's commission surprisingly in his pocket, while the whole scene, begun
so sombrely, ends gaily with the earl's song and a cheerful chorus.
Ulrica, indeed, looks as much forward to the lively Preziosilla
in *La forza del destino* as backward to Azucena.

Hand in hand with this greater command of characterization
goes a far more complex musical texture. Not only is the orchestration fuller and more consistently varied than in any of the
preceding operas—*Boccanegra* again being excepted, on account of
its later revision—but the whole style of the work is more contrapuntal. Verdi is no longer content to rely on simple arpeggio
accompaniments and bare harmonies, lit up though they often
were with flashes of dramatic intuition. The orchestra moves
more freely with genuinely independent parts, and, although the
human voice remains the paramount vehicle of dramatic expression, it no longer entirely monopolizes the interest of the
audience.

Finally there is a great advance in the suppleness of the ensembles. The conspiracy may owe something to the example of
Meyerbeer's *Les Huguenots*, but it is far more sensitive than anything Meyerbeer achieved. In this connection it may be remarked
that, although Verdi was contemptuous of *L'Étoile du Nord*,
Meyerbeer's melody had at this period a great influence upon his
own. In *Un ballo in maschera* and the operas that succeeded it
we are continually coming across this type of tune:

MEYERBEER, *Étoile du Nord*

The *cantabile* section of Renato's 'Eri tu' is of this type. But, whereas Meyerbeer's melody has all the air of having been consciously made up, Verdi's seems to flow spontaneously from an imagination white-hot under the pressure of emotion.

Like the other operas of this period in Verdi's career, *Un ballo in maschera* has its weak patches, among which must be included nearly the whole of the first scene in Act I. The opening chorus presents the opposition of the two parties at Riccardo's court effectively enough, but it can hardly be called first-rate. Riccardo's *romanza* is no more than a pleasant melody without great distinction, and Renato at his first entry echoes the musical style of father Germont in *La Traviata* without achieving his dignity and pathos. The entry of the judge, too, is accompanied by the kind of music that had served for the courtiers in *Rigoletto*. Only Oscar's song, a delightful piece of soubrette music, redeems this scene from being second-rate. Elsewhere the weaknesses are rare, and I am not certain that the sort of tarantella to which Riccardo makes his escape from his enemies in Act II should be included among them. For it has an effective urgency that redeems it from absurdity.

Verdi arrived in Rome only a month before the first performance of *Un ballo in maschera*, having been detained in Naples for the production there of *Simon Boccanegra*, which was substituted for the new opera when the impossibility of satisfying both the censorship and the composer was realized. This visit was the occasion of the first of the series of caricatures made by Melchiorre Delfico, whose witty pencil has recorded some of the amusing incidents without which no opera can be produced. These drawings range from the impressive disembarkation of Verdi and Giuseppina accompanied by Lulu, their *cagnolino*—why has English no diminutive for dog?—to the general rehearsals, and, if one may judge from them, this visit must have been singularly happy. Even Verdi's moments of rage and depression seem but passing shadows that could be comically treated. Any one who can get access to Luzio's *Carteggi Verdiani*, where the whole series is reproduced, will be well rewarded.

Arriving in Rome so soon before the first performance, Verdi seems to have had less say than usual in the production of *Un ballo in maschera*. Indeed, we may fancy that he was so weary of the struggle to get the work produced at all, that he was glad to have it off his hands anyhow, and took less interest than was his custom in the details of casting and staging. In the event he was dissatisfied with the performance, which had an unfavourable reception from a section of the press. To Vincenzo Jacovacci, the impresario, who had secured the production of the opera he wrote some months later:

You are wrong to defend the *Ballo in maschera* from the attacks of the press. You should do as I always do: refrain from reading them and let them sing what tune they please. . . . For the rest, the question is this: is the opera good or bad? If it is bad and the critics say so, they are right; if good and they have not thought it so owing to their own prejudices, etc., one must let them have their say and not take it to heart. Besides, you should be defending yourself in certain matters connected with the spring season. The company you provided was unworthy of me. Listen to the voice of conscience and confess that I was a model of rare restraint in not taking my score away and going in search of dogs who would howl less painfully than those you offered me. But *post factum* and for what followed, etc.

Verdi was not the only composer to profess that he never read nor took any notice of criticism, and perhaps he was more sincere than most of his kind. The brutality of his own criticism of the company may, perhaps, be accounted for in the following paragraph of his letter, where he flatly declines Jacovacci's proposal that he should reduce the rate of his royalties in view of the failure of the opera to attract the public. Verdi was stern in the exaction of his rights and touchy about even a proposal for their curtailment.

The streak of rather cantankerous boorishness in Verdi's temperament made itself felt in another direction when he returned to Sant' Agata. The municipality of Busseto had decided to build a new theatre and not unnaturally desired to enlist the support of their most distinguished fellow-citizen. Verdi disapproved of the expenditure of money upon such a project at a time when every penny was needed for the furtherance of the national cause. In spite of his objection, the building was begun and, on its completion, in 1868, was named after the composer. In the meantime a tactless mayor had stated that the theatre was being built for Verdi's benefit and that he had promised to secure the engagement of the finest singers in Italy. Verdi was furious and refused ever to enter the new theatre, to the cost of which he did, however, subscribe 10,000 lire. He further exacerbated public opinion by pointedly giving away the box that was allotted to him for his own use. This hostile attitude towards the people of Busseto may have been due in part to a rankling memory of the dispute about his appointment to the organist's post in his early youth. But it is more probable that it was the unkind gossip of a country town about his living with a woman to whom he was not married that made Busseto so distasteful to him that he never entered the town if he could avoid it.

Yet he allowed himself, though only under pressure from Cavour himself, to be nominated in 1860 as a local candidate for the national Parliament which was to be convened in accordance with the new Constitution. Verdi had at first flatly refused to stand, and only changed his mind after a visit to Cavour, who impressed upon him the importance of securing as members of the new Parliament all the available men of talent and prestige. In the meantime, Verdi's refusal being regarded as unalterable, another candidate had been nominated, Giovanni Minghelli Vaini, a personal friend of the composer's. On his return to Busseto Verdi characteristically refused to stand down or transfer to another constituency, and he was duly elected. Minghelli Vaini immediately wrote Verdi a generous letter acquitting him of intrigue—a word which, Verdi protested in reply, did not exist in his dictionary. His letter proceeds caustically with a Falstaffian series of questions about 'intrigues' on his behalf during the election, which reads rather ungraciously, as from victor to vanquished. But one fancies that Verdi's instinctive tendency to dramatize any situation often led him to express his feelings more strongly than he really intended, and so exaggerated his appearance of 'bearishness.'

Verdi took his responsibilities as a member of Parliament seriously and attended the sittings at Turin with regularity. He does not seem to have taken part in the debates, and his administrative contribution to the new regime was confined to consultations with Cavour about the co-ordination of the musical institutions in Italy and their relations to the state. He proposed that the three principal theatres (in Rome, Milan and Naples) should receive a Government subsidy and that the conservatoires of music in these cities should be similarly taken over by the state and linked with the theatres. 'Had Cavour lived,' Verdi commented later, 'the plan might have been realized. With other ministers it was impossible.'

Cavour's death in 1861 affected Verdi deeply; he could not 'restrain his tears and wept like a child.' It was, indeed, only his admiration for the statesman that induced him to remain a deputy. He had wished to resign, but acceded to Cavour's entreaty that he should retain his seat at least until the seat of government could be moved to Rome. After Cavour's death, his attendance became less assiduous, partly owing to absence abroad and partly because he became bored with politics, or rather with the politicians.

Later he remarked to Piave that, when the history of that Parliament came to be written, it should be stated that 'there were in
fact not 450, but 449 members, since, as a deputy, Verdi was non-
existent.' He resigned his seat at the election of 1865, declining
to stand again.

This period of his political career provides an interesting piece
of evidence about Verdi's methods as a composer. Next to him
in the chamber sat Quintino Sella, for whom Verdi had a great
respect and friendship. Sella recorded later the following conversation, which alone proves Verdi's regard for his fellow-
deputy, since he rarely discussed music outside the circle of his
intimates and usually snubbed any inquiries about his work:

Sella: When you are composing one of your stupendous pieces of
music, how does the idea present itself to your mind? Do you think
out the principal theme first, and then combine it with an accompaniment, and afterwards consider the nature of the accompanying voices,
whether it shall be for flutes or violins and so forth?

Verdi (interrupting): No, no, no. The idea presents itself complete,
and above all I feel the colour of which you speak, whether it should be
the flute or the violin. My difficulty is to write it down quickly enough,
to express the musical idea in its integrity as it comes into my mind.

It is recorded, too, that on one occasion Verdi amused himself
by setting to music some outburst of feeling in the Assembly. Is
it possible that these experiences suggested the scene in the
council chamber which he and Boito added to the second version
of *Boccanegra*?

Apart from his political activities Verdi occupied himself
during the years after *Un ballo in maschera* with the management and
improvement of his estates. He directed the work of making an
artificial lake and of sinking an artesian well, which was a failure.
He went duck-shooting in the marshes, and was less scrupulous than English sportsmen about what constitutes game. He
ordered from Genoa ten *magnolia grandiflora,* 'about five feet high
. . . and see that they are carefully dug up and wrapped in straw
the day before they are sent.' There were drains to be laid, and
new iron lattices, 'without too much ornamentation so that they

will let in light and air, and adequately strong,' to be made for the ground-floor windows. He was an exacting master and rated his steward for allowing a new piece of agricultural machinery to be used in his absence and for allowing the horses to be idle and get fat and out of condition. For the most part his letters are genial and full of humorous sallies. He shut himself off from the world at Sant' Agata and would have nothing to do with local society, but with his chosen friends he was far from being the morose bear he seemed to casual acquaintances.

Among these friends at this time the chief was Angelo Mariani, who bought shrubs for him, exchanged a gun he had bought in Genoa for another without so much kick, and shared his shooting expeditions at Busseto. Mariani was at this time the conductor of the Carlo Felice Theatre at Genoa, and a musician of outstanding ability. Before his appointment to Genoa in 1852 at the age of thirty, he had travelled much abroad. He was conductor of the Court Theatre at Copenhagen when the revolutions of 1848 broke out, and he returned to Italy in order to join the volunteers. Subsequently he went to Constantinople, where he was honoured by the Sultan, for whom he composed a hymn. As a conductor, he seems to have been the first of a line whose greatest ornament is Arturo Toscanini. Chorley recorded that he gave 'the only good orchestral performance I have encountered in Italy,' and a more recent writer, summing up his qualities, says:

> Mariani exercised an extraordinary personal fascination on all those who were under his direction. For him, no matter the name of the composer, the music he conducted at the moment was always the most beautiful, and he threw himself into it with all his soul. . . . At rehearsal nothing escaped him in the orchestra or on the stage.

Verdi made his acquaintance when he conducted the first performance of *Aroldo* at Rimini, and from that time the two became close friends. When arms were required for the volunteers in the Duchy of Parma during the war of 1859, it was with Mariani that Verdi arranged for their import from England through the port of Genoa. Later, perhaps as a souvenir of this event, he sent the conductor a gun as from 'a Deputy of central Italy who for many years has had the cheek to write music'! When Verdi was in Turin on parliamentary business, he usually managed to slip away to Genoa to see Mariani, and Mariani was a frequent visitor at Sant' Agata. Years later they quarrelled miserably. But for the time there was no one whose society gave Verdi greater pleasure.

CHAPTER XI

THE FORCE OF DESTINY

IN June 1861 Cavour died. Verdi was about to leave for Turin when the news reached him. He was so overcome with grief that he felt unable to attend the funeral and he confesses that at the memorial service at Busseto he cried like a child. He was already conscious of a growing disgust with politics and with the inadequacy of Cavour's successors, and from a letter of Giuseppina's written at a rather later date it appears that he was beginning to be bored with shooting. Gardening alone survived as an abiding hobby till the end of his life. The arrival of Achille Tamberlik, son of the famous tenor, from St Petersburg with a commission to write an opera for the Imperial Theatre was, therefore, opportune and Verdi once more turned eagerly to composition.

The contract was signed at Turin in June. *Ruy Blas* was suggested as a possible subject, but Verdi was given a free hand, the only restriction made (unofficially) being that he must not insist on the tsar's proclaiming a republic! Verdi rejected Victor Hugo's drama. He remembered having read some years before a romantic Spanish tragedy by the Duke of Rivas, *Don Alvaro, o La fuerza del sino*, and the bookshops of Turin were vainly ransacked for a copy. In the end one was procured from Milan. That this subject had been in Verdi's mind at least ten years before is evident from a letter written in 1852 by de Sanctis who says: 'I begged you to let me know, as a favour, what subject you have chosen for Venice, but you have not gratified me. Is it to be *Faust* or *Kean* or *Pagliaccio*, or *La forza del destino*?'

This tragedy, which Verdi justly described as 'potente, singolare e vastissimo,' was written by the duke, who was a liberal politician as well as a distinguished man of letters, during a period of exile in France, and was produced in Madrid shortly after his return to Spain in 1834. During his exile Rivas visited England, where he came under the influence of Walter Scott. *Don Alvaro* is an extreme example of romantic melodrama. The action concerns a noble Spanish family caught helplessly in the toils of fate. It is full of accidents and coincidences, none of them beyond the bounds of possibility, but producing in the sum an effect of extravagant improbability. The fantastic activities of Alvaro and the de Vargas family in pursuit of their vendetta was, however, set against a background of minutely observed Spanish life during one of the interminable civil wars that have been the curse of Spain. For this background Rivas had plenty of first-hand material, for he had served against the French in the Peninsular War and had no doubt witnessed many of the horrifying scenes that have been preserved for us by Goya's scathing pencil.

Inevitably much of this most interesting local colour had to be sacrificed in the process of reducing the drama to operatic proportions—a task undertaken by the faithful Piave. Indeed Verdi's choice of the subject is the most striking instance of his blindness to certain aspects of opera. So long as a subject presented him with a series of striking situations which could be made theatrically effective, he was content. He did not very much care what happened between these situations nor whether they were joined together by a convincing chain of cause and effect. No doubt, having the original of his libretto in his mind, he imagined that the action was being set forth in an intelligible manner. Or perhaps he did not very much care whether the spectator understood what was happening, so long as he felt the powerful emotions aroused by the dramatic situations. If, however, an opera is to be regarded as a work of art, it must be self-contained and self-explanatory. It should not be necessary to go to outside sources in order to understand the motives of the characters and their actions. Verdi's tendency to dismiss an important dramatic point in a couple of lines of recitative has already been observed in discussing *Macbeth* (the fight between Macbeth and Macduff) and *Simon Boccanegra* (the scene between Simon and Paolo in the first act). This jumping from climax to climax was of less importance in the earlier operas, as for instance *Il Trovatore*, in which it may indeed be considered an element of strength. But in the later works, which aim at genuine tragedy as Shakespeare understood it and not at conventional melodrama, these inadequacies seriously detract from the design and go some way towards cancelling their subtlety and depth of emotion. It is this weakness, which amounts to a serious flaw in Verdi's literary and dramatic sense, rather than the occasional lapses of the music into triteness, that has deprived such works as *Simon Boccanegra*, *La forza del destino* and *Don Carlo* of the success they deserve on musical grounds. For the difference in musical quality between these operas and *Otello*, considerable though it often is, is not sufficiently great to justify our setting them on an altogether lower plane. But the difference between their librettos and Boito's masterly compression of Shakespeare's tragedy is enormous.

By July 1861 Verdi was at work with Piave at Busseto, and in September Giuseppina wrote to Tamberlik on his behalf—'he is absorbed in composition and has not a minute to spare'— about the production, 'which is his province and not Piave's.' By the end of October Verdi was able to announce that 'this accursed *Forza del destino* is practically finished, apart from the orchestration, which is no great matter. Any quarter of an hour serves to get on with the work. I write to you in fret and fury and must run back to my martyrdom.'

Early in the following year Verdi visited St Petersburg to supervise the production of the new opera, but the illness of the *prima donna*, La Grua, and the impossibility of finding a substitute necessitated its postponement until the autumn. Verdi and his wife took the opportunity to visit Moscow, and returned to Sant' Agata, whence he wrote on 15th April:

I am here on business. To-morrow or the day after or the day after that I go to London to join Peppina, who has been there for the past fortnight. The bearer of this is a young man from the village, good, honest, very willing and exceedingly shy—so do look kindly on him or he will be scared out of his wits. . . . On the way back from London

I shall stay in Paris: in September back to St Petersburg. You see what an infernal life it is!

The occasion of the visit to London was an invitation to compose a work for the opening of the exhibition of 1862. Rossini having excused himself on the grounds of his age from representing Italy, Verdi was asked to take his place. His acceptance is rather surprising in view of his dislike of such commissions and his general disinclination to write occasional works. It is possible that Enrico Tamberlik had something to do with the matter. The tenor divided his time between St Petersburg, where he sang in the winter, and London. The solo part in Verdi's festival work was designed for him. But undoubtedly patriotism was the chief motive that dictated acceptance. It was important that Italian claims to musical eminence among the nations should not go by default. England was to be represented by Sterndale Bennett who set an official ode by Tennyson; France by Auber who offered a march; and Germany, oddly enough, by Meyerbeer who wrote an overture.

Verdi's popularity in England had grown since his previous visit, despite the vigorously expressed criticisms of Chorley and Davison. All his operas were produced in London soon after their first appearance in Italy or in Paris. *Un ballo in maschera* was given in 1861 with success, though the two critics were of opinion that it was vastly inferior to Auber's *Gustave III*. 'I was never fully aware of the value of Auber's music,' wrote Chorley, 'till I heard the assault made by Signor Verdi on the same subject.' So completely could two honest and by no means unintelligent men be blinded to what was fine and original in Verdi's music by their prejudice in favour of the refined and gentle melodies of an earlier generation and their dislike of what they thought a vulgar brutality. It is, even so, difficult to understand how they could prefer the more blatant vulgarity of Meyerbeer or the empty glitter of Auber to Verdi's obvious strength.

Verdi's contribution to the festivities in London was a cantata, *Inno delle Nazioni* (*Hymn of the Nations*), which is remarkable only for the fact that its text was by Arrigo Boito and that its finale consists of an apostrophe to England, France and Italy, which was set to a contrapuntal combination of 'God save the Queen,' 'La Marseillaise' and Novaro's 'Inno di Mameli.' In the event this extraordinary farrago was not performed at the exhibition. The excuse given was that the score was not delivered in time—which was untrue. Mr Toye suggests that the true reason for its non-appearance was political, Her Majesty's Commissioners taking exception to the use of the revolutionary 'Marseillaise,' which had not yet achieved the respectable status of a national anthem outside France. It was as if to-day a composer should use 'The Red Flag' as a theme in an official composition for some royal occasion. Possibly, too, the aspirations for a free and united Italy expressed in Boito's poem were considered impolitic. The hymn was eventually given after a performance of *The Barber of Seville* at Her Majesty's Theatre, the soloist being Mme Tietjens. It was encored, Verdi was called before the curtain, and the critics praised the vigour of the choruses and the 'pompous and brilliant instrumentation.' Even the combination of the three national melodies was hailed as a piece of polyphonic ingenuity 'rarely heard in his operas.' *The Times* incidentally stigmatized the text as 'the somewhat bombastic stanzas of the poetaster whom it has been the fortune of the popular Italian composer to immortalize.' Immortalize him he did, but not with this hymn.

Boito, who was the son of a Paduan miniature-painter and a Polish lady, Countess Josephine Radolinska, was born in 1842 and studied music at the Milan Conservatorio, where he formed a close friendship with Franco Faccio, a fellow-student who became a famous conductor. The two friends collaborated in the composition of *Le sorelle d'Italia,* a cantata of which each wrote a part. Its success earned them a travelling scholarship, and they went to Paris where it is probable that Verdi met Boito at Rossini's house, which was the resort of all artists on a visit to Paris. Boito was an intellectual young man. During his residence in Milan he had studied poetry as well as music and practised himself in literary composition. His musical taste centred in an admiration for Beethoven and he subsequently became, for a time, an enthusiastic admirer of Wagner. It is not surprising, therefore, that he had no great opinion of the debased medium of Italian melodrama, in which Verdi was expending his genius. In the year after his first collaboration with Verdi he published a poem which heralded the advent of a new composer who should once more restore the honour of Italian music 'upon the altar now befouled with the filth of the brothel'—a callow effusion which was probably intended rather as a puff for Faccio than as an attack on Verdi. Such expressions, however, could not but offend the leading Italian composer of the day. To Ricordi he suggested that if the altar needed purifying, Boito had better show how it might be done, and he (Verdi) would come and light the first candle in his honour. To Piave he wrote acidly two years later:

> Do not be afraid of this Babylonian music of the future, as you call it. . . . These apostles of the future would initiate something sublime. It is necessary to *cleanse the altar fouled* by the swine of the past. These gentlemen want music to be pure, virginal, holy, to be spherical music![1] I look up at the heavens and watch for the star that will show me where the Messiah is born, so that, like the royal Magi, I may go and adore Him.

Thus unhappily began the relations of the two men whose ultimate collaboration was to rival that of Mozart and da Ponte as the happiest and most fruitful in the history of opera. Boito's unfortunate lampoon was merely the effusion of a sanguine young man giving vent to a passing distaste by way of showing enthusiasm for the music of his own generation. He had no real and deep-seated dislike of Verdi's music, as is proved by his eventual conversion to a whole-hearted admiration, which included a special affection for 'Quando le sere al placido' in *Luisa Miller*. In the event, Boito's learning, culture and literary taste were the perfect complement to Verdi's intuitive genius. It is unfortunate that a youthful ebullition of the poet's should so long have kept them apart.

---

[1] This refers to an article by Boito in which, contrasting the *Beautiful* with the *Sublime*, he wrote: 'The Sublime consists of the grand design . . . spherical form. . . . Beethoven is spherical.'

The summer of 1862 was spent at Sant'Agata upon finishing the orchestration of *La forza del destino*, and at the end of August Verdi and his wife set out for St Petersburg via Paris and Moscow. The new opera was produced on 10th November, and four days later Giuseppina wrote gaily to the de Sanctis:

I have been silent, thou hast been silent, he has been silent, we have been silent, and so on. It is true I have not written, Verdi has not written and you have mislaid pen, paper and inkstand. This reciprocal silence is no cause for reproach since, if sin there is, we are both guilty. However the silence of the pen does not imply silence in the heart, and I hope that you and your dear wife love us as we love and always have loved you. I hope you admire my skill in conjugation and the wealth of my vocabulary.

But to come to ourselves. The proverb says: 'No news is good news,' not always with accuracy. But I give you on this occasion news and good news! *La forza del destino* has been produced with great success. A good performance by every one, singers, chorus and orchestra. The emperor had an attack of bronchitis and severe ophthalmia, and was unable to be present until the fourth performance.

Your friend lost nothing on that account however, for the emperor applauded, himself called out his name and had him presented by the minister in his box. There he was, so to say, buried under an avalanche of compliments, especially from the empress who was most gracious and appreciative in all she said. You imagine that this presentation in the temple was the end of it? *Niett*, as they say in Russia; on Satur-day Verdi received the imperial and royal order of St Stanislas (the commander's cross to hang round his neck), and that without any suggestion or intervention from outside, but *per moto proprio* of the Emperor of all the Russias! Doff your hat and bow to the emperor, to the cultured public and to the Illustrious Night-gown, and so good-night!

We leave shortly for Spain where Verdi has accepted a pressing invitation to produce the new opera. . . . We shall be in Madrid at the end of December.

It was natural that Madrid should wish to see Verdi's setting of the popular Spanish drama, which had given a new impetus to national poetry and ousted the French classics from the Spanish stage.

The enthusiasm for *La forza del destino* in St Petersburg was not unanimous outside the court. The Russian musicians, growing conscious of national ideals and impatient of the long domination of foreign composers, regarded Verdi as yet another interloper, and ruefully contrasted the large fee of 20,000 roubles he received with the 500 they were usually paid for an opera. This opposition even made itself audible in a demonstration at one of the per-formances. Nor was even the Italian press exactly enthusiastic, the critics concentrating on the progress Verdi displayed in his orchestration and on the beauty and originality of the choruses, and leaving unsaid the things that would indicate a high opinion of the opera as a whole.

Apart from what has already been said about the weakness of the libretto, due to the reduction of Rivas's vast canvas to the size of an opera, the chief criticism that may be made against *Forza* is its atmosphere of gloom and horror. It is certainly relieved, unlike *Simon Boccanegra*, against which a similar charge may be sustained, by the genre-scenes that survived from the original— the choruses of soldiers and peasants, the picturesque scene in the monastery and the comic figures of Melitone, the friar in whom the weakness of the flesh is more obvious than the devotion of the spirit, and of Preziosilla, the fortune-telling *vivandière*.

It is odd that the early critics of the opera made no mention of Fra Melitone, for he is the most original and remarkable creation in this opera. He is, indeed, a character unique in Verdi's tragedies, for though he had introduced the sardonic Sparafucile into *Rigoletto* and the impertinent Oscar into *Un ballo in maschera*, this is the only occasion on which a character derived from *opera buffa* introduces a note of farcical comedy into a serious opera. In conception Melitone owes something to such figures of fun as Don Pasquale and Rossini's Dr Bartolo, especially in the earlier scenes, but in the punning sermon delivered to the troops and in what may be called the soup-kitchen scene he comes near to Falstaff. Oddly, too, he will remind any one who has seen Moussorgsky's *Boris Godounov* of that more rascally and intemperate monk, Varlaam, and one cannot help wondering whether

Mussorgsky, whose opera was first produced at St Petersburg in 1874, did not see and profit by Verdi's handling of a similar character.

Preziosilla is a more conventional figure for whom precedent can be found in *opéra comique*. She is even given a 'rataplan' song with chorus which is clearly derived from the imitation-band choruses that were a popular feature of French comic opera at the time. The example most familiar to modern audiences is the chorus of *gamins* accompanying the arrival of Don José and his troop in *Carmen*, which is a refinement upon the broad humours of Auber's *Fra Diavolo* and Meyerbeer's *Étoile du Nord*, where this kind of thing is carried to ridiculous lengths in imitations of a full brass-band, of the rattle of dice in the box and so on. The inclusion of this kind of music and of a character like Preziosilla in an Italian tragic opera is worthy of remark, revealing, as it does, how far Verdi had travelled from the narrow limits of the world of *opera seria*.

In his earlier operas Verdi moves in a strictly circumscribed world inhabited entirely by characters under the ban of some extraordinary fatality. In *Rigoletto* this world had been enlarged to include the tragi-comic figure of the protagonist, and in *La Traviata* we are introduced to a more intimate world in which the characters, for all their conventionality of utterance, are closer to ourselves and our own experience. But, notwithstanding the pertness of Oscar and the human villains in *Un ballo in maschera*, it is in *La forza del destino* that Verdi achieves something like universality for the first time, comprehending in it so wide a variety of types that the opera comes near to being a microcosm of the world we live in, despite the strain put upon our credulity by the extravagant romanticism of the drama. The choruses of peasants, muleteers, pilgrims, monks, soldiers and gipsies, for all that they are sometimes trivial as music, have an individuality that rarely makes itself felt in the earlier operas, with occasional exceptions in *Il Trovatore*. Those earlier choruses are, from the dramatic point of view, no more than part of the scenic background before which the chief characters move. Musically they serve merely to provide a contrast to the solos and a means of making a resounding climax in the finales. In *Forza* the crowd has a life and a character of its own, for a contemporary parallel to which we must go to *Boris Godounov*.

This extension of Verdi's musical resources is evidence of his readiness to take over and turn to his own account whatever he found useful in the music of other composers. This is not, however, a foundation for a charge of plagiarism. Any artist has the right, even as any scientist has, to make use of the discoveries and inventions of his colleagues, provided always that he does not merely reproduce them as tricks, but absorbs them into his own being, makes them a starting-point for fresh adventures, and so endues them with the force of his own individuality that, though their origin may still be recognizable, the result is far from being a literal copy. It is not to be forgotten, either, that at any given moment in the history of art there are certain ideas, certain tendencies, as it were, in the air, which may be seized upon and developed by a man of genius so that they are ever afterwards associated by historians with his name as though he were their sole originator. In the nineteenth century the tendency of opera was to develop in the direction of symphony. The self-contained arias joined by recitative gave place to a more continuous musical style, in which aria and recitative are less and less clearly differentiated until they become an unending melodic declamation that rises at the dramatic climaxes to a more formal lyrical style. This manner was most rapidly developed in Germany, where the modern symphony originated and naturally had the most powerful influence upon operatic composers, and Wagner was of course its great exponent. But the same process was at work elsewhere, and in Verdi's operas there is a gradual advance from a rigid scheme of air and recitative towards a more flexible and coherent style until in *Otello* we are hardly conscious of the transition from recitative to air and in *Falstaff* there is actually nothing that can be torn out of the opera for exhibition on the concert platform.[1]

[1] Except the miniature 'Quand' ero paggio,' which is hardly an exception since it loses its effect out of its context and becomes a mere test of the singer's ability to sing a patter song very fast.

As a composer Verdi was, no less than Leonora and Alvaro in his opera, subject to the force of destiny as manifested in the musical developments of the age in which he lived.

It is important, therefore, to examine Verdi's attitude to other composers, and of this we fortunately have first-hand evidence in a letter written in 1869 to Filippi, the critic of *La Perseveranza*, who thought he had discovered a similarity between a passage in Leonora's music and Schubert's 'Ave Maria.' [1] After assuring Filippi that he bore him no ill-will for tempering his praise with criticism of certain details, and declaring that he neither complained of censure nor thanked those who expressed admiration for his music ('wherein,' he adds, 'I am possibly wrong'), he continues:

I can well believe that Ricordi, who, unless I am mistaken, has a high opinion of Leonora's *cantabile*, was disconcerted by your suggestion that it was an imitation of Schubert. If it is, I am not less astonished, for in my profound musical ignorance I cannot remember how many years it is since I heard Schubert's 'Ave,' and it would therefore be difficult for me to imitate it. Do not imagine that when I write of 'my profound musical ignorance' I am joking. It is the simple truth. In my house there is very little music, and I do not go to musical libraries or publishers to look at scores. I go now and then to the better contemporary operas, not as a student, but to hear what they are like in the theatre, from motives which you will appreciate. I repeat that of all composers, past and present, I am the least learned. I mean what I say in all seriousness, and by *learning* I do not mean *knowledge* of music. It is true that in my youth I studied long and laboriously. In that way I acquired sufficient ability to bend the notes to my will and to realize without difficulty the ideas of my imagination. If I am guilty of breaking rules, it is because I cannot get what I want by a strict adherence to them, and because I do not believe in the infallibility of all the accepted theories. The treatises on counterpoint badly need rewriting.

Verdi was much too honest to write in this vein if he did not mean it, and we need not waste time upon a sterile argument about whether the alleged resemblance to the 'Ave Maria' may or may not have been due to an unconscious memory of Schubert's

[1] The reference is presumably to Leonora's music at the opening of the last act ('Pace, pace'), though the resemblance is not marked.

phrase. To this kind of criticism Brahms had the perfect answer
when he retorted to those who perceived a resemblance between the
tune in the finale of his first Symphony and that in Beethoven's
ninth: 'Any ass can see that!'

It will be more profitable to examine Verdi's relationship to his
great German contemporary. For it has been too frequently
assumed, especially in England, where German views about
music for so long dominated scholastic and critical opinion, that
anything in Verdi's music in which a remote resemblance to
anything in Wagner's could be found, must have been lifted by
the Italian from the German. This was a not unnatural result
of the impact of Wagner's novel, not to say revolutionary, procedure
and of the enthusiastic propaganda of his pamphleteers (among
whom he must be himself accorded the first place). Now that
the dust has settled we can see more clearly, and the first fact that
leaps to the eye is that until 1865 Verdi had heard not one note of
Wagner's music. He had missed the historic Paris production of
Tannhäuser in 1861, whose failure to please the patrons of the
Opéra is described with malicious glee in a letter to Verdi from
Léon Escudier. When he was in Paris for the rehearsals of
Don Carlo he went to a concert at which the overture to *Tann-
häuser* was played. 'È matto' ('he is daft') was his comment to
Arrivabene, and to the Countess Maffei he wrote: 'So I know a
little of everything and nothing about anything!'

It is certainly not of anything in the *Tannhäuser* overture that
Verdi's orchestration at this period reminds us. There are
passages for the brass, particularly in *Don Carlo*, that recall
Wagner's use of those instruments in the *Ring*. But of that it
is quite safe to say that Verdi knew nothing at all. He did not
hear even *Lohengrin* until 1871 (after *Aida* was written), when
Mariani conducted it at Bologna. Of course there were scores.
Tristan was published in 1860 and the pianoforte score of *Die
Walküre* appeared in 1865. But as we have seen Verdi did not
study scores. To the evidence of his letter to Filippi may be
added his declaration that music is meant for the ears and not for
the eyes and his warning to a visitor to Sant' Agata that 'we do

not discuss music here and you will probably find that the pianoforte is not only out of tune but without any strings!'

The origin of the 'Wagnerisms,' with which Verdi was reproached at the time by critics in Italy—for they fell into the same fallacy—must be sought elsewhere. It will be found in the sources from which Wagner himself drew. These included, besides Beethoven, Schubert and Schumann, who are not to our purpose, Meyerbeer and Berlioz. About Meyerbeer Verdi could be as caustic as Wagner himself, as for instance in the criticism, quoted above, of *L'Étoile du Nord*. But that he was greatly influenced by his example has already been shown. For Berlioz the man he felt at first an affection based upon an elective affinity. But as the French composer's cantankerousness developed, until at the end it passed the bounds of reason, Verdi, himself always sane and well-balanced, modified his judgment. In 1882 he wrote to Arrivabene:

Berlioz was a poor sick man, rabid against every one, bitter and malignant. He had great genius, a keen sensibility and a feeling for instrumentation. He anticipated many of Wagner's orchestral effects, though the Wagnerians will not admit it. He was without restraint and lacked the calm and that equilibrium which produces perfect works of art.

Still less did Verdi owe anything to Wagner's structural procedure. The repetition of certain themes in Verdi's operas has been seized upon as evidence of an indebtedness to Wagner's *Leitmotiv*-principle. But that is to misunderstand that principle completely. For the *Leitmotiv*, when it is not a mere label tied to some character or object upon the stage, is a short symphonic theme whose dual purpose is to provide material for the weaving of a continuous and coherent musical texture and to evoke in the hearer emotions aroused by the previous associations of the theme. At its best the *Leitmotiv* can be the means of achieving at once the most powerful dramatic effect, the most subtle characterization and the most highly organized musical texture imaginable. In the third act of *Tristan* the themes previously stated are subjected to changes and to combinations that present to us with the utmost psychological truth the hero's disordered imagination. Such subtlety, which goes far beyond the delineation of 'character' and penetrates into the inmost soul of man, has never been achieved elsewhere in opera, nor elsewhere outside the works of the greatest novelists. For the process ends in bringing Wagner nearer to Henry James than to Shakespeare.

There is nothing of the kind to be found in Verdi. When he repeats a theme, it is with only the simplest and least subtle intention. The nearest he comes to a psychological use of the repetition is when he wishes his characters to recall past happiness (and so to remind the audience of it) at a moment of crisis. Otello kisses Desdemona for the last time to the same music which accompanies their embrace in the first act. Don Carlos recalls in his misery the melody he had sung at Fontainebleau when Elizabeth was his betrothed. This is allusion in its most direct and simple form. The music never suggests, as Wagner's often does, what lies behind their words or actions in the inmost thoughts of his characters.

More often the repetitions have not even so much dramatic character as that, but simply serve to accompany or signal the approach of the character with whom they are associated, just as Figaro sings a snatch of 'Se vuol ballare' as he enters the countess's boudoir. No one has ever suggested that there is a use of *Leitmotiv* by Mozart. Verdi's repetitions are, in fact, no more than reprises, sometimes in the most literal sense of the term, as when Aida repeats the final phrases of 'Ritorna vincitor' at the end of her stormy scene with Amneris in the second act. How little conscious, as compared with Wagner's, Verdi's method was may be seen from the fact that it is impossible even to be certain whether the recurrence of a phrase from Manrico's first song in his contribution to the 'Miserere' scene is deliberate or not.

It seems strange at this time of day that Verdi should ever have been accused of Wagnerism, for his melodies are wholly unsuitable to the Wagnerian manner of symphonic development, even had he wished to resort to it. As a composer he was Wagner's equal and opposite. He believed in concision even to a fault and, where Wagner expands his mighty themes ever more fully in the process of explaining the motives of the action until he brings the drama dangerously near a standstill, Verdi passes so rapidly from one salient situation to the next that we have some difficulty in perceiving what are the connecting links of the story. It is significant that the whole of *Falstaff*, which may be taken as the most complete and satisfactory realization of Verdi's ideal, could be played through with something to spare in the time occupied by the last act of *Die Meistersinger*.

It is high time that we returned from this lengthy digression to the proper subject of this chapter. Our excursion was not, however, so irrelevant as it may have seemed. For at the very outset of *La forza del destino* Verdi states a theme whose use exemplifies what had just been said about his method. It admirably characterizes the agitation of the unfortunate heroine and accompanies her faithfully throughout her many vicissitudes:

This unusually concise theme, whose essential feature is the phrase marked A, is exceptionally adapted for symphonic treatment, and it is in fact used in the *andante* section of the overture as a counterpoint to Leonora's other main theme, the wonderfully strong, yet pathetic, melody for her air, 'Madre, pietosa Vergine':

La forza del destino is one of the few operas for which Verdi
wrote a full-blown overture, and the form of this very malleable
theme may well have been dictated by the use to which it was to
be put as a counter-subject. To depict the fury of Amneris in
Aida he wrote a very similar theme, whose use as an accompaniment to Radamès's 'Nè d'Amneris paventi il vindice furor'
comes as near as anything in Verdi's operas to resembling Wagner's
use of *Leitmotiv*—and still remains in its simplicity and lack of
subtlety far removed from it.

The example last quoted incidentally exhibits several other characteristics of Verdi's mature style. There is the strong rhythmic
bass, so different from the simple harmonies marking the strong
beats in the earlier operas, which carries the music forward on its
undercurrent. There is the bold and beautiful line of the melody
at the top, devoid of ornament and relying solely upon its broad
curve. Compared with it the melodies given to Gilda ('Caro
nome'), Violetta ('Ah! fors è lui') or even to the heroine of *Il
Trovatore* ('D' amor sull' ali rosee') seem short-winded and almost
fussy in their elaborate vocal ornaments. Verdi had developed a
plainer and more virile melodic manner, which (it should be
remembered) laid him open, no less than Wagner, to the criticism
that he was ruining the art of singing. To us nowadays his music
seems the last mainstay of that sadly neglected art. But to conservative admirers of Rossini, Donizetti and Bellini his shrieking
sopranos and bawling tenors were monstrous negations of *bel
canto*. Even in the 1890's Bernard Shaw, in his paradoxical desire

to prove that Wagner could write for the voice, conclusively proved to his own satisfaction that Verdi could not:

Any one who knows how to sing can go through all the solos proper to his or her voice in *Messiah*, and feel not only free from fatigue, but much the better for the exercise. The same experiment in *Il Trovatore* or in *Un ballo* would leave them tired and, as regards a considerable part of their compass, almost toneless. The *reductio ad absurdum* of the Verdi style is the music-hall style, which is simply the abuse of a particular part of the voice carried to its furthest possible limit. Signor d' Andrade at Covent Garden, who can shout all the high G's of the Count di Luna with the greatest gusto, fails as Figaro in *Le Nozze*, exactly as the vivacious lady who sang 'Woman, poor, weak woman' at the Alhambra the other night would fail if she were to try, 'Eccomi alfine in Babilonia,' or 'Return, O God of Hosts.' No doubt she would protest that Rossini and Handel did not know how to write for the voice, quite as vehemently as the Verdi screamers did when Wagner went back to the old plan and revived the art of singing for us.

Elsewhere Shaw inveighs against Verdi for 'his habit of taking the upper fifth of the compass of an exceptionally high voice, and treating that fifth as the normal range,' and there is certainly some truth beneath his exaggerated statements. It is almost as difficult to find an adequate Manrico or Othello as it is to find a Siegfried. But Shaw forgot that Verdi was writing for Italian voices and Wagner for German, and that they are not the same thing. He also ignores the fact that Rossini's *tessitura*—for example in the case of Figaro in *Il Barbiere di Siviglia*—is often quite as high as Verdi's, even though his music may make less demands upon the singer's robustness. It is certainly most surprising to find this advanced radical joining forces with the old conservatives of a generation earlier and completely missing the real point. It is also odd that these champions of the old *bel canto* never seem to have condemned in Meyerbeer, whose tenor in *Les Huguenots* is expected to possess a high C♯, the sins that they anathematized in Verdi. Even Mozart himself is open to the criticism of employing a *tessitura* too high for any tenor's comfort in Don Ottavio's airs and of writing for the Queen of Night music that really demands, even more than Violetta's, two different types of voice.

The Leonora of *La forza del destino* is own sister to Amelia in *Un ballo*, but she is drawn on a more heroic scale. Her music is austere in its rejection of all bravura, of all the trills and roulades of her namesake in *Il Trovatore*.[1] Not for her the gay *cabaletta* nor, even in the moment of her last desperate meeting with Alvaro, any note of 'dolce giubilo.' She has little enough cause for jubilation. From the very rise of the curtain she is a doomed and unhappy figure. Her story depends so much upon arbitrary accidents and coincidences, and so little upon actions and motives within the control of the characters, that it fails to qualify for the title of tragedy, if by that term we mean something more than a tale of disaster. Even the Greeks did not accept a view of destiny so blind and motiveless as this. Fate might strike the apparently innocent, but there was always some hereditary taint, some primal sin that must be expiated. Theoretically, at least, Leonora should be the least interesting of heroines. For it is difficult to feel any interest in, and therefore any sympathy with, a merely passive victim of senselessly cruel circumstance, whose character and actions have no influence upon the course of the drama. But music has a provoking way of upsetting theories and falsifying the deductions of logic. The greater intensity of musical expression, as compared even with that of all but the finest poetry in Shakespeare, can give to an opera an essential truth and a convincingness that would be lacking in a play upon the same theme. Verdi's music, compounded of strength and pathos, does clothe the dramatic nullity of Leonora with the cloak of the authentic tragic heroine. To our intellect she may remain a lay figure, but to our emotions she is a living human personality.

The same considerations apply to Don Alvaro, her lover, who is characterized only by a certain noble if rather perfunctory idealism, and to Don Carlo, her brother, whose desire for revenge seems, perhaps, less extravagant in the hot-blooded south than it

[1] In a letter to Luccardi concerning the production of *La forza del destino* in Rome (February 1863) Verdi says: 'There is no need [in this opera] for vocal exercises [*solfeggi*], but the singers must have souls and understand the text and be able to express it.'

does to us. The accidental discharge of a pistol which sets in train the woeful sequence of events makes a weak beginning from the theatrical point of view. For while such an accident can be effectively described in a narrative form, it is not easy to make it clear to an audience in the theatre that it is an accident, and the literal adherence to the stage direction—'Don Alvaro throws down his pistol which on striking the ground goes off and mortally wounds the Marquis'—raises practical difficulties of stage-management and is apt to produce the unfortunate effect that Alvaro has thrown a squib. The final catastrophe is no less unhappy from the dramatic point of view. For Carlo is killed and Leonora is stabbed by him before he dies off stage, while Alvaro is left alive to curse his fate.[1] Not even the beauty of the final trio can wholly palliate the ineffectiveness of this ending.

Yet when all has been said against the absurdity of a hero whose acts are always contrary to his intentions and who is so fantastically negative, and of Don Carlo, who sets his sense of family honour so high that he disregards his own, these two puppets are given at least the semblance of flesh and blood by the splendour of their music. Their two great duets are as fine as anything Verdi wrote for tenor and baritone. Carlo even shows something approaching a sense of humour, which never reappears in the later acts, during his first scene when he is disguised as a student. His narration here is an effective piece of characterization, even though we may feel that it does not accord with what we learn of him elsewhere.

Throughout the opera the recitative has a flexibility and an aptness of the highest order, while the instrumentation shows yet one more advance in the command of orchestral colour upon anything Verdi had previously achieved. Nothing could be

---

[1] This is one of the modifications made by Verdi and Ghislanzoni for the revival of the opera at Milan in 1869. In the original version the duel was fought on the stage and Alvaro committed suicide at the end. The alteration, due apparently to a feeling that the stage was overloaded with corpses, is a particularly unhappy application of the old classical principle: 'Ne pueros coram populo Medea trucidet.'

better done than the opening scene in which the Marquis of Calatrava is saying good-night to his daughter. Verdi contrives to invest it with a sense of tragic foreboding that foreshadows the intensely pathetic scene between Desdemona and Emilia in the last act of *Otello*, yet without giving a disproportionate emphasis to the commonplaces of the domestic colloquy. The dialogue between Leonora and Fra Guardiano, to quote but one more passage, is another instance of the naturalness and freedom of the recitatives.

But when all is said, the greatness of *La forza del destino* lies in the succession of great and noble melodies, and in the beauty and masterly handling of the concerted numbers. The ensemble in the second act, where the chorus of pilgrims is contrasted with that of the visitors at the inn by the opposition of minor and major keys, while Leonora's voice soars independently above the rest in great, sweeping phrases, can bear comparison with the finest things of its kind in *Aida*, the *Requiem* and the revised version of *Boccanegra*. Even more beautiful, because more profound in its feeling, is the finale of the second act, where Leonora takes her vow in the Franciscan monastery. Indeed the whole of this scene, which begins with the lovely aria, 'Madre, pietosa Vergine,' and ends with the no less beautiful 'La Vergine degli angeli,' ranks very high among the best individual scenes in Verdi's operas, and is alone sufficient to give this work an exceptional distinction.

CHAPTER XII

'DON CARLO'

AFTER his visit to Madrid Verdi returned to Sant' Agata by way of Paris, where he discussed with Léon Escudier, director of the Théâtre Lyrique, various projects, including the production of *La forza del destino*. He felt so dissatisfied, however, with the original ending of the opera that he preferred to withdraw it from performance until some more satisfactory solution could be found. It was arranged instead that Verdi should revise *Macbeth*. Something has already been said about this revision, which included the addition of a ballet (for Hecate and the witches), without which no opera was considered complete in Paris. It is easy to smile at this ballet music, which includes a tarantella and a waltz, so inapt does it look on paper for the infernal characters who perform it. But Verdi was very serious about it.

The apparition of Hecate, the goddess of night [he wrote to Escudier], is well conceived, for it interrupts the infernal dances and provides an opportunity for a calm and severe *adagio*. I need hardly say that Hecate should not dance, but mime her part. Nor need I insist that this *adagio* must be played, as it is written, by a bass-clarinet which, in unison with the violoncello and bassoon, will produce the deep tone, dark [*cupo*] and severe, that the situation demands. . . . You realize that the dances are continually changing in tempo. (At the Opéra, for instance, I should say that the tarantella cannot be danced as I should wish. A street urchin from Sorrento or Capua would dance it best of all with the tempi I want.) If the tempi are not observed, this ballet of witches will lose all its character and will not produce the effect that I believe it has.

There was some disagreement about the French translation, which was at first entrusted to Édouard Duprez, who had made versions of other operas by Verdi. Duprez's brother complained to Verdi that Carvalho, Escudier's partner, had unjustly criticized the translation, though others approved it. Verdi supported Duprez, in whose judgment he had confidence, but the task was, nevertheless, transferred to Nuitter and Beaumont, who had made the translation of *Tannhäuser*.

From the interesting correspondence about this production the following passages deserve quotation:

You must adhere strictly to the instruments composing the small orchestra beneath the stage at the apparition of the eight kings. This little orchestra of two oboes, six clarinets in A, two bassoons and one contra-bassoon produces a sonority that is strange and mysterious, and at the same time calm and quiet, such as other instruments cannot do. They must be under the stage, but beneath an open trap large enough to allow the sound to come out into the theatre, but in a mysterious way as though from a great distance.

You will smile when you see that for the battle I have written a fugue! I who detest all that smells of the school! But I tell you that in this case the musical form fits the occasion well. The rushing to and fro of the subject and counter-subject, and the clash of the dissonances express a battle well enough. Ah! if you could only have our trumpets with their brilliant, sonorous tone! Your *trompettes à piston* are neither flesh nor fish ... I see the newspapers are already talking about *Macbeth*. But, for the love of God, *ne blaguez pas trop*.

Verdi always disliked the puff preliminary.

The opera was produced in April 1865. Although both Escudier and Carvalho sent enthusiastic telegrams to Verdi after the first performance, it failed to achieve any great success. Verdi was bitterly disappointed, but, as usual, accepted reverse philo-sophically. Only the criticism that he did not understand Shakespeare wounded him. He may be acquitted on that charge, but it is odd that he did not yet understand his Parisian audience with its passion for smartness and novelty, its impatience of serious art. For *Macbeth* is the most serious of Verdi's early operas, and, for all its obvious inequalities, it has virtues that have had to wait for recognition until our own day.

At this time Verdi finally abandoned politics and resigned his

seat as deputy. He had become increasingly bored with the pro-
crastinating debates and disgusted by the vanity and self-interest
of his colleagues in Parliament. But he took the trouble to secure
that his successor should be a good Liberal and an honest man.
'There is need,' he wrote, 'of serious minds in our Parliament.'

Despite the failure of *Macbeth* and Verdi's dislike of 'the big
shop,' 'la grande boutique,' as he called it, it was for the Paris
Opéra that he wrote his next new work. He and his wife spent
the winter of 1865-6 in the French capital, and the idea of producing *La forza del destino* was again debated. The project was
abandoned, however, in favour of a new opera based upon
Schiller's *Don Carlos* with a French libretto by Méry and du
Locle, one of those pairs of theatre hacks by whom Verdi, as he
remarked on an earlier occasion, seemed always to be haunted
in Paris.

Schiller's tragedy is on a very different plane from that of the
romantic melodramas of Gutiérrez and the Duke of Rivas, in
which the springs of action are not a part of the mechanism of
human character but high-flown abstractions, sentiments of love
and honour and revenge put into the mouths of puppets with no
inner life of their own. Whatever his faults of imagination as a
poet—and they do not really concern us here—and whatever his
position relative to Shakespeare and the Attic masters in that
august line, Schiller belongs to the great tradition of tragic drama.
He understood that a tragic action must arise from the conflict
of personalities, real and convincing as presented within the conventions of the theatre, and that the sense of tragedy is created
precisely by the web of circumstances, inevitable only because they
are conditioned by the conjunction of these particular personalities,
in which the actors are caught. This is from our point of view
the most important fact about *Don Carlos*, and beside it the question of historical accuracy is irrelevant, and even a certain clumsi-
ness in the construction of the drama is unimportant for the good
reason that Schiller's structure had to be pulled to pieces and
put together again by the librettists. Schiller's drama provided
Verdi with a genuinely tragic theme and with a set of, for the

most part, psychologically convincing characters at a moment when his craftsmanship as a musician had become equal to the greater strain that such a subject, as compared with that of, say, *Il Trovatore*, put upon it. He might have been able to compose *Don Carlo* five years earlier, perhaps, but certainly not in 1857, as the earlier version of *Simon Boccanegra* shows.

Although historical accuracy is irrelevant in poetic drama, which is concerned not with the facts as they occurred in life, but with their reaction upon the creative imagination of the poet, the poet is on that very account laid under a great responsibility. His invention need not square with the history books, but it must square with the imagined 'facts' of the ideal world in which we live in the theatre. It must be, in a word, convincing. And paradoxically the poet may carry least conviction when he is keeping most closely to the spirit, if not to the established facts, of the historical period he has chosen. It is possible, for instance, to believe that a king of Spain in the sixteenth century might, for political reasons, marry the bride intended for his own son—though, even so, it is not easy to see why marriage with the king should put an end to a war more surely than marriage with his heir. But while this is historically possible, it is unconvincing and, what is worse, repellent to a modern audience. We may suspect Schiller of an obsession with the classic Oedipus-Jocasta theme, which he was inhibited by contemporary notions of propriety from handling frankly in all its horror; so he cast over it a cloak of romance that may have sufficed for his audience, ready to be moved by a spectacle of suffering innocence. But in the process the tragic motive is weakened and the whole situation becomes false. In his part of lover Carlos makes an unsatisfactory tragic hero, though Schiller manages to arouse our interest and sympathy with him as a political idealist. It is not surprising, therefore, that some of Carlos's music in the opera, where the librettists were obsessed by the same idea of the importance of a 'love-interest' that preoccupies the film producer, is by comparison with the rest conventional.

The real interest of Schiller's drama lies, however, not in Carlos and Isabella (Elisabetta in the opera), but in Philip and Posa.

It is their tragedy that holds us, however much we may pity the unhappy queen. In order to make this clear the facts must be briefly narrated. The action of the opera takes place in Spain about 1559.[1] In that year Philip II, already twice widowed and having failed to persuade Queen Elizabeth of England to take the place of her sister Mary as his consort, married Elizabeth (Isabella in Spain), daughter of the French king. There is no historical warrant, as I have said, for Schiller's idea that Don Carlos, the king's son by his first wife, had been affianced to Isabella. Carlos was, in fact, a malformed epileptic, but we need not complain of his transformation into a personable, if rather neurotic young man whose humanity sets him in opposition to the ruthless policy of his morose father. For this is the Philip of the Inquisition, the Spain of El Greco, the period of the cruel oppression of Flanders by the Duke of Alva.

Alva plays an important part in Schiller's drama as the protagonist of the party opposed to Carlos. The Princess Eboli, whose unrequited love for Carlos turns to fury, is his tool in the intrigue that brings about the catastrophe. But Alva is eliminated from the opera with much else that is important for a proper understanding of the action. The motives of the Marquis of Posa, for example, are hard to divine from the libretto, though Schiller makes them clear enough. He is the real leader of the opposition to the Inquisition. It is he who inspires the vacillating Carlos with his ideals. That he is an anachronism in sixteenth-century Spain, as Verdi remarked, is beside the point. He is the mainspring of the action or at least of its most interesting aspect. His astuteness is great and the scene where, by refusing to ask for any favour from the king, he gains the confidence of the suspicious Philip, unaccustomed as he is to a courage that will not stoop to flattery, is magnificently dramatic. The reasons for his assassina-

[1] Schiller placed his drama in 1588, the year of the Armada, in order to bring in, by way of historical decoration, a pointless little scene for the defeated Duke of Medina Sidonia. Isabella has a small daughter, whose presence adds a touch of unnecessary horror and false sentiment to the scene in which Philip taxes the queen with infidelity.

tion are again insufficiently brought out in the libretto, though it is made clear that he has sacrificed himself for Carlos, and it must be said that the manner of his self-sacrifice is hardly convincing enough to makes its omission a matter for regret.

So long as MM. Méry and du Locle adhered closely to their original text, e.g. in the scenes between Carlos and Isabella, Posa and the king, and the greater part of the fourth act, they at least provided the composer with a series of unusually interesting dramatic situations. The interest is unusual, from our point of view as students of Verdi, because it arises in each case from a conflict of characters observed and presented with a subtlety not to be found in any of the earlier operas. It has been truly remarked that all we need to know of Manrico and di Luna is that they are rivals in love, and the same is true of the tenor and baritone in *Un ballo in maschera*. Nor do Carlo and Alvaro in *La forza del destino*, though their situation is different, interest us as individual human beings who have an existence outside the simple emotions they represent. In *Don Carlo*, on the other hand, our interest is deeply engaged in six important characters caught in a complicated web of public and private antagonisms—between church and state (Philip and the Grand Inquisitor), between Catholic Spain and Protestant Flanders (Philip against his son, Carlos, and the Marquis of Posa), between Philip and his son over Queen Isabella, and between Isabella and Eboli over Carlos. Not one of these figures is conventional in the sense that it presents only one facet of character to the audience. Their love or hate, jealousy or self-sacrifice are but a part of their being. Philip is so remarkable a creation that he comes near to being the real hero of the opera. His fanaticism and cruelty are shown to be the result of his isolation as a man, and his loneliness arouses real sympathy. He can be politic as well as harsh. He is in fact a real king, not a lay figure in a crown. The queen, too, is well drawn—a happy, sweet nature crushed by the oppressive etiquette of a gloomy court. Carlos, in turn, is much more than the operatic tenor-in-love, for all that his revolt against the king's policy is subordinated by the librettists to his love for the queen. He is a 'weak' character, vacillating and neurotic even to the point of lacking the dignity usually associated with a tragic hero. Indeed he yields that position, for all that he gives the title to the play, in Schiller's drama to the Marquis of Posa.

Even though his part is severely curtailed in the opera and his motives are, as we have seen, far from clear, Posa retains something of his importance. He is far from being the mere 'friend and confidant' of the hero, a colourless convenience for dramatic exposition. The Grand Inquisitor, for all that he appears only twice and that his second scene is sometimes cut in modern performances of the opera, is an immensely impressive figure, as he must be if he is adequately to represent all the forces ranged against Carlos and Posa. Most remarkable of all is the Princess Eboli. She has been likened to Amneris in *Aida*, but, unlike Amneris, she has more than one stop to play on. She is not actuated all the time by the fury of a woman scorned. She is by turns coquettish, jealous, vindictive and self-sacrificing; in short, a human being.

If I may record a personal experience, I have never been so interested, on seeing one of Verdi's operas for the first time, in the details of the situations between the characters, as I was at *Don Carlo* — in what they had to say to each other and in their reactions to each other's words. In this respect *Otello* and *Falstaff* must be left out of account, because an Englishman at least does not come to them without some knowledge of the Shakespearian originals. They have an even greater psychological interest than *Don Carlo*, but not its novelty for those who have not been brought up on Schiller.

Where Verdi's librettists departed from Schiller's text, they went, for the most part, woefully astray. They had good reason for adding a preliminary act, in reality a prologue, showing the meeting of Carlos and Isabella as affianced lovers in the forest of Fontainebleau. It was the only way in which to establish clearly in an opera a situation which could be satisfactorily revealed after the event in the more leisurely exposition of a spoken drama. It is one of the faults of the opera, as it is still often presented without the original first act, that the fact of Carlos having been

engaged to Isabella before her marriage to his father is not plainly
indicated—though there are references to it intelligible enough to
those who have made themselves acquainted with the story before-
hand—until the scene between Philip and Isabella in Act IV.
The scene of the *auto-de-fé* was another reasonable addition,
regrettable though it is for other reasons yet to be stated, in that it
provides for a grand spectacular finale to the second act and serves
to show what Carlos and Posa are up against.

Less fortunate is the librettist's handling of the rendezvous
between Eboli and Carlos, who is led to believe that it is Isabella
who has made the appointment. Into this scene they have
introduced the well-worn operatic device of the veiled lady whose
voice and figure remain unrecognized until her partner in the
scene has deeply committed himself. Even in *Il Trovatore*,
where Leonora has at least heard Manrico's voice and di Luna
has not uttered a word to her, the mistake of identity is apt to
provoke a smile. In *Don Carlo* this stale *coup de théâtre* makes
the audience laugh audibly.

Worst of all is the alteration of the catastrophe of Schiller's
play, where Carlos visits the queen in order to say farewell to her
before his intended flight to Flanders. To this end he disguises
himself as a friar, in which form the ghost of his grandfather,
the Emperor Charles V, is reputed to walk abroad. Seizing
upon this hint and upon the historical fact that Charles V retired
before his death to a monastery, leaving his son to reign, Méry and
du Locle transferred the final scene to a cloister and introduced
the emperor in Franciscan habit to spirit his grandson away from
the vengeance of Philip and the Inquisition. By way of preparing
for this feeble denouement the friar is introduced into the second act,
where his cryptic utterances merely serve to puzzle the audience,
since the emperor is definitely referred to as dead. Modern producers of the opera have attempted to improve upon an impossible
situation by turning the friar into the emperor's ghost, whose
appearance is such a shock to Carlos that he incontinently dies.
This remedy is as bad as the disease, and nothing will serve but
the restoration of Schiller's ruthless ending, which could be done

by a slight arrangement of the music or even by cutting out the friar's brief appearance altogether.

It is strange that Verdi, who took such pains with his Italian librettists and bullied Piave into providing what he wanted, should have accepted the libretto of *Don Carlo* as it stands apparently without question or murmur. Perhaps he felt that the French librettists knew best what would 'go' at the Paris Opéra. It is difficult to believe, in face of the grandeur and originality of a great part of the music, that he did not greatly care. That he was ill and worried during its composition may account for the serious inequalities of the work. He suffered at this time from throat trouble, which was at times serious enough to make work impossible. Then, in the spring of 1866, war broke out between Prussia and Austria with Italy as King William's ally. The Austrians were finally defeated at Sadowa, but in the meantime Italy had been ignominiously beaten. As a result the province of Venice was added to the kingdom of Victor Emmanuel not by direct cession, but in the most humiliating way through the good offices of Napoleon III. Verdi was so disgusted with the proceedings that he wished at one time to cancel his contract with Paris.

From what has been said about the libretto it will be understood that *Don Carlo*, or at least those parts of it that are faithful to Schiller, demanded for its proper presentation as an opera a different musical treatment from that which suited the clear-cut situations of, say, *Il Trovatore*. Although in the operas immediately preceding it Verdi's musical style had been growing in this direction, *Don Carlo* is the first of his works which may be correctly described as, in its best scenes, a true music-drama. In it the evolution of Verdi's genius reached the solution of the operatic problem for the Italy of his time, even as Wagner, with greater independence from public support and in a more radical spirit, was engaged upon solving it for Germany in his *Ring*. That *Don Carlo* is not the complete masterpiece it might have been is due to Verdi's misfortune in being supplied with so unequal a libretto, which presented him alternately with scenes requiring the finest subtlety of characterization and with others that were part of the stock-in-trade of every conventional composer of grand opera. The inevitable result is that, Verdi's inspiration responding like some sensitive scientific instrument to the varying intensities of the drama, the music similarly alternates between a profound psycho-logical insight, that makes the listener hang upon every note in order to arrive at the last fineness of shade in the meaning, to the most blatant commonplaces against which he would willingly shut his ears.

A charge that has been made against *Don Carlo*, as against *Simon Boccanegra* and *La forza del destino*, is its too consistent atmosphere of gloom. This impression is due in part to the sacri-fice of the original first act, to which Verdi found it necessary to resort in order to reduce the opera to reasonable dimensions for audiences less voracious that those of the Paris Opéra in the 'sixties. This omission is unfortunate not only from the dramatic point of view, as has already been stated, but also because it involves the loss of almost the sole relief from the oppressive sombreness of the story. Carlos and Isabella are shown at the moment of their brief happiness hunting in France. In what remains, the only ray of light is the scene for Eboli in the second scene of the original Act II—her 'Song of the Veil' and her gossip-ing with Posa about Paris fashions. The song with its bolero rhythm and its characteristically Spanish roulades shows the influence of popular Spanish music that Verdi must have heard during his visit to Madrid. From the gay chatter of the duet with Posa, which serves as a background to Isabella's reading of Carlos's letter, I quote the cadence to show that, even in so skilfully worked a scene, Verdi was still not immune from lapsing into commonplace:

Verdi

Of the original first act all that remains is an abbreviated version of Carlos's romance, which is spatchcocked into the first scene of the second edition and deprived of its semiquaver ornamentations (e.g. in the second bar where the *gruppetto* marked A becomes a dotted crotchet on E):

The plainer version is an example of Verdi's careful attention to detail, since it undoubtedly fits Carlos's mood of dejection better than the original which was designed to express his happiness. This beautiful melody is used again in the prelude to Act III, where it is given to the horns and is worked out with a contrapuntal and instrumental skill that shows as well as anything in the opera the enormous advance Verdi had made in the art of composition.

The brass plays a very important part throughout the score of this opera. The horns are used to introduce the hunting chorus in Act I with their cheerful calls, and to them is given the tragic theme that serves as a prelude to the chorus of monks at the tomb of Charles V. It is the brass again that gives its startling colour to the astonishing modulation which, even in these days, makes the whole audience 'sit up' during the scene between Carlos and Isabella—that most unconventional of love-duets in which the relations of the two characters as queen and subject, as mother and son, and as lovers subtly alternate, while Eboli and Posa promenade round the garden producing at their appearance on the stage a sudden check to passion and a return to cold formality. Even more impressive is the sudden darkening of the harmony and orchestral colour at the point in the scene between Posa and the king when Philip warns the marquis to beware of the Inquisition:

The unprepared modulation from F sharp to A minor produces a most blood-curdling effect which very adequately establishes the feeling of awe connected with that terrifying institution, the age and dignity and ruthlessness of whose chief officer are again wonderfully summed up in the sombre theme that accompanies his entrance in the fourth act:

It is unfortunate that this effect of horror is completely destroyed in the finale to Act III, where the Inquisition is displayed before our eyes at its dreadful work. It is true that the burning of heretics was, by definition, regarded as an occasion for public rejoicing and for making holiday. But could anything be more trumpery than that dreadful choral melody which pounds up and down the scale in even quavers supported by the brass in unison? Verdi seems to have set himself here to outshine the tawdry brilliance of Meyerbeer's grand ensembles, and he has unhappily succeeded only in producing something as empty as his model at his worst. The whole scene, with its contrasting choruses of rejoicing populace, intoning priests and supplicating Protestants (with an all too dreary Lutheran kind of melody), is musically on the lowest level of achievement. Carlos's defiance of the king and his disarming by Posa provides a moment of dramatic excitement, and a word of praise is due to Verdi's masterly skill in handling the assembled forces of soloists, chorus and band upon the stage in the final pages of the scene. The part-writing here is remarkable for its independence and flexibility. But for the rest the scene depends entirely upon its spectacular staging. In its general structure it resembles the finale of the second act in *Aida*, but one has only to mention the resemblance to perceive at once how far it falls short of that triumph in musical splendour and dramatic power.

It is pleasant to turn from this failure in the grandiose style to the airs which are among the chief glories of this opera. They are conspicuous for the breadth and nobility of their melodies, and they mark a further advance in Verdi's development as a composer. For these airs are highly organized symphonic movements, in which the orchestra has a share in the interest only a little less important than the voice. Philip's 'Ella giammai m' amò' is an extended movement worked out with the greatest possible sense of musical form and dramatic propriety. As an expression of the king's loneliness in his high station, of his bitter disappointment and passionate longing for the peace that only death can bring, it wrings the listener's heart. But it also moves him to admiration as a musical composition and as an example of euphonious orchestral writing. The scene which it begins ends with Eboli's no less beautiful and even more famous 'O don fatale,' the measure of whose quality is the fact that it provides a

VERDI'S BIRTHPLACE AT LE RONCOLE

MS. OF THE QUARTET IN 'RIGOLETTO,' ACT III

VERDI IN MIDDLE LIFE, FROM AN ETCHING
BY C. GEOFFROY

CARICATURES BY DELFICO

(above) Rehearsal of *Boccanegra*.   *(below)* Verdi and Lulu

CARICATURE BY DELFICO (SEE APPENDIX D)

THE VENERABLE VETERAN OF SANT' AGATA

VERDI AND HIS DOGS AT SANT' AGATA

magnificent climax to a scene which from its first bar has remained consistently upon the heights. Between these two airs come first the Inquisitor's audience with Philip, in which the technical difficulty of giving interest to a colloquy between two basses is so completely overcome that we are not even conscious of its existence, and then the appeal of Isabella to the king and his accusation of her, which foreshadows, even if it does not equal, the terrible poignancy of the corresponding scene in *Otello*. The duet leads to a quartet for the queen, Eboli, Posa and Philip, which is remarkable for the suppleness of the four parts, and so to Eboli's confession to the queen—a passage in which passionate entreaty and penitence are balanced by the icy dignity of a character in whom all passion is spent. No other individual scene in any of Verdi's previous operas displays so consummate a mastery of musico-dramatic technique combined with so profound an expressiveness.

The scene which follows this magnificent achievement shows us Carlos under arrest for his defiance of the king at the *auto-de-fé*. To him comes Posa, still in power but already condemned by the Inquisition. He is assassinated by a shot fired through the prison window, and his death song is one of Verdi's most moving inspirations. I quote the accompaniment to the opening of this beautiful passage:

To the pathetic melody in thirds for two trumpets, whose muted tone by itself produces an effect of the utmost poignancy, the oboe adds its sob on an off-beat, while the bassoon's chromatic skirl portrays with terrible imaginative power the slipping away of man's consciousness into faintness and death. The effect is not strictly original. Beethoven had used it in the coda of the first movement in the ninth Symphony, where it is the whole universe that seems to be sliding away from under our feet towards inevitable cataclysm. No parallel less august will serve to set off the high merit of Verdi's inspiration. It is further to be remarked that the instrumentation of this passage exhibits the finest sureness and economy of means. No other instruments could produce exactly this effect of colour, and nothing is added to what is needed to produce that effect. Even the rhythm has an extraordinary subtlety as a result of the syncopations (note the entry of the drum-roll one quaver after the oboe) and the accents on weak beats.

This mood of exaltation is unhappily not maintained to the end of the scene. Before Posa dies Verdi recalls the melody, to which he and Carlos had sworn their vows of friendship in the second act:

Sung in thirds by tenor and baritone with a fine ringing tone this tune will pass as an exciting piece of vocalization. Allotted to a wind band with a tonic-and-dominant accompaniment in the bass it provides a sad example of the depth of banality to which Verdi could still descend.

Let us emphasize the point by a glance forward to the comparable duet in which Othello and Iago make their devilish pact:

The superficial similarity of this melody to that of the duet in *Don Carlo* is obvious enough. But the greater spring of its rhythm, due to the substitution of a crotchet for a minim on the first beat of each bar, and the wider span of its intervals replacing a rather crabbed compass, give it a greater distinction that is enhanced by the freedom with which it is worked and by the suppleness of the supporting bass, which is not confined to marking the rhythm with the most rudimentary harmony.

It will be noticed that in both these examples triplets are used to give an added swing to the rhythm. This is a characteristic feature of Verdi's melody and may be found from the outset in the famous 'Va, pensiero' chorus in *Nabucco*. This simple device of setting a compound against a simple metre, 6–8 against 4–4, rarely fails of its effect and its use becomes more and more frequent.   There is hardly a page in *Don Carlo* in which it does not occur and the following example is quoted for comparison with the duet and as yet another instance of the inequality of this score:

This is the march from the finale to Act III.   It is scored for wind and, like the march accompanying Duncan's entry in *Macbeth*, is the kind of thing that Verdi might have heard played by the Busseto town band on a Sunday afternoon.

At the other end of the scale of quality is Isabella's air, which with a duet with Don Carlos occupies all but the three final pages of the last act.   Here is its most salient melody, whose range incidentally confutes Bernard Shaw's charge that Verdi used only one part of the voice:

Here is a great nobility exceeding even that of Leonora's in *La forza del destino*, combined with a sweetness that reminds us of Amalia's lovely 'Vieni a mirar la cerula marina' in *Simon Boccanegra*:

Happy the composer who could weave so much enchantment from arpeggios of the common chord and the successive notes of the major scale!

Like the other airs in *Don Carlo*, Isabella's is a highly organized musical composition. These airs still generally adhere to the old ternary scheme of two contrasting sections—one pathetic and one brilliant or agitated according to the dramatic circumstances—with a return to the first section at the end. But Verdi has made this scheme much more flexible and less formal by the addition to the two main sections of subsidiary material and by incorporating dramatic declamation into a context originally reserved exclusively for lyrical melody. In this way the air is liberated from its obvious formality and at the same time enlarged to symphonic dimensions so that it equals a sonata movement in length and comprehensiveness. The sonata was at last paying back from its accrued interest the debt it owed in the beginning to the operatic air, not by making over to the air its essentially instrumental scheme of contrasted yet interlinked subjects and keys within one tempo, but by providing a model in the variety and suppleness it had acquired through independence from the human voice and exact dramatic ideas. It is necessary only to compare even so fine an example of Verdi's earlier style as Violetta's 'Ah! fors è lui' — where, by the way, the reprise of the second section is introduced (it is one of his most wonderful dramatic strokes) not by Violetta herself but by Alfredo's voice singing off the stage—with this air of Isabella's or Philip's 'Ella giammai m'amò' to perceive at once how enormously Verdi's technique as a composer had advanced. The bare bones of the ternary form no longer stick out visible to all; they are clothed with a solid flesh that consists of subsidiary and often declamatory material, of a wider harmonic range and an instrumentation that responds most eloquently to every change of mood. We are no longer so much aware of the skeleton that, nevertheless, makes these airs entirely satisfying to the sense of musical form. To take one point, the two sections of Violetta's air are joined together by a frank lapse into conventional recitative. In *Don Carlo* recitative in that sense has completely disappeared and in its place there is a style of declamation, more fully supported by the orchestra and more definitely melodic. It is difficult to say where recitative ends and lyric begins.

It must be added that Eboli's 'O don fatale' breaks away altogether from the old aria form. There is no reprise of the open-ing section, but an entirely free sequence of contrasted sections culminating in a tremendous dramatic climax. The situation here would have been weakened by any return to the opening phrases, however skilfully the convention might be veiled. The same process is used in Aida's 'Ritorna vincitor' which, unlike Eboli's aria, is more accurately entitled a *scena* in the score.

In complete contrast to these elaborate dramatic pieces are the lyrical strophic songs allotted to Eboli and Isabella in the second act. Eboli's is the 'Spanish' song already mentioned. Isabella's is a charming lyric in which she offers consolation to her dis-missed lady-in-waiting. Musically it is not of great importance or even merit, but it does serve to display the gentleness of Isa-bella's character and to lighten the general atmosphere of severity and gloom.

The concerted numbers, excepting the grand finale of the third act and the not more than adequate ensemble at the end of Act I, are conspicuously fine. The lovely duet for Carlos and Isabella in the first act is one of the chief losses due to the excision of that act. But even better is their final duet in which they renounce their love and in a *marziale* movement, which has been unjustly condemned by some critics, give expression to their ideals. The trio for Carlos, Eboli and Posa, which occupies most of the first scene in Act III, is magnificently dramatic. The quartet in the fourth act, though somewhat conventional from the dramatic point of view, is a splendid piece of vocal writing. Verdi's earlier ensembles, for instance in *Il Trovatore*, have been criticized for the poverty of the basses which too often resemble those of a brass band in their slavish adherence to tonic and dominant. In this quartet each of the four voices has a real part and moves with freedom and independence. The flexibility of the music is due to the use of Verdi's favourite contrast of simple and compound metres interchanged from one bar to the next between the various parts. The effect of pathos is obtained by a chromaticism, most conspicuous in the beautiful descending phrases in octaves for the soprano and mezzo-soprano, which reminds us that chromaticism, usually regarded as typically Wagnerian, was in reality characteristic of the whole of music in the latter half of last century. It had not yet, in Wagner, Brahms or Verdi, become over-ripe or reached the point of disturbing the sense of key, but served in their hands as an enrichment of music's expressive power.

There remains the short finale to Act III, in which after the death of Posa all the main characters, except the queen, the court and a rebellious mob of citizens, are with little show of probability brought into Carlos's prison-cell. The choral ensemble is finely handled from the dramatic point of view and displays the new freedom from formality which we remarked in other parts of the opera. The musical interest of this scene may not be very great, but the swiftness and assurance with which the dramatic points are made and the clash of the opposing parties is presented make it extremely effective in the theatre. Unfortunately, owing to the length of the opera even without the original first act, this finale is often sacrificed to the impatience of audiences who yet will tolerate the immensities of Wagnerian music-drama.

On its merits, which far outweigh its defects, *Don Carlo* deserved a resounding success, especially as those defects, arising as they do from an adherence to the popular conventions of the time, would be (and were) less apparent to a contemporary audience than they are to us. The *auto-de-fé* was, indeed, acclaimed even by critics like Reyer and Théophile Gautier, who acknowledged the superior musical quality of the scene between Philip and the Inquisitor. But, in spite of the praise lavished upon the opera by the more intelligent writers, Verdi writing to Arrivabene on the morrow of the first performance (11th March 1867) had to admit that *Don Carlo* was not a success. Various explanations have been given of its failure to please the Parisian public. The heretical doctrines of the Marquis of Posa were said to have offended the Catholics headed by the Empress Eugénie, who turned her back to the stage at the fall of the curtain, to show her disapproval. The Italians, as a nation, were suffering from one of their periodic bouts of unpopularity with the French. And there was the usual feeling of jealousy among native musicians aroused by the fuss made about even so distinguished a foreigner.

Apart from these external considerations, the general feeling seems to have been that the opera was consistent neither in style nor in musical quality. For this judgment there is, as we have seen, a solid basis. But it seems that the quality of the performance contributed, more than anything else, to the opera's failure to achieve a resounding success—for complete failure it certainly was not. Verdi complained of a lack of real enthusiasm on the part of the singers. The opera went better in London under Costa's direction, though it had to wait for a revival at Covent Garden until 1933, when it was given three poor performances, and failed to achieve any real popularity here until it was given, for the first time in English, at Sadler's Wells in 1938. Mariani, who had expressed his dissatisfaction with the Parisian performance, produced it with great success at Bologna in the summer of 1867, and the opera subsequently went the round of the Italian cities, but, like the other products of this period in Verdi's career, it never achieved the wide popularity of his three earlier masterpieces. Like *Boccanegra*, it has always been rewarded with the respect and admiration of musicians rather than with the affection of the larger public, at least until recent years.

Don Carlo was certainly composed under trying circumstances. Verdi was in poor health at the time and was compelled now and again to knock off all work upon it. Giuseppina writes of the anxiety and extreme fatigue induced by its composition. It was a sad time, too, for Verdi's father was seriously ill, and his death, which occurred in January 1867 while Verdi was in Paris, affected him so deeply that for a time the rehearsals had to be abandoned. Yet it would be a mistake to take too sombre a view of Verdi's mood at the time. He could write gaily enough to his intimate friends, and there is an amusing letter purporting to come from his dog, Black, to Arrivabene's dog, Ron-ron. Without the companionship of Black, the successor to the faithful Lulu, he wrote later, *Don Carlo* could not have been written. At the same time Giuseppina was writing in the best of humours to Cesare de Sanctis, whom she addresses with affectionate abuse as 'Animal, assassin, brigant-scellerato.'

CHAPTER XIII

THE MAKING OF 'AIDA'

THE year 1867 brought other griefs. Antonio Barezzi, Verdi's father-in-law and patron, became gravely ill while Verdi was in Paris, and on 20th July he died. At the end of January he wrote to the Countess Clarina Maffei from Sant' Agata, whither he had returned to visit the dying man:

You know that to him I owe everything, absolutely everything. To him alone and to none other, as some have thought. I seem to see again all those years ago, when I had finished my studies at the Gymnasium at Busseto, my father saying that he could not possibly keep me at the University of Parma and deciding that I must return to my native village. This good old man said to me: 'You were born for something better than to sell groceries or work on the land. Ask the Monte di Pietà to award you their small pension of twenty-five francs a month for four years and I will provide the rest. You shall go to the conservatoire at Milan, and, when you can, you shall repay me what I spend on you.'

So it was. You see how generous, how kind and good he was! I have known many men, but none better than he. He loved me as one of his own sons, and I loved him as much as my father.

Then in December Verdi's faithful collaborator, Piave, had a paralytic seizure, which deprived him of speech and movement, but not of the power of thought or the ability to recognize his friends. For eight years the unhappy man lingered on in this helpless condition, his mind occupied with two ideas: Verdi and the future of his young daughter. Verdi did what he could to relieve the anxieties of his friend by helping him financially and by arranging to provide an income for the little girl. He also organized the publication for Piave's benefit of an album of six songs by various composers, including Mercadante, Auber and Thomas. His own contribution to this album was the *Stornello*.

This effort to obtain the collaboration of his colleagues was more successful than the ambitious project of a joint tribute to Rossini from the leading composers of Italy. Rossini died in Paris on 13th November 1868. Verdi not only revered Rossini as the greatest Italian composer of the previous generation, but was on terms of friendly affection with him. Despite his dislike of Olympe Pélissier,[1] Rossini's second wife, he never failed to visit her salon whenever he was in Paris. Two letters only from Rossini survive out of what was probably a larger correspondence with Verdi. The first, dated 1845, is addressed to 'Signor Giuseppe Verdi, Celebre Compositore di Musica'; the second (1865) opens 'Illustre collega' and is subscribed 'Rossini, ex-compositeur de musique, pianiste de quatrième classe,' and is addressed to 'M. Verdi, Célèbre Compositeur de Musique, Pianiste de cinquième classe!'—which gives the measure of their relations. But it was the public figure, the respected doyen of Italian composers, whom Verdi wished to commemorate, and he proposed that a Requiem Mass should be composed by himself and a dozen of his contemporaries, each providing one movement, for performance in Bologna, Rossini's spiritual home.

Verdi had no illusions about the artistic result of his proposal. The Mass was to be a public tribute to the dead composer from his successors, and, once performed, the score was to be deposited in the Liceo Musicale of Bologna and never used again except at the celebration of future anniversaries. Above all no one was to make any money out of it. It was upon this last rock that the generous if ill-considered project foundered. It presupposed that every one else concerned would view the matter in the same unselfish way, that no one would push for a place or feel sore at his exclusion. In the event the Mass did not progress beyond the committee stage. The municipality of Bologna took no interest

---

[1] The dislike was apparently mutual, for Verdi writing to Countess Maffei says that the proposal to bury Rossini in Italy would come to nothing if Mme Rossini had a say in the matter, since 'while no Frenchman loves the Italians, she concentrates in her own person the detestation of the whole French nation.'

in it; the manager of the opera declined to permit his company to participate without payment; and—the unkindest cut of all—Mariani, Verdi's intimate friend, gave him the impression of being less than enthusiastic in his arrangements for the performance, which he was to conduct. This was the first cause of that unhappy breach that was soon to be irreparably widened by a more personal offence.[1] Of the contributions to the Mass only Verdi's has survived. This was the 'Libera me' which became three years later the base upon which was built that splendid monument to Manzoni, the *Requiem*. It is interesting to note that, in deploring Rossini's death, Verdi wrote: 'His reputation was enormous, the most popular in our time, and a glory to Italy! When that other who still lives [Manzoni] is no more, what will remain? Our ministers and the exploits of Lissa and Custozza?'

In the meantime Verdi was occupied with the revision of *La forza del destino* for Milan. In default of Piave, now incapable of rendering assistance, the alterations to the libretto were entrusted to Antonio Ghislanzoni, who visited Sant' Agata in the summer of 1868 in order to discuss the revision with Verdi. The main change, apart from the addition of the overture, was the provision of a new ending. In the original version, as in Rivas's drama, Don Alvaro committed suicide by jumping over a precipice after the deaths of Carlo and Leonora. He was now permitted to survive. The most important outcome of this change was the beautiful trio which compensates us for the dramatically rather ineffective ending.

Ghislanzoni, who became an important member of Verdi's circle during the next few years, was a remarkable character. He had been by turns a medical student, a performer on the double bass, an operatic baritone, a journalist, a novelist and a playwright. He was without respect for the conventions and his conduct brought him notoriety as an 'original.' On one occasion he startled the Milanese by appearing on the cathedral square in the uniform of an ancient Roman general, having omitted to change into mufti after the opera. But, apart from his unaccountable-

[1] See Supplement II, p. 314.

ness, his theatrical and literary experience made him a suitable collaborator for an operatic composer.

In its new form *La forza del destino* was produced with great success in Fenbruary 1869. The press was favourable, the public enthusiastic, and, most satisfactory of all, Verdi was delighted with the performance. His succession to Rossini as 'a glory to Italy' was shortly afterwards officially recognized by his appoint⸍ ment as Cavaliere to the Order of Merit of Savoy, to which was attached a pension of 600 lire. With characteristic generosity Verdi used this pension to help needy and deserving scholars in the school at Busseto where he had been in so great need of such assistance.

At this time Verdi was approached by an agent of the Khedive, Ismail Pasha, with a proposal that he should compose an opera to be performed at Cairo in celebration of the opening of the Suez Canal. The progress of the negotiations is best set out in Verdi's own words taken from a letter to Ricordi written in June 1870:

Towards the end of last year I was invited to write an opera for a distant country. I refused. When I was in Paris [in the spring of 1870], du Locle opened the question anew and offered me a large sum of money. Again I refused. A month later, he sent me a printed sketch, saying that it was the work of an important personage (which I do not believe), that he thought it good and I ought to read it. I found it absolutely first⸍rate, and replied that I would write the music on certain conditions. Three days later came his acceptance by tele⸍ gram. Du Locle himself then came here unexpectedly and we ampli⸍ fied the terms and discussed the scenario, making some modifications that seemed necessary. Du Locle departed to submit the terms and modifications to the important and unknown author. I have studied the scenario again and am making some further changes in it. Now I must think about the libretto or rather about its versification. For all we need is the verses. Do you think Ghislanzoni would undertake this work? It is not original work . . . it is only a question of versification, for which you are to understand he would be well paid. . . Do not talk about this matter, as the contract is not yet signed.

It will be seen that Verdi makes some mystification about the proposal, referring vaguely to a distant country and an important personage. But we need not attribute this to anything but caution. As the last sentence shows, he wished to avoid any premature talk about it, and he knew well that the fewer the people who know a secret, the less likelihood there is of a disclosure. From a letter to du Locle, written twenty years later, it appears that Verdi was led to believe at first that the important and unknown author was the Khedive himself, whose contribution to the work was confined to a request for an Egyptian story and the approval of the scenario submitted to Verdi through du Locle. The author of this scenario was Mariette Bey, who was the Khedive's agent in the negotiations with Verdi. Mariette was a French Egyptologist who had been in charge of the Egyptian antiquities at the Louvre and was at this time Inspector of Monuments in Egypt with the title of Bey. He was consulted upon all the archaeological questions connected with *Aida*, as the new opera was called, and was responsible for supervising the designs for the scenery and costumes, in which strict attention was paid to historical accuracy. So well and thoroughly was this work done that after nearly seventy years little modification has been made in the staging of the opera, except in matters of detail, at the larger opera houses. The original scenario is referred to by Verdi as consisting of four pages, but he had also a complete French version of the text to work upon, and to this he makes frequent reference in his correspondence with Ghislanzoni.

The financial terms were extremely favourable to the composer. He was to be paid 150,000 francs and retain the rights in the opera in all countries excepting Egypt. But it is clear from the letter quoted above that the monetary reward did not tempt Verdi and that it was only when his imagination was fired by the proposed subject that he consented to discuss terms.

Ghislanzoni readily undertook the task of writing the libretto and sent a characteristic message by Ricordi to say that he would be arriving at Sant' Agata accompanied by a Nubian slave, who would carry him to the door so that his own legs might be saved, and who could then be thrown as food to the dogs! The dogs at this time included three large mastiffs, gigantic successors to 'poor little Lulu,' who might well have appreciated such a meal.

During the summer of 1870 *Aida* began to take shape. Ghislanzoni proved an ideal collaborator, as willing as Piave to take his orders from Verdi, but at the same time capable of making sensible suggestions. The progress of the work, which proceeded with great rapidity, is fully documented in the correspondence, albeit one-sided, from Verdi to the librettist. These letters are so revelatory of Verdi's methods and views about operatic composition that a digest of them is here appended. Verdi treated his collaborator with a respect that he had never shown towards Piave, whom he bullied with merciless good humour, and it is amusing to note that his more exacting criticisms are tempered by the addition to Ghislanzoni's name at the beginning of the letters of flattering adjectives ranging from *caro* through *egregio* to *gentilissimo*. Comments and explanations are added in square brackets.

12th August 1870. . . . Mariette tells me that we can have as many priestesses as we want [Verdi had inquired whether Egyptian religious ritual was celebrated exclusively by priests], so they can be introduced in the scene of the consecration. . . . The hymn [following Radamès's appointment as general] is good as it stands, but you will see that Radamès and Amneris ought to take part in this scene, otherwise these two will appear to stand coldly outside it. . . . Amneris might take a sword, a standard or some other devilry and address her strophe to Radamès, warm, loving and warlike.

16th August. . . . We must revise the scene of consecration to give it more character and greater dramatic importance. It must be not a cold hymn, but a real scene. The characters do not express themselves as they should and the priests are not sufficiently priestly. . . . In the meantime let us get on with the second act upon which I can also get to work. There is no time to lose. The first chorus is cold and insignificant. It is a narration that any messenger might deliver. I know it is not an action, but with a little skill something can be made of it. There is no action in the scene in *Don Carlo* where the ladies are waiting for the queen in the convent garden. . . . [The parallel between these two scenes for mezzo-soprano and women's chorus will be obvious to anybody who has seen the two operas.] We need here a scene with a *lyrical* chorus, while the girls dress Amneris and with a dance for Ethiopian boys. [Verdi then proceeds to sketch the scene as it stands in the opera.] There should be two couplets of ten lines each, the first strophe of four lines warlike, the second amorous and then two voluptuous lines for Amneris. And without straining the rhythm, could you write some lines of seven feet . . . and, if it is not too trouble-some, a number of lines ending with accented syllables, which are most useful now and then from the musical point of view. The melody of 'Di Provenza' in *La Traviata* would be less tolerable if the lines were all equal.

17th August. . . . In the duet [Aida-Amneris in Act II] the beginning and end are excellent, though too long. . . . But when the scene warms up, it seems to me to lack the *parola scenica* . . . by which I mean the word that clinches the situation and makes it absolutely clear. For instance the lines:

> *Amneris.* Per Radamès d' amore
> Ardo e mi sei rivale.
> *Aida.* Che? voi l' amate?
> *Amneris.*   Io l' amo
> E figlia son d' un rè.

seem to me less dramatic than: 'Tu l' ami? ma l' amo anch' io, intendi? La figlia dei Faraoni è tua rivale! *Aida*: Mia rivale? E sia: anch' io son figlia,' etc.

But what about the verse, the rhyme, the strophe, you exclaim? . . . When the action requires it, I should abandon rhythm, rhyme and strophe altogether, and use blank verse to say exactly and clearly what the action requires. There are moments in the theatre when poets and composers must have the talent to write neither poetry nor music.

22nd August. . . . I have an idea for the consecration scene . . . which should consist of a litany chanted by the priestesses, to which the priests respond. Then a sacred dance to slow and sad music, followed by a short recitative, energetic and solemn like a biblical psalm. Finally a prayer of two strophes for the Chief Priest and repeated by every one. You will see that it would have a quiet and pathetic character, dis-tinguishing it from the other choruses at the end of the first scene and in the second finale, which smack a little of 'La Marseillaise.'

By the end of August the greater part of the first two acts was finished and Verdi summoned Ghislanzoni to Sant' Agata to discuss the final adjustments of detail. A glance at the libretto will reveal how closely Ghislanzoni followed Verdi's suggestions, making a further improvement here and there, as in the final version of the Aida-Amneris duet in Act II.

On 15th July the Franco-Prussian war broke out and, though it distracted Verdi's attention from his work only for a few days, it caused a delay in the production of the opera, which had to be postponed from the beginning to the end of 1871. Verdi's sympathies were with the French. 'I am desolated by the news from France,' he wrote. 'Poor country and poor us!'

The correspondence with Ghislanzoni was soon resumed:

8th September. . . . Since your departure I have done very little, only the march which is very long and full of detail. . . . You must alter the first eight lines [of the chorus] and add eight more for the priests to the effect that 'We have conquered with the help of divine providence. The enemy is delivered into our hands. God is henceforward on our side.' (See King William's telegram.)[1]

10th September. . . . The last words of your letter sent a shiver down my back. 'I can let you have the beginning of the third act.' How's this? Isn't it finished? I am waiting for it from hour to hour. I have finished the second act. Send me the text as soon as possible. In the meantime I will do some polishing here and there.

The verses of the finale are all right, but I cannot make sense of the strophe for the priests at the end. Ramfis is a person of importance and should be given something to say for himself.

28th September. . . . This third act is very good indeed, though there are one or two points that in my opinion need touching up. But, I repeat, the whole is very good and I congratulate you.

I see you are afraid of two things: of any bold theatrical strokes and of *not* writing cabalettas! I think the cabaletta should be reserved for a situation that demands it. In neither of these duets is it appropriate to

---

[1] A reference to the King of Prussia's message to his queen announcing the victory of Sedan which was turned into verse by some ribald spirit of the time:

> The war is won, my dear Augusta,
> In fact, we've had a perfect buster.
> Ten thousand Frenchmen sent below—
> Praise God, from whom all blessings flow

the situation, especially in the duet between Aida and her father. . . .
Aida in her state of terror and moral abasement cannot and should
not sing a cabaletta. There are two extremely dramatic moments in this
scene, truthful and fine opportunities for acting, which are not well
brought out in your verses. The first follows Amonasro's 'Sei la
schiava dei Faraoni,' where Aida can only utter broken phrases. The
other is when Amonasro reveals his identity as King of Ethiopia, where
Radames must hold the stage with strange words of mad exaltation. . . .
The first of these is weak at present and I think Aida's patriotic
enthusiasm strikes a false note here. After the terrible scene with her
father she would be, as I say, incapable of speech. So she should have
broken words uttered in a low and stifled tone. . . . I should forgo
rhythm and formal verses, for I do not think that the situation can be
given its full value except in recitative, though Amonasro might be
given a lyrical phrase to sing when he urges Aida to think of her native
land. In short I would keep as closely as possible to the scenario.

30th September. . . . The choral chant [at the beginning of Act III]
is in slow (*grave*) time; eight lines are too many; six would be enough.

The *cantabile* part of the Aida-Radamès duet is very beautiful, but in
my opinion it fails to develop the dramatic side of the situation and to
make it sufficiently clear. I should prefer a recitative at the beginning.
Aida should be calm and dignified, and might utter with clear articula-
tion some sentences that would be theatrically effective, for example:
'Do not swear oaths to me; I would not have you perjure yourself . . .
How can you turn away from the caresses of Amneris, the will of the
king, the wishes of the people?' etc. The *cantabile* should begin at
Radamès's 'Aida, ascoltami' [in the final text, 'Odimi, Aida'],
though these two words should be mortised into the preceding recitative.
[If the reader will refer to the vocal score, he will see how exactly
Ghislanzoni complied with the composer's wishes and how beautifully
Verdi has set the whole scene, bringing out the dramatic and psycho-
logical situation with the utmost clearness and precision.] . . .

In the scene that follows you are afraid of making Aida appear unsympathetic. But consider: Aida is justified by the duet with her
father and, one may add, by his concealed presence, of which the
audience is aware. I do not think the situation is dangerous, though it
might be. So more should be made of Aida's demands, which are
natural and true to life. But there must be not a word too much . . .
only a vivid and very brief dialogue. Try above all to get Radamès

well into the foreground. . . . After this duet you want to have a trio, but this is not the place for them to stop and sing. We must go on at once to Amneris's entrance.

To the end of the act Verdi wished to give the minimum of words and the maximum of action. He suggests reducing the verses provided by the librettist to single words exclaimed by each character in turn, and at the end of this long and detailed letter he writes:

The final verses are excellent:

> 'Io qui resto, su me scenda
> Il tuo vindice furor.'

But would it not be better still and more dramatic to say simply: 'Io qui resto, sacerdote'?

This was further improved to the magnificent declamatory phrase that brings down the curtain:

Radamès   Sa-cer-do-te   Io   re-sto a te

6th October. . . . I think some of the words given to Amonasro are out of place, and I suggest that after Radamès's line 'Tu Amonasro, tu il rè!' the king should have a phrase, uttered with ferocious joy: 'Anche i miei saranno nelle gole di Napata,' or words to that effect. [This phrase was put in before, not after, Radamès's exclamation and is most effective as well as dramatically necessary.]

In the next passage two lines of strong invective against Aida should be given to Radamès. Then take out Aida's two lines which are not to the point . . . here Amonasro should say: 'I have faithful friends waiting by the Nile. You must fly with us,' etc. The next six verses are excellent and very dramatic, but the 'Die' to Amneris is too bare. I would add: 'You would undo my work? Die.' But he should not say: 'Die by my dagger.'

I crave your diligence.

7th October. . . . I have received your verses [the revision of Act III] . . . Amonasro should not speak to Aida at his entrance. It would be better if she suddenly sees him. . . . Also I do not like the line:

'I read the secrets of your heart,' in the mouth of this proud and cunning king. 'Nothing escapes my eyes' would be better.

What follows is good, but the end of the scene still does not meet the situation. Perhaps you have not fully understood my previous letter, in which I think I explained that this is a dramatic moment on which we must dwell. The part of Aida must be more fully developed . . . she needs four very *dramatic* lines. You will appreciate that here ordinary commonplaces will not do.

8th October. . . . Please understand that I do not intend to criticize your verses which are always good, but to express my views on their theatrical effect. The duet for Aida and Radamès seems to me vastly inferior to that for Aida and Amonasro. This may be because the situation, or possibly the form it takes, is more ordinary. I am certain that the succession of lyrical stanzas of eight lines each, given to one character and then repeated by the other, do not make for vivid dialogue. . . . Some of the lines are not dramatic, that is to say they afford no scope for acting; the attention of the audience is not held and the situation loses its effect. . . . [Verdi proceeds to sketch the kind of sentiments he would put into the mouths of the singers. His suggestions were embodied in the lines given to Aida, beginning 'Nè d' Amneris paventi il vindice furor?'] You may say: this is silly. . . . Silly it may be, but it is a fact that such phrases as 'Cadrà su me, sul padre, su tutti,' etc., if properly accented, hold the attention and hit the mark *every time*.

16th October. . . . In his duet with Aida Radamès is not given an equal share of the interest. I think he should answer her: 'Leave my country, my gods, my birthplace, where I have won glory,' etc. But, if you do not care for these *roles of honour*, we must think of something else. [This suggestion resulted in the verse, embodying Verdi's ideas but raising them to the plane of genuine poetry, beginning: 'Sovra una terra estrania teco fuggir dovrei !'] . . .

As to Aida's *romanza* ['O patria mia, mai più ti rivedrò !'], we need not consider the singer; she will certainly not complain, though, if she found it too exacting, she might neglect the duets that follow. But there are other considerations: the first chorus is solemn, and so is the scene for Amneris and the priest; then the solemn chorus is repeated. If to that we add a scene and *romanza* in slow time and solemn mood, we shall come to grief. I have written this *romanza*, but it will not do ! . . . It should be idyllic, you say, I agree with you absolutely, but it

must *be* an idyll. We must have the smell of Egypt in our nostrils and
avoid 'orphan,' 'the bitter cup of misfortune' and similar ideas. We
must find a newer form. [And find it they did, though it did not take
its final form until nearly a year later, in that lovely idyll aquiver with
the fragrance of the hot Egyptian night.] . . .

I know you have rewritten Radamès's stanza many times. Your time
has not been wasted, for
> 'Il ciel de' nostri amori
> Come scordar potrem?'

is quite extraordinarily happy. But I will tell you with my usual frankness that I am not passionately enamoured of the line: 'È fuoco, è
febbre, è folgore.' And I am annoyed that you have not kept 'L' are
de' nostri dei' with Aida's reply. But we can talk this over, when I
have the pleasure of seeing you. Then we will adjust and polish up
and make the stage directions clear and so on. In the meantime get
busy with the fourth act. I have nearly finished the third.

The scene for Radamès and Amneris at the beginning of
Act IV was the subject of even more extended discussion, but,
as the gist of Verdi's argument is again directed to making the
text more pointed in dramatic effect, more characteristic in diction,
and to the avoidance of weak and flat verses, we may pass on to
the last scene of all. It is interesting to note, however, that Verdi
did not overlook the resemblance to Bellini's *Norma* in the passage
where Amneris offers to plead for Radamès's life if he will
renounce Aida, but thought that there was no danger of the resemblance being obvious owing to the different form of the verses.

3rd November. . . . Directly I had posted my letter yesterday, I
set to work on the serious consideration of the final scene. In inexpert
hands this might become either throttled (*strozzata*) or monotonous.
It must not be throttled because with so much scenic apparatus, if it is
not well developed, it will be a case of the mountain and the mouse.
Monotony must be avoided by devising an unusual form. . . . The
two solo passages for Radamès and Aida [beginning 'Morir, sì pura e
bella'] would have the same form and character, even though each were
set to a different melody. The French often use lines of different lengths
even in the stanzas of an aria. Why should not we do that? The whole
of this scene must consist of lyrical song, pure and simple. A form of
verse in a strange metre for Radamès would compel me to find a different

sort of melody from that to which verses of seven or eight feet are usually set. And so I should have to change the tempo and time signature for Aida's solo which would be almost in the nature of an air. So with Radamès's unusual *cantabile*, another in the manner of an air for Aida, the dirge of the priests, the lovers' farewell to life and Amneris's 'pace,' we should have a varied and well-developed whole. And if I can contrive to bind it all together in the music, we shall have accomplished something good, or at least something out of the ordinary.

Courage, then, Signor Ghislanzoni; we have the fruit almost in our hand; you, at any rate. I send you a string of ideas unrhymed, of which you can make good verses as you have made so many others:

> *Aida.* E qui lontana da ogni sguardo umano
> . . . sul tuo cor morire (a very pathetic line)
> *Radamès.* Morire! tu innocente?
> Morire! tu, sì bella?
> Tu nell' april degli anni
> Lasciar la vita?
> Quant' io t' amai, no, no 'l può dir favella!
> Ma fu mortale l' amor per te.
> Morire! etc.
> *Aida.* Vedi? di morte l' angelo, etc.

You can hardly imagine what a lovely melody can be made of this unusual form, and what grace the five-syllable line coming after three of seven syllables will give to it, and what variety will result from the hendecasyllabic lines that follow! . . . See if you can turn this into poetry and keep 'tu sì bella' which makes such a good cadence.

It is evident that Verdi must have had the melody of this passage already in his head, and was sketching out words that would fit it. Ghislanzoni served him most loyally and produced a stanza that retains the metrical form with a modification at the end, but flows more easily and works the ideas together more compactly. He gave Verdi the required cadence on 'bella,' without however repeating the first two lines as Verdi suggested:

> Morire! sì pura e bella?
> Morir! per me d' amore?
> Degli anni tuoi nel fiore
> Fuggir la vita?

The Final Scene

T' avea il cielo per l' amor creata,
Ed io t' uccido per averti amata!
    No, non morrai,
    Troppo t' amai!
    Troppo sei bella!

. . At the very end you must take out the customary agonies and avoid
such expressions as 'I faint; I go before you; wait for me! death! I still
live!' etc. I want something sweet and vaporous, a *very short* duet, a
farewell to life. Aida should fall gently into Radamès's arms as Amneris
kneels on the stone above the vault and sings her *Requiescant in pace*.

These extracts from the immensely lengthy correspondence with
Ghislanzoni will, I hope, have given the patient reader who
troubles to refer to the vocal score an insight into the mystery of
operatic composition, such as no theoretical exposition could so
vividly provide. That is my excuse for placing before him the
discussion of so many seemingly trivial problems of versification
and diction.

From this discussion two main points emerge: Verdi's enormous
punctiliousness in the minutiae of the text and his quite extraordinary mental vitality, that could seize upon what was essential
and reject what was feeble or inappropriate in any form of words
or any dramatic situation. Of his scrupulousness one more
example may be cited. In the scene of Radamès's trial Ghislanzoni
had given the accusing Ramfis the words: 'Taci? taci?' ('You
are silent?'). This will not do, says Verdi, for the interrogative
cannot be expressed in music. And he proceeds to suggest the
substitution of 'Difenditi!'—a pause—'Tu taci? Traditor!'
('Defend yourself!—You are silent? Traitor!). But, he adds,
the *ti, tu, ta, ci* is dreadful. From this Ghislanzoni evolved the
admirable: 'Discolpati' (which avoids the *di ti* of *difenditi*) —
'Egli tace; traditor!'

It would not be overstating the case to say that there is not
one dramatic stroke in the whole opera which Verdi did not
himself suggest or in some way improve upon. It was he who
insisted that the relationship of Aida to Amonasro should be
clearly brought out at the moment when the Ethiopian king enters

in the triumph scene. Aida must cry out 'mio padre,' not the more ordinary 'o padre mio,' in order to get the emphasis and musical accent on *padre*. It was again Verdi who suggested that after Radamès's condemnation the priests should return to the stage and so afford the opportunity for Amneris's effective appeal for mercy and for her outburst of fury against them when it is rejected.

It is to be observed, too—since *Aida* might nowadays be taken as the very type of conventional grand opera—that he is never weary of insisting upon the necessity for avoiding commonplace expressions or of demanding from the poet new and unusual forms of verse. Ghislanzoni was evidently inclined to abide by convention and at first served up cabalettas in all the usual places and lapsed into poetic clichés at the big dramatic moments. Verdi would have none of them. Everything must be vivid and to the point; the actor's words must be in character and, above all, must be such as would heighten the dramatic effect of the scene.

There was no musical device that he was not prepared to employ, if it seemed to suit his book; and if he could give to its use a novel and original turn, so much the better. His acceptance of everything, his readiness to lay any style under contribution, is avowed in a letter written in 1882 to Opprandino Arrivabene:

Opinion on musical matters should be liberal, and for my part I am very tolerant. I admit the melodists, the harmonists, the bor⸍ —shall we say those who would bore us at any price for the sake of *bon ton*? I admit the past, the present, and I would admit the future, if I knew it and thought it good. In a word, melody, harmony, declamation, florid vocalization, orchestral effects, local colour (a much⸍used term that too often serves to cover up a lack of ideas) are only the raw material of music. Make of these materials good music, and I will admit them one and all, of whatever kind. For example, in the *Barber* the phrase, 'Signor giudizio per carità,' is neither melodic nor harmonic; it is declamation, exact and truthful—in fact, music.

From one point of view *Aida* is, indeed, the very type of grand opera. It is the last and greatest example of that species created by the reaction of the Parisian taste of the Second Empire upon the romantic drama of the nineteenth century, born of the union of the German passion for size with the Italian feeling for lyrical melody, and admirably adapted for performance amid the glittering magnificence of Charles Garnier's opera house. But the reason why *Aida* has not merely survived, but has lost none of its vitality, is that within the grand framework of its spectacular and patriotic theme it contains a set of human characters, subtly observed and truthfully drawn. The main outlines of the action may seem conventional after seventy years—what drama of that period would not so appear?—but Aida and Amneris and Radamès engage our interest and excite our sympathy as fully now as they engaged those of their early audiences, because Verdi clothed their skeletons, originally indistinguishable from any other set of the usual operatic bones, with individual flesh and blood.

This result was achieved by Verdi's conscientious attention to all the details he discussed with his librettist. In our enjoyment of the long succession of bold and beautiful melodies and powerful dramatic strokes in *Aida* we are apt to overlook the subtleties of characterization and the precision with which the dramatic points are made. But it is these imponderables that have secured its survival in an age which sees in the once famous operas of Meyerbeer, so grand and effective when they were new, only tawdriness and sham sentiment.

There have been found critics, on the other hand, who dismiss *Aida* as a vulgar and pretentious work, a mere sequel, inflated to even more grandiose proportions, of Meyerbeer's *L'Africaine*. But such writers, correct though they may be in noting Verdi's indebtedness to Meyerbeer, too often lay themselves open to the suspicion that their judgment is affected by the degree of popularity enjoyed by a composer, and that they are always ready to assert what is contrary to general opinion. So they rate Liszt above Wagner, Berlioz above Brahms, and *Les Huguenots* and *L'Africaine* above *Don Carlo* and *Aida*. Such paradoxes may have their utility in shaking us out of a too complacent submission to accepted opinions; but the attraction of their smartness, their novelty and their usefulness as clever debating points too often blinds those who propound them to their perversity.

To what in *Aida* does the charge of vulgarity really apply? Let us concede to the critics the tune 'Su! del Nilo' in the first scene—yet how noble is the second strain of it sung in turn by Ramfis and Amneris!—and the chorus 'Gloria all' Egitto' with its bang on the big drum on the weak beat in every third bar. I will even admit that the whole of the triumph scene up to Amonasro's entrance wears thin after, perhaps, fifty hearings. But the similar scene in *Don Carlo* sounds tawdry the very first time, and I fancy that one's loss of interest in the *Aida* scene is largely due to the shoddiness of the spectacle in the average performance. The ballet, too, in this scene is apt to be boring, for all that it contains the best ballet music Verdi ever wrote, because the art of ballet has made such enormous strides since it was devised. Let us throw in, not as vulgarities but as un-deniable weaknesses in the music, the oddly sanctimonious tune given to Amonasro at the end of Act III ('No, tu non sei col-pevole'), the incongruous triviality of the phrases in which Radamès's dreadful sentence is pronounced, and the rather tedious little chorus of the Priests when they return to the stage and reiterate the word 'Traditor!' But, when all these are added up, they amount to only a very few bars in an opera of large dimensions and quite exceptional imaginative power.

At the risk, then, of seeming to drive along a well-worn rut, I shall subscribe to the opinion that *Aida* is of all the operas com-posed by Verdi up to this time the most consistently fine in con-ception and execution. It has all, and more than all, the grandeur of *Il Trovatore* without its crudity and violence. If it contains nothing that surpasses the third act of *Don Carlo* in psychological interest, neither does it contain such serious musical and dramatic flaws as mar that great but uneven work. If it lacks the variety and comic relief of *La forza del destino*, it makes up for that want by its coherence and spectacular interest. It exhibits, more than any other, Verdi's inexhaustible melodic inspiration, which was capable of pouring out one great tune after another, without ever repeating ideas already used elsewhere, whatever family likeness there may be between them.

It is necessary to emphasize the originality of thought that went to the making of *Aida*, for the simple reason that, owing to our very familiarity with the opera, we are apt to overlook it in our simple enjoyment of its melodic riches. When all the indebted' ness to Meyerbeer has been acknowledged and all the similarities between Verdi's handling of cognate situations in this and the previous operas have been allowed for, there remains an enormous residue of individual character that belongs to *Aida* alone. Verdi himself points out the parallel between the scene of Radamès's trial and the 'Miserere' in *Il Trovatore*; but it is not a resemblance that will immediately strike the spectator, because the composer has not been content to repeat an effect once successfully made, but has approached a similar situation with a fresh mind and an eye for its particular circumstances and local colour. Manrico, the troubadour, naturally gives voice to his heroic grief in his dungeon; Radames is, as naturally, silent in the face of his accusers. The priests sing the 'Miserere' to a liturgical strain that is obviously Roman Catholic; the chant of the Priests of Isis is, if not authenti' cally ancient Egyptian, at least oriental and exotic. And, finally, what a vast difference there is between Leonora's lyrical lament and Amneris's declamatory outpouring of her agony of grief and self' reproach! It would not be possible to assert that the one scene is more dramatic than the other, or more 'beautiful.' They really cannot, for all their similarities, be compared. Each is *sui generis* perfect in its own context.

Local colour, one of those ingredients of which Verdi avowed his readiness to make use, plays an important part in *Aida*. Yet this colour is not produced by the deliberate application of exotic harmonies and rhythms to Verdi's native Italian manner, which would have produced an impure style like that of Puccini's *Madame Butterfly*, in which the Japanese and American tunes were never completely absorbed into the texture of the music but stick out of it like so many almonds on top of a trifle. In *Aida* it is extremely difficult to define exactly how the Egyptian atmosphere is created. Indeed, were it not for the marked peculiarity of this score, which differs from more than it resembles any other of Verdi's, it might be thought that this 'atmosphere' was a hallucination created by our association of the music with those megalithic statues and Ramessid temples on the stage. The orientalisms on which one can lay a finger are rare, the most obvious being the chromatic figure with its strongly accented appoggiatura of the Priestess in the second scene, which one might hear, sung with a more nasal whine than would be tolerated at the opera, in any 'native village' at any International Exhibition:

The same influence may, perhaps, be seen in the unbarred and unaccompanied invocation of the priests at the beginning of the trial scene in Act IV.

The local colour in *Aida* is not, however, confined to points like these. It is almost all-pervasive, except perhaps in the triumph scene where the brass band plays stirring patriotic tunes that would suit any Latin military parade. Even here Verdi nearly hit, quite by accident, upon a piece of archaeological exactitude. One of the most striking things in this scene is the successive entry of two sets of 'natural' trumpets, the one pitched a minor third higher than the other, the one playing in A♭ the other in B♮. With the entry of the second set he achieves that sudden lift of the music into an even greater brilliance by the unprepared transposition of the fanfare into the higher key which must stir even the least musical listener. I have already suggested that this device, used over and over again in vocal duets and exceptionally frequent in *Aida*, originated in the necessity for adapting the *tessitura* of a given melody to voices of a different pitch. But Verdi found the device so effective in heightening the dramatic tension that he used it in this and other passages in *Aida* for its own sake. It is an odd coincidence that in the tomb of Tutankhamen there were found two trumpets, one of silver twenty-eight inches long and one of copper twenty-five inches long, which respectively produce the notes C, E, G, C, and D, F#, A, D. Owing to the shortness of the instruments—the natural trumpet in D is about eighty-eight inches long—their pitch is high and the number of notes obtainable limited. When a broadcast of these instruments was made, they proved to have a shrill but not disagreeable tone. It is interesting to know that in ancient Egypt there existed trumpets capable of producing the notes of the harmonic series one tone apart in the modern diatonic scale. Verdi's instruments three semitones apart are historically justified.

Let us examine two other passages in which Verdi uses this harmonic 'step-up' to heighten the musical and the dramatic interest of scenes that might in themselves have been, in one instance, commonplace and, in the other, flat and boring. They will serve also to show that his attention to detail in musical composition was no less scrupulous than in the construction of the libretto, of which examples have already been given. The two things are really complementary and indivisible.

Here, then, is an excerpt from the trial scene in Act IV:

This passage is repeated note for note three times, but at each repetition the pitch is raised one semitone. Ramfis begins his first charge to Radamès on A, the second on B♭ (in the last bar of the passage quoted), and the third on B. The harmony accompanying the last two bars of Amneris's appeal to the gods is:

The tonic note of the new key of B♭ is inserted into the unexpected chord of E major without warning or preparation, and so lifts the tonality up a minor fifth with a violence that must startle the ears even of those who do not know B♭ from a bull's foot.

The tonality of the whole of this passage is extremely fluid, passing through A major—C sharp minor—E major—E minor —E major in a dozen bars. All these keys are closely related, but their sequence is carefully graded to produce a growing sense of climax up to the shout of 'Traditor,' upon whose C♮ Amneris abruptly imposes the tonality of E major by way of the chord of

The Diminished Seventh

the diminished seventh, which makes the transition less violent than the switch from E to B♭ five bars later. Her descending phrase is in E minor, but the harmony of her cadence returns to the major key with the F♯.

This ever-shifting kaleidoscope of tonality within a nearly related group of keys is one of the characteristics of Verdi's mature style, and indeed of music generally in the middle of the nineteenth century. But Verdi turns the kaleidoscope in his own individual way, which differs completely from Wagner's chromaticism and sequential development of his themes. Verdi uses chromaticism mainly as an ornament to his melody, for pathetic effect or for purposes of local colour, as in the incantation of the Priestess quoted above. His favourite resource for modulation is, as he confessed, the diminished seventh, which offers so wide a choice of direction that it has been nicknamed the musical Clapham Junction. But his resort to this protean device became less facile as his style matured and his selection of the particular direction to be taken from this harmonic junction more judicious and so less commonplace. His use of it does not remind us of Wagner, to whom it was no less an ever-present help. For Wagner tends to use it melodically. Play the notes B, D, F, [A], A♭ as an arpeggio and you have the basis of the Siegmund-Sieglinde music in *Die Walküre* and of much else in Wagner's works.

The second passage to which I want to draw attention exemplifies a rather different kind of harmonic step-up. It is taken from the temple scene in Act I:

I have reduced this to its bare harmonies. The priestesses with their accompanying harp having stated the key of E flat major, the priests, as is the way of unaccompanied male choirs, let the pitch drop to A flat major and finish their chant on the chord of

191

the dominant (E♭), which the harps promptly seize upon and turn into the tonic chord of E♭. The procedure is extra-ordinarily simple and its effect is out of all proportion to the means employed. Personally I can never hear this scene without being taken by surprise at the re-entry of the harps on the E♭ chord, for all that I know it is coming. Part of the effect is due no doubt to the sudden imposition of the treble notes upon the bass of the choir, which exaggerates the upward change in the pitch of the tonality. In this way Verdi gives an interest which is little short of miraculous, so disproportionate are the means to the effect produced, to a scene that might well have seemed flat and mono-tonous after the stirring patriotic chorus followed by Aida's dramatic scena ('Ritorna vincitor!') at the end of the preceding scene. In *Don Carlo* he had achieved the same result in a similar context by giving to the monks at the tomb of Charles V a chant that alternates between the major and minor chords of F♯. That this chorus, sung off stage, makes a rather drab beginning to the opera in its revised version (without the original first act) is not to be denied. But it was designed as a contrast to the brilliant scene at Fontainebleau, and immediately established the oppressive gloom of the Spanish court which weighs so heavily on the un-happy Isabella. In *Aida* the purpose of the temple scene is rather different, being designed to impress upon us the solemnity of Radamès's dedication to his country's service and so to emphasize the enormity of his unwitting betrayal of his oath.

The libretto of *Aida* has been criticized on the grounds that the main action of the drama does not begin until the third act, the first two acts being occupied with expository matter which a competent dramatist could have compressed into one short scene, and with other matter concerning the war between Egypt and Ethiopia which is not very relevant to the personal relations of Radamès, Aida and Amneris. But *Aida* is something more than yet another theorem upon the Eternal Triangle. Its real subject is the conflict between love for Aida and love for his country in the heart of Radamès, and Aida herself is torn by a like emotional struggle. To the exposition of this conflict all the 'patriotic' scenes as well as the solemn ritual of the priests are absolutely essential, even if the triumph scene were not a necessary spectacular element in an opera designed in the 'grand' manner for a state occasion. Never before, even during the stirring times of the *Risorgimento*, had Verdi given such splendid expression to his own patriotism, and *Aida* may not unfairly be regarded as a musical celebration of the final realization of Italian unity which was achieved, at the expense of the Vatican, during the year of its composition. It is, to put it at the lowest, a worthier monument than its conscious and visible memorial, the statue of King Victor Emmanuel, which serves only to show in what shallows of pretentiousness the art once glorified by Donatello, Verrocchio and Michelangelo had grounded. That Verdi wished to emphasize the true nature of the dramatic conflict in *Aida* is surely made evident in the prelude to the opera, in which the melody associated with Aida is opposed, not to that of Amneris, but to that which accompanies the Priests of Isis who stand for Egyptian law and morality and are the final judges of Radamès. It is also to be observed that Verdi, with Ghislanzoni's help, was successful in suggesting the warlike background to *Aida*. It is one of the faults of *Il Trovatore* that we are never sufficiently aware that there is a civil war in progress, while even in *La forza del destino* the state of war is only brought to our notice spasmodically and, owing to its length, these references are too often eliminated in modern productions of the opera. But in *Aida* we are never allowed to forget the danger to Egypt from the savage Ethiopians.

Such criticisms of the libretto, mistaken though they are, have some foundation, perhaps, in the undoubted fact that with the appearance of Amonasro towards the end of the second act the dramatic interest of the opera is greatly enhanced. For Amonasro, whose sole motive force is a burning patriotism, is the finest baritone part Verdi had so far created. It is also true that the third act is musically the most beautiful (with the possible exception of the last act in *Rigoletto*, which is, however, not on the same plane of musical inspiration) and the most flawless individual act in any of his operas up to this date.

The beauty of Aida's aria ('O patria mia'), of the great duet with Amonasro, one of the most powerful scenes in opera, and of the passionate love duet that follows, is too self-evident to need underlining. But Verdi had written beautiful airs and duets before; what was new was the continuity of the music throughout the whole act and the perfect balance achieved between voice and orchestra. He had approached this perfection occasionally in *Don Carlo*, in the revised scenes of *Macbeth* and even, at rare intervals, in earlier operas still. But never before had he given so sure and sustained a homogeneity to a whole long act. Not only are the old formal cadences at the end of individual movements abolished or, at least, disguised by the skilful dovetailing of one movement into the next, so that there is no dead halt, at which the auditor is held up, as at a junction of many roads, while he has time to consider along which of them the composer may choose to take him—not only is he carried along smoothly, though at varying emotional speeds, according to the tightening or relaxation of the dramatic tension, but the difference between the lyric aria style and the dramatic recitative style has been narrowed down to vanishing-point. Verdi's vocal line had at last achieved perfect flexibility. This is evident throughout the opera, but nowhere does his mastery serve him so well as in this third act. There is not a phrase in the whole act—with the exception already mentioned—that has not some rare distinction of melody, sometimes developed at length into strophic tunes like Amonasro's 'Rivedrai le foreste imbalsamate' or Aida's seductive 'Là tra foreste vergini,' sometimes compacted into a single phrase. Amneris, conducted to her vigil in the temple of Isis to an accompaniment of chanting priestesses, has but two lines to sing:

In those two lines Verdi reveals, for the only time but so completely that we need no other confirmation, the womanly tenderness within that hard and passionate nature. I can think of no better instance, even in the later operas, of Verdi's mastery of the pregnant phrase that at one stroke defines character and situation, while ravishing our ears with its beauty.

Of the orchestration of this act it would be difficult to speak too highly. It is never obtrusive or 'clever'; it is always exactly right. How else establish the scene, the shimmer of heat and moonlight in the Egyptian night, than by staccato semiquavers for the violins on the note G rising and falling through four octaves? The scene, as well as the varying moods of the dramatic situations, seems always to have been at the back of Verdi's mind, dictating the warm and tremulous figurations of the low flute notes, that also provide the characteristic 'colour' of many pages elsewhere in the score, accompanying Aida's 'O cieli azzurri,' the keener oboe tone in 'Là tra foreste,' and, most magical touch of all, the soft trumpet fanfares of Radamès's 'Nel fiero anelito.' Verdi had used the trumpet to achieve an effect of poignancy in Posa's death scene; here it is the voice of passion at its tenderest whispered by a soldier (Verdi forgets nothing) into the summer night.

The Franco-Prussian war failed to interrupt the composition of *Aida*, but it delayed its production. Mariette with all his designs for the scenery and costumes was shut up in Paris during the siege, which lasted until January 1871. The inevitable postponement caused some anxiety in Egypt, for it was feared that the opera would be given for the first time in Italy, since Verdi had stipulated that it should be produced at the Scala immediately after the original date fixed for the production in Cairo. But Verdi, hard bargainer though he was and insistent upon adherence to the terms of his contracts, was an honourable and reasonable man. In the circumstances he suggested on his own initiative that the Milan production should also be postponed. Incidentally it may be mentioned that sympathy with France's sufferings under the Prussian invasion quite overcame the antagonism aroused by the failure of *Don Carlo* in Paris and by Napoleon III's betrayal of Italy a few years before. He instructed du Locle to pay out of the royalties on *Aida* 2,000 francs to a fund for the benefit of wounded French soldiers.

In the event *Aida* was produced, with enormous success, in Cairo on 24th December 1871. Mariani had been invited to conduct the work, but he was by this time, unfortunately, too ill to undertake it. Muzio, engaged in his place, was unable to go to Egypt at the later date. So it fell to Giovanni Bottesini, the celebrated double bass player, who had for some years been director of the Italian Opera in Cairo, to conduct the performance. Verdi was curiously indifferent about the first production, saying, that if Mariani would not conduct, it did not much matter who did. He did not go to Egypt himself, and expressed his disgust at all the preliminary publicity to which his new work was subjected. For *Aida*, written at the command of a foreign potentate in order to celebrate the completion of a great engineering enterprise, had 'news value' in the eyes of journalists and newspaper proprietors, and news value implied standards of judgment that had no validity for an artist of Verdi's integrity. To Filippi, the correspondent of a Milanese paper, he wrote indignantly:

You in Cairo? That is one of the finest imaginable advertisements for *Aida*! It appears to me that in these days art is no longer art, but a trade . . . something that must achieve, if not success, notoriety at any price! I feel disgusted and humiliated. In my early days it was always a pleasure to come before the public with my operas, almost friendless and without a lot of preliminary chatter or influence of any kind, and stand up to be shot at; and I was delighted if I succeeded in creating a favourable impression. But now what a fuss is made about an opera! Journalists, singers, directors, professors of music and the rest must all contribute their stone to the temple of publicity, to build a cornice out of wretched tittle-tattle that adds nothing to the worth of an opera, but may rather obscure its true merits. It is deplorable, absolutely deplorable! . . . All I want for *Aida* is good and, above all, *intelligent* singing, playing and stage production.

What, one wonders, would Verdi think of modern standards of news value in regard to music, which make front-page copy of a concert that does not take place and ignore what happens on the platform or the stage in favour of some irrelevant incident in the auditorium? *Aida* started its triumphant career in Europe at the Scala Theatre six weeks after the first performance in Cairo. Here it was conducted by Franco Faccio, who had atoned for his youthful association with Boito's scurrilous poem by becoming a devoted admirer of Verdi and a first-rate conductor of his music. The singers included Teresa Stolz (Aida) and Maria Waldmann (Amneris), who were from now onwards associated with so many great performances of Verdi's music. It was at one time put about by those whose motto is always *cherchez la femme* that an intrigue with Stolz was the cause of the breach between Verdi and Mariani. Stolz was Mariani's mistress during the years before *Aida* and, when the Verdis visited Genoa, they occupied a flat in the house where Mariani lived with the singer. What more natural than to suppose that, as other musicians have done, Verdi fell in love with the singer who did him so much credit, that there were quarrels with the jealous conductor, who turned against his friend in a fit of pique, when deserted by his mistress, and became an ardent Wagnerite? There is little concrete evidence to support this commonplace, if romantic, explanation of the affair. The correspondence between Verdi and the singer is full of affection, but it is the affection of mutual friendship and admiration, not of passionate love. The publication of Giuseppina Verdi's correspondence seemed to destroy the whole basis of the scandal—unless we are to suppose her an unusually complaisant wife—for it reveals the closest friendship between the two women.[1]

The truth of the matter seems to be that Mariani had treated his mistress abominably. He promised her marriage and, on the strength of that promise, she entrusted to him a large part of her savings, which she had difficulty in recovering. To a man of Verdi's absolute honesty Mariani's conduct and his inability to arrive at any decision about his marriage appeared absolutely inexcusable. Verdi took Stolz's part and vainly intervened on her behalf with Mariani. Thereafter, though he continued to respect him as a musician, he could feel only contempt for him as a man. Even when Mariani died miserably in 1873 of the cancer from which he had so long been suffering, Verdi was unable to relent. He sent a formal message of condolence, indeed, but did not attend the funeral.

During the months after the production of *Aida* in Milan Verdi was pestered with invitations to attend performances of the opera in cities all over Italy. His reaction was characteristic. To the management at Trieste he replied, thanking them for their courtesy, but pointing out that his presence in the theatre could make no difference to the artistic quality of his opera and that he had no taste for being exhibited to the public as a curiosity. Even when he was in London for the performance of the *Requiem* in 1875, he refused an invitation from Covent Garden to be present at the first production of *Aida*. Possibly he was actuated in this instance by pique; for he disapproved of Gye's choice of Patti to sing the title-part although Stolz was in London and available. Yet he had received the *prima donna* at Busseto and run through the music with her. He was not of the pusillanimous kind that cuts off its nose to spite its face; but, if he would be helpful where help was really needed, he would not give the added advertisement of a personal appearance for the benefit of impresarios.

To his refusals he made two exceptions. He honoured Parma, as the capital of his native duchy, and received the acclamations of his fellow-citizens. He went to Naples because he did not

[1] See Supplement III, p. 317.

trust the management to do their job properly. Here the production was delayed owing to the illness of Stolz, and Verdi amused himself during this period of enforced leisure (March 1873) by composing a string Quartet. Of this Quartet in E minor, his sole essay in chamber music, he wrote that it was 'of no importance.' Once it had been played at his lodgings in the presence of a few intimate friends, he laid it aside and refused at first to have it printed or publicly performed.

In this 'pastime,' as he called it, Verdi was, whether consciously or not, exercising himself, enlarging his command of a purely instrumental technique and of a mode of musical thought independent both of literary and dramatic associations. It might even he called a sketch for *Falstaff*, as yet unthought-of, for the bubbling humour of the fugal finale is in the very vein of Sir John's tormentors. Much of it, especially the first *allegro*, whose main theme reminds us of Amneris, is quite clearly the product of a mind that had so long been concentrated upon *Aida*. But its style is wholly light and free from anything in the nature of bombast. The Quartet is not 'great' music in the sense in which we apply the adjective to Beethoven's. But it deserves occasional performance, not merely as an interesting excursion by the composer into a strange field of music, but on its own merits because it makes delightful hearing. There is nothing here for tears, but a great skill in handling the medium of the string quartet, a melodic charm, and an all-pervading sense of happiness and well-being that would be surprising in the composer of so many 'pessimistic' operas, were it not that we had his letters to correct the impression of a gloomy temperament and of the 'bearishness' which Verdi was apt to parade.

CHAPTER XIV

IN May 1873 Italy lost that 'other glory,' Alessandro Manzoni, whose death affected Verdi as profoundly as had the deaths of Rossini and Cavour. He felt unable to face the funeral, but made a pilgrimage to Milan a few days later to pay homage in private at the poet's grave. At the same time he wrote to the municipal authorities in Milan offering to compose a *Requiem Mass* for performance in Manzoni's native city on the anniversary of his death. He waved aside the expressions of gratitude contained in the municipality's letter of acceptance; the idea of commemorating, in a great musical composition, the poet whom he regarded as the purest, the most saintly and exalted manifestation of the Italian genius, sprang from 'an impulse or, rather, from a heartfelt necessity.'

Verdi had by him, it will be remembered, the movement composed for the abortive commemoration of Rossini. Verdi himself seems to have forgotten about it, for there is a letter of February 1871 from Alberto Mazzucato, the director of the Milan Conservatoire and a member of the Rossini Memorial Committee, reminding him of its existence, praising it as 'the most beautiful, the most immensely poetical page of music imaginable,' and urging Verdi to do his duty to the world and complete the Mass himself. To this appeal the composer replied, not without a twinkle in his eye:

If at my age I could still decently summon up a blush, I should go crimson at the compliments you pay my piece—compliments that, I do not fail to appreciate, coming from a master and a critic of your standing, have the greatest importance and flatter my self-esteem. And—behold the ambition of a composer!—these words of yours have almost awakened a desire to write, at some later date, the whole Mass, especially as in making this larger expansion I should find the 'Requiem' and 'Dies irae' ready-made, as their reprise in the 'Libera me' is already composed. Consider, then, with due remorse, the deplorable consequences that your praise may have! But keep calm; it is a temptation that will pass, like so many others. I have no love of useless things—Requiem Masses exist in plenty, plenty, plenty! It is useless to add one more to their number.

The occasion that would make such an addition 'useful' had now arisen, and upon the foundation of the 'Libera me,' composed for Rossini, rose the great structure of the monument to Manzoni.

It is important to note that Verdi's letter clearly states that the reprises of the 'Requiem aeternam' and of the 'Dies irae,' which occur in the 'Libera me,' had already been composed, the implication being that the music already written for these passages could be made to serve for the 'Requiem aeternam' and 'Dies irae' in the Mass proper. This implication has, so far as I know, been swallowed hook, line and sinker by every biographer and critic of Verdi. And, on the face of it, there seems to be no reason for questioning the accepted idea that the 'Libera me,' as we know it, is what Verdi wrote for the Rossini Mass. If, however, we consider the matter more closely, it will appear as not the least strange feature of this extraordinary work that it could have been written backwards, that its climax, both musical and emotional, could have been created before the material out of which the climax is made had been considered at all. This is a complete reversal of the normal process of musical composition, as though a composer were to write the development of a symphonic movement before the exposition had been conceived.

Let us see exactly what happens in the score as we have it. The opening movement of the Mass begins with a setting of the words:

'Requiem aeternam dona eis, Domine, et lux perpetua luceat eis.'

Verdi

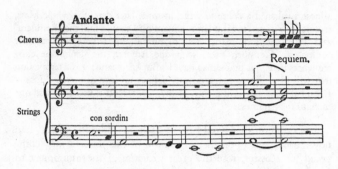

The melody and harmony are given wholly to the muted strings, the chorus whispering the prayer, for the most part on one note, in broken declamation. The words recur again in the 'Libera me' and here they are set for unaccompanied voices, the melody being given to the solo soprano:

-nam do - na e - is, do - na e - is, e - is,

-nam do - na,_____ do - na,_____ do - na,

Domine, do - na, do - na e - is, Do - mi-

ppp

do - na e - is, do - na e - is, do - na e - is,

- ne. Et lux per-pe-tu-a lu ce-at

cresc. *ppp*

Do - mi - ne. Et lux_____ per - -

e - is, lu - ce - at e - is, lu
-pe-tu - a lu-ce at e - is, et lux per - pe - tu -

- - ce-at e - is. 1. Requi-em ae - ter - nam
2. Do-na e - is, Do-mi-ne

a lu-ce-at e - is. 1. Requi-em ae - ter - nam
2. Do-na e - is, Do-mi-ne.

Et__ lux_____ per - pe - tu - a lu-ce-at

Et lux, et lux per - pe - tu - a lu-ce-at

Now it is possible that Verdi could have composed this second passage for the Rossini Mass and then evolved from it the simpler, shortened version with which the Manzoni Mass begins. But I find it extraordinarily difficult to believe. It involves the sup⁄ position that the composer could divest his music of its final beauty, could refrain from using, for example, the lovely extension (bars 10–13 in the soloist's part) of the appeal for peace, and that he could, like a child keeping the best plums in the pudding for last, reserve the new, yet inevitable, development of it all for his final stroke. If we do accept these things as having happened, contrary to all reasonable assumptions about the workings of a composer's mind, then we must credit Verdi with an even more remarkable eye for propriety in expression and for musical structure than his greatest admirers have allowed him. For it need hardly be emphasized that one of the chief beauties of the Mass is this elaborated reprise of the 'Requiem aeternam,' which so perfectly rounds it off as a whole composition, and that any full anticipa⁄ tion, at the beginning, of its final form would greatly diminish its effect. It is precisely because at the outset this melody is pre⁄ sented in a comparatively simple and unobtrusive form, that the revelation of its potentialities in the last movement is so overwhelming. In honesty I must confess, however, that in bars 8–11 of the first example the string parts do look as if they had been designed for voices. An experienced choral conductor, whom I consulted on the point, however, did not think there was much in it either way.

If the 'Requiem aeternam' raises a doubt that cannot, in default of the manuscript of the 'Libera me' as composed in 1868, be definitely resolved, but must remain a matter of opinion, the setting of the 'Dies irae' gives us internal evidence that is, at least, some- thing to go upon. The *Dies irae*[1] proper is a long metrical sequence of which the first verse is:

> Dies irae, dies illa
> Solvet saeclum in favilla,
> Teste David cum Sibylla.

(Day of wrath, that day shall reduce the universe to ashes, as David and the Sibyl bear witness.)

In the 'Libera me' there is a reference in *prose* to this poem:

Dies irae, dies illa calamitatis et miseriae, dies magna et amara valde.

(A day of wrath, that day of calamity and anguish, a great and bitter day in truth.)

Both these passages are set to identical music by Verdi, and it is extremely difficult to believe that he would, in the first instance, have set the prose sentence to music that fits the metrical verse like a glove. What, in fact, does happen is that in order to get in music that could only have been imagined for 'Solvet saeclum in favilla,' he has to go on repeating the words: 'Dies irae, dies illa,' because 'calamitatis et miseriae' can by no means be made to fit the notes. Fortunately they could be made to fit the next bars, though only so if 'calamitatis' were repeated. If ever there was a clear case of a text being fitted to music originally suggested by another text, this is one.[2]

---

[1] To avoid confusion I italicize *Dies irae* when referring to the whole poem. 'Dies irae' refers to the musical setting of the first verse of it or its reprise in the 'Libera me'.

[2] I am indebted to Dr H. C. Colles for directing my attention to this clinching point in the argument. I had always been bothered by the discrepancy in the reprise of the 'Dies irae,' but, not having referred to the Missal, I had not realized that it was in prose and so missed the point.

From this I venture to deduce that when he came to complete
the *Requiem*, Verdi found that the reprises of the 'Requiem
aeternam' and the 'Dies irae,' which he had thought would
'come in' and save him the trouble of composing music for part
of the first two movements, did not, when it came to the point,
prove satisfactory. He, therefore, scrapped his original ideas and
introduced the new ones into the 'Libera me' in order to give
coherence to the whole composition. If this suggestion is accepted,
it will also explain why a certain discrepancy of style, which I have
always felt to exist between the 'Libera me' and the rest of the
Mass, is most noticeable as between the 'Libera me' and the
'Requiem aeternam' which now forms a part of it. For, if my
deduction is correct, all that we now have of the movement composed in honour of Rossini is the dramatic introductory recitative
—the most operatic passage in the whole *Requiem*—and the
final fugue.

The fugue may be admirable as a fugue—and it has been
praised as such by the most respectable critics—but its movement
has always seemed too jaunty and its style too trivial to make it a
satisfactory coping-stone to the great edifice. It is always difficult
at a performance of the *Requiem* not to regret that the work
does not end, as it began, with the quiet prayer for peace that
precedes the fugue. After that beautiful passage with the solo
soprano's voice soaring ever more softly above the unaccompanied
chorus until it disappears from hearing, like a bird from sight, on
the *pianissimo* high B flat, the strongly accented fugue-subject
accompanied solely by a loud orchestral chord on the weak beat
of its last bar in the manner of the Egyptian march in *Aida*,

always seems out of key with the mood of the *Requiem* sustained up to this point on a consistent plane of grandeur and tragic emotion. It is, indeed, customary for military bands returning from a funeral to relieve their feelings after the mournful business is over with gay marches, and Verdi may have felt that something cheerful would be an appropriate last thought to leave in the minds of a congregation gathered to do honour to that great comedian, Rossini. But as an ending to the Manzoni *Requiem*, as we know it, the fugue produces a sense of anticlimax. Not even the great beauty of its final pages, where, after the fugue has been worked out, the solo soprano re-enters with large phrases (an augmentation of the fugue-theme) above the chorus and then in the last bars repeats the muttered, fearful prayer for deliverance from eternal death, can wholly redeem the movement.

I realize that I am in a minority in holding this opinion of the 'Libera me' fugue. But previous writers have been so concerned with either attacking the 'theatricality' of the work or defending it from that charge, that they seem to have overlooked the defects of the fugue, not as a fugue, but as an adequate finale to the *Requiem*. The charge of theatricality must be faced. In so far as the word implies insincerity, it may be rebutted with a firm negative. Never was there music so patently sincere. Verdi was no orthodox churchman, but he was in the truest sense a Christian and in this work he was paying tribute to a man he profoundly loved and respected.

Let us then use the less pejorative word, 'dramatic.' It has always been the custom of southern peoples to dramatize their religion. Greek tragedy, itself, the very fount of European drama, originated in ritual, and the Roman Catholic Church is giving true expression to a national tendency when it surrounds its services with the glamour of dramatic effect. For that reason it was found to be temperamentally unsuited to the colder and more austere non-Latin people of northern Europe, once they developed their national consciousness. The political motives which induced authority to support the Reformation could not alone have established the permanent breach with Rome.

We are faced, then, in Verdi's *Requiem* with a work whose style is fundamentally alien to the traditions of English Church music—the one branch of the art in which we have maintained a consistent national tradition from Tudor times until the present day. It was particularly difficult for Victorian, Evangelical England to swallow a 'sacred' work, that was so vivid and exciting, so little contemplative and austere, whose melodies, moreover, were so strongly redolent of the opera house. An English audience, even at this day, approaches the *Requiem* with a knowledge of Verdi, the composer of *Aida*, not through a general knowledge of Italian music and culture, in which the sacred and the profane have never been segregated like the sheep and the goats of the parable. In Catholic countries it has never been considered improper for the operatic composer to make offering in his own kind to the Deity. The juggler could find no better way of honouring the Virgin than in the performance before her altar of his most skilful feats.

There is a further consideration. The longest section of the Requiem Mass is the thirteenth-century Latin poem, *Dies irae*, which is the counterpart in words of the contemporary pictures of the Last Judgment that still survive faintly upon the walls of many pre-Reformation churches. If this presentation of the alternate joys and horrors of that dread day is not dramatic, it is difficult to see what meaning that adjective can have. It is true that among all the settings of the poem none is more beautiful than the traditional plain-song melody which so fascinated the minds of nineteenth-century composers that one after another they made it the basis for their own particular ideas of hell and, incidentally, in the process so vulgarized it with their clever instrumental apparatus that the very sound of the melody has become corrupted for modern ears by an ineradicable association with all those tubas, bells and gongs. A composer, however, who tackles the problem of setting the *Dies irae* must solve it in his own way along the lines of his own musical style, if the result is to be anything more than a still-born exercise in composition. Giuseppina Verdi really said the last word upon this aspect of the subject when, commenting upon certain adverse criticisms of the Mass, she wrote:

They talk a lot about the more or less religious spirit of Mozart, Cherubini and others. I say that a man like Verdi must write like Verdi, that is according to his own way of feeling and interpreting his text. The religious spirit and the way in which it is given expression must bear the stamp of its period and its author's personality. I would deny the authorship of a Mass by Verdi that was modelled upon the manner of A, B or C.

If we accept, then, the premiss that the Requiem Mass containing these dramatic verses was to be set by a nineteenth-century Italian composer, it is absurd to criticize him for not turning out a composition in the manner of Bach or Byrd or whoever may be the critic's ideal of a 'religious' composer, or to complain that he uses all the resources of his period and of his own experience in order to heighten the dramatic effect of the work. If the result were merely theatrical, that is to say, were the dramatic effect to be created by the use of meretricious tricks in default of a genuine stimulus to the artist's power of imaginative creation, condemnation of the result could not be too severe. But we need not, in our turn, wise after the event, be too severe upon critics of the *Requiem*. For, where religion is concerned, the forces of conservatism are always most strongly entrenched, and any breach with tradition is resented. It is hardly surprising, therefore, that in England and Germany the Mass was at first misunderstood, that the resemblance of some of its melodies to Verdi's operatic music should have been more obvious than their difference, and that the essentially religious spirit of the work should be obscured by its dramatic power. A man like Hans von Bülow, all the more because he was a great musician, brought up in the tradition of Bach and Beethoven and at this time an ardent Wagnerian, might well be excused for honestly failing to perceive the merits of the Mass, even if he had not twenty years later made an honourable recantation. Yet Brahms, the author himself of a very different *Requiem* as thoroughly German as Verdi's is Italian, had from the first admired Verdi's work, and is said to have instigated the change in Bülow's opinion which found expression in the following letter to Verdi:

Hamburg, 7th April 1892.

ILLUSTRIOUS MASTER,

Deign to hear the confession of a contrite sinner! Eighteen years ago the writer committed the crime of making a great—a great journalistic howler [*gran BESTIALITÀ giornalistica*] against the last of the five kings of modern Italian music. How often he has bitterly regretted it! When he committed that mistake (for which your magnanimity will perhaps have made allowances) he was out of his senses, if you will forgive the mention of this extenuating circumstance. His mind was blinded by fanaticism, by an ultra-Wagnerian prejudice. Seven years later he gradually came to see the light. His fanaticism was purged and became enthusiasm. Fanaticism is an oil lamp; enthusiasm, electric light. In the world of the intellect and of morals the light is called justice. Nothing is more destructive than injustice, nothing more intolerable than intolerance, as that noble writer Giacomo Leopardi says. . . . A recent performance of the *Requiem,* though it was a poor one, moved me to tears. I have now studied it not only according to the letter which kills, but according to the spirit which quickens. And so, illustrious master, I have come to admire you and to love you! Will you absolve me and exercise the royal prerogative of forgiveness? . . . Faithful to our Prussian motto, *Suum cuique,* I cry: Long live Verdi, the Wagner of our dear allies![1]

To this somewhat high-flown effusion Verdi replied with characteristic calm, countering the compliment of the quotation from Leopardi with one from Wagner, and ignoring the reference to a former version of the Axis, which was unpopular in Italy:

There is no shadow of sin in you, and there is no need to talk of penitence and absolution. If your opinions have changed, you have done well to say so; not that I should have dared to complain. For the rest, who knows? . . . perhaps you were right in the first instance. However that may be, your unexpected letter, coming from a musician of your worth and standing in the world of art, gave me great pleasure. And that, not out of personal vanity, but because it shows that really great artists can form judgments without prejudice about schools and

---

[1] The Triple Alliance had recently been signed.

nationality and period. If the artists of the north and south have different tendencies, well, let them be different! Every one should maintain the peculiar characteristics of his own nation, as Wagner has most happily said. Happy you, who are the children of Bach! And we? We too, children of Palestrina, once had a great school—and to-day? Perhaps it is corrupt and in danger of falling in ruin! If we could only turn back to the beginning!

The mention of Palestrina, whose music might on the face of it be regarded as at the very antipodes to Verdi's, shows a red light to easy generalizations. Verdi was no learned scholar, but he had genius's uncanny knack of being able to lay a hand upon whatever materials or sources of inspiration or processes of composition he might need for a particular purpose. How much he knew by the time he was seventy-four is evident from a letter to Boito, who had consulted him about the curriculum of a proposed state school of choral music:

If you will promise not to give me any credit (or blame) in the matter, I send you some names, the first that come into my mind. There are more than the six you ask for, but there are so many good composers in each period that one does not know how to put them in any order of merit:

1500	*Palestrina (first and foremost),
	Victoria,
	Luca Marenzio (a very pure stylist),
	Allegri (of the *Miserere*),
	and many other good composers of this century, excepting Monteverdi, whose part-writing is poor.
1600	*Carissimi,
	Cavalli,
Later	*Alessandro Scarlatti (also a mine of harmonic wealth),
	*Marcello,
	Leo.
1700	*Pergolesi,
	Jommelli,
Later	*Piccinni (the first, I believe, to write quintets and sextets, etc. Author of the first real *opera buffa*: *Cecchina*).

If you really want only half a dozen, I suggest those I have marked with an asterisk as being the most important.

Verdi

Later we have: Paisiello,
Cimarosa,
Guglielmo Pietro, etc.
And then Cherubini, etc.

Elsewhere the most tuneful composer of his age could write:

Music must not be exclusively melodic. The more harmonic
interest there is, the greater will the melodic interest be. That is music!
Do I seem to speak in riddles? I explain: Beethoven was not a melodist,
nor was Palestrina—in the sense we give to the word.

Again, surprisingly and nearer our particular mark, he wrote to
Ricordi during the composition of *Aida* saying that he was
substituting a new chorus for

a four-part chorus worked out in the manner of Palestrina, that might
have won me applause from the bigwigs and earned me a post in some
conservatoire or other. But I had scruples about writing *alla* Palestrina
in the middle of so much Egyptian music! There it is—I shall never
be a musical *savant*, only a mar-trade!

The composition of a *Requiem Mass* naturally offered a much
more suitable occasion for writing *alla* Palestrina, if we take
the expression to mean an adherence to the spirit and not an
imitation of the letter. For we shall certainly look in vain for
anything in the nature of that smooth, homogeneous texture, as
devoid of obvious surface-incident as marble rubbed down and
polished to the last degree, yet, like marble, amazingly responsive
to the artist's touch, which is the hall-mark of the Palestrinian
style. Even when he sets 'Te decet hymnus' as a four-part
unaccompanied chorus, and uses a theme that is colourably like
plainsong, Verdi gets no farther than bringing in three of his
four voices in contrapuntal imitation, after which he reverts to a
more homophonic style. It is not that he was incapable of writing
strict fugue, but that his mind, his way of thinking musically, did
not actually take that direction. He was writing living music
according to his own individuality and the manner of his time,
not an archaic exercise. When, therefore, he did set himself the
problem of a fugue, his solution never bore any resemblance to
the accepted models of the classical masters—any more than

their fugues, of which the pedants make a pattern, followed the procedure laid down by earlier composers.

If, then, we put aside the expectation of hearing something that conforms to a conception of 'sacred' music based upon styles of composition created by men of different nationality and creed, living in another age; if we recognize that it is unreasonable to ask the composer of *Aida* and *Don Carlo* to do what we do not demand of the composer of *Fidelio* and the Mass in D—that is to shed his personality or cloak it under a factitious style according to whether he is writing for the church or the theatre; if, in short, we approach the *Manzoni Requiem* without prejudice and listen to what is really there in the music instead of allowing casual resemblances to arouse in our minds operatic associations that are largely imaginary, we shall find that the favourite smart paradox about the *Requiem* being 'Verdi's finest opera' is a superficial judgment quite deeply false to the facts. It may be that the 'Kyrie,' whose broad initial phrases announced by the solo quartet in turn (each voice, by the way, having its own individual variation of the cadence) certainly wear a liturgical air, settles down to something like a typical Verdian ensemble. But there is this difference, which holds elsewhere throughout the Mass, that, whereas in most of his operatic ensembles Verdi is portraying a conflict of emotions in the personalities on the stage, here there is no such conflict but a unity of spirit in prayer. In that sense the 'Kyrie' is not at all dramatic, despite the superficial resemblances in the vocal writing to that of the operatic ensembles.

It is, naturally, in the sequence of the *Dies irae* that the dramatic element is most conspicuous. But if it is dramatic to present the coming of the Day of Wrath with all the thunder of drums and brass and with all the whirlwind of rushing strings, and then, by way of a wonderfully conceived *decrescendo* full of ominous mutterings, to usher in the Great Judge in an awed whisper, is the drama out of place? And, if the subsequent fanfares of trumpets, at first distant and then blared out by the full force of orchestral brass, are naïve, what other adjective can we find for this medieval conception of the Last Judgment? The effect is, in any case, so tremendous, quite literally shaking the hearer to the very core of his being, that he is little inclined to bother about the naïvety or otherwise of the actual procedure adopted. The device itself may have been suggested by Berlioz's even more elaborate apparatus of brass bands in his setting of the 'Tuba mirum,' but, if so, Verdi has gone one better, producing a more potent effect with a greater economy of means.

A great part of the remaining verses of the *Dies irae* is allotted to the soloists, but the whole is held together by the repetitions of the tremendous opening verse, in whose downward chromatic phrases the whole universe seems to slide to ruin—an effect that has the highest precedent in the coda of the first movement of Beethoven's ninth Symphony, which produces by the same means the same sense of total collapse and disintegration. The reprises of the 'Dies irae,' sometimes reduced to monotoned mutterings by the chorus of the two words alone, serve to punctuate the enormous movement and to hold together as a single entity what would otherwise be a succession of independent solos, quartets and choruses. Verdi had acquired, through his operatic experience, the art of giving unity to a vast design, not by using the symphonic method of development, but by carefully placed repetitions of or references to his initial theme, which serve to hold the various sections together. The procedure may be compared to that of the painter who by repetitions of certain figures, shapes or curves gives unity to his picture, and the larger the picture the greater the need for the bold use of such repeated forms so that the spectator's eye may the more easily take it in as a whole and not be confused by a jumble of unco-ordinated detail. In effect, the *Dies irae* is a composition of Michelangelesque grandeur, power and *terribilità*.

The literal illustration of the words in music is, of course, the first thing that strikes the newcomer to the *Dies irae*. He observes the brass 'spargens sonum'; the stupor of death portrayed by the dull thud of the big drum (with cords slackened) and *pizzicato* double bass, that punctuates the monotone of the bass solo; the majestic tread of the Great Judge; the pastoral *obbligato* of the

oboe that introduces the tenor's air, 'Inter oves locum praesta,'
though Verdi leaves to Strauss the imitation of bleating sheep
and goats; and the heartrending sobs of the 'Lacrymosa' that have,
it may be, their origin in the profaner griefs of Violetta and
Leonora. But there is more to it than that. The spirit of the
words is made music, too, and therein resides its greatness. It is
not easy to lay a finger upon quotable examples to show how it is
done, for the context is always important. But this join between
'Quid sum miser' (for solo trio) and 'Rex tremendae majestatis'
gives some measure both of Verdi's feeling for mood and of his
sure mastery of contrast:

The whole of 'Quid sum miser' has a quiet, resigned pathos,
set off by the lamenting figure for two clarinets and the flowing
solo of the bassoon, the strings being used for the most part to
double the voices. And then when the three solo voices, un-

accompanied, have wrung the last drop of pathos from the melody, in bursts the whole orchestra, without preparation, as we are told His coming may be, to announce the awful majesty of God.

Or, again, turn to the last page of the 'Lacrymosa,' that is to the end of the whole *Dies irae* sequence. The movement had begun with the most childlike of all the melodies in the *Requiem*, a tune that really might belong to one of Verdi's earlier operatic mezzo-sopranos:

But out of this, with its lamenting counterpoint, a choral movement of solemn beauty and musical complexity has been woven until the soloists utter, unaccompanied and in a style nearer to the Palestrinian than usual, the final prayer to Jesus—a rhymeless couplet probably added by some later hand to the sequence:

This text again has been taken up by the chorus, who transfer to it the original melody of the 'Lacrymosa,' and then all the voices sink to a quiet monotone, the melody fades out of the accompaniment leaving only a suggestion of its rhythm behind, and with one of those magical unexpected modulations that never fail to take us by surprise, however many times we hear them, the final Amen is reached:

This sudden imposition of the chord of G major upon the tonality of B flat produces an effect of sunlight suddenly gleaming —we must not use any word expressive of so much violence as 'breaking' implies—through the lamentable clouds of a tearful sky. There is, after all, some hope of peace and quiet in the grave. It should be observed that in bar 4 the choral sopranos and altos are silent for half the bar and add their volume to the tone as the *crescendo* grows and then are silent again half-way through the next bar. The four soloists and the choral tenors and basses sing the G♮ in octaves through the whole of these two bars. The string harmony is also enriched at the entry of the choral sopranos. In this way the *crescendo* is given a wonderful reinforcement at the right point. And, be it noted, the movement ends on the chord of B flat major—that is the relative major of G minor which is the main key of the *Dies irae*. So at one stroke and in half a dozen bars Verdi has managed both to give sublime utterance to the poetic idea and to round off the whole vast composition with the satisfying musical 'last word.'

The remaining movements of the Mass—the Offertorium, 'Sanctus,' 'Agnus Dei' and 'Lux aeterna' — are, as has already been noted, not dramatic in their themes, and Verdi does not dramatize them, unless the entry of the solo soprano at the words 'sed signifer Michael' in the Offertorium is to be so qualified:

222

Offertorium

But as this shining appearance of the Archangel to defend the righteous from the 'mouth of the lion' and the depths of Tartarus is in the nature of a dramatic intervention, Verdi's very restrained dramatization of it is hardly open to criticism. It amounts to no more than bringing in his soloist on a high E, held over five slow bars while two solo violins play the lovely main theme of the movement, and thereby lifting the tonality and orchestral colour out of darkness into light. It is, in fact, one of the sublime moments in the work and in all music.

There is in this movement none of that sense of physical terror which is displayed in the soprano's agitated recitative with its shuddering accompaniment in the 'Libera me,' for all that the poetic idea is at one point the same. The words 'libera eas de ore leonis' are set to the main melody treated in imitation by the solo quartet, and the darkness of the mood is suggested by the tonality and by the sombre colour of the orchestration, of which the chief feature is the doubling of the violoncello part by the bassoon. Its character may be seen in the first bars of the example just quoted.

The following sentence, 'Quam olim Abrahae,' had almost invariably been set as a fugue by previous composers. Verdi after making a feint at fugue—the first glance at the page with its successive entries for the four soloists from the bass upwards suggests a fugal subject treated in imitation, but a second glance shows that it is nothing of the sort—settles down to a homophonic style. This section is one of the few in the work that depend upon the judgment of the conductor. If he interprets the direction *Allegro mosso* as meaning a quick *allegro* the movement becomes jerky and the whole effect is insignificant. Taken at a pace leisurely enough, without dragging, to give spaciousness to its two-bar phrase, it sounds dignified and fervent. It is a case of giving the singers time to expand their tone on the notes, instead of hustling them from one to the next as is done in nine performances out of ten.

If any one still doubts Verdi's ability to express genuine religious feeling, the setting of 'Hostias et preces' must surely convince him.

The melody clinging to one note and only once straying outside the interval of a major third, is as pure an expression of faithful offering and oblation as it is possible to imagine. It is the same imagination that invented Manrico's first entry in *Il Trovatore*; yet what worlds away from that passionate declaration it has travelled!

The melody is accompanied by string *tremolandi* in the middle of the compass with no treble and very little bass. The movement develops in the same quiet and dispassionate mood as a solo quartet, and when the voices reach the words 'fac eas, Domine, de morte transire ad vitam,' the first violins add a long-held harmonic note to the already ethereal texture. It is a touch of pure genius. The whole orchestration of this movement is a model of delicacy and reticence, as transparent as Mozart's own. The very introduction, where the violoncellos climb up an arpeggio from low C to E♭ at the top of the treble stave, to be answered by a brief phrase for the wood-wind, seems, after the hectic ardours and endurances of the 'Dies irae,' to realize the unimaginable, 'the peace that passeth all understanding.'

The 'Sanctus' is set as a double fugue for chorus, introduced by a fanfare of trumpets and a great shout of 'Sanctus' from the whole chorus and orchestra. The sopranos of the two choirs announce the fugue, which takes in its stride the 'Pleni sunt coeli,' 'Benedictus' and 'Hosanna':

The accents on the off-beats in bar 4 are an important feature, and though, as in Verdi's other fugues (cf. the battle fugue in *Macbeth*, the 'Libera me' and the finale of *Falstaff*), the subject does not flow over the four-bar measure and has a dance-like rhythm, the result is neither jerky nor trivial. Indeed, as a hymn of the Cherubim and Seraphim, it is not unworthy to be set beside Bach's—a judgment that will be no doubt frowned upon by those who regard it as a blasphemy to mention any other composer, and especially a composer of popular 'blood-and-thunder' operas, in the same breath as John Sebastian. But odious comparisons apart, there are few passages in music more angelic in sound than that where the theme is set in augmentation (*pianissimo* and *dolcissimo*) to the words 'Pleni sunt coeli.'

After the jubilant shouts of 'Hosanna' with which the fugue ends, we return to earth and the body on the bier in the 'Agnus Dei,' intoned by two soloists in octaves without accompaniment:

Like so much of the melody in the *Requiem* (cf. that of 'Hostias et preces' and the opening of the 'Lux aeterna'), this seems to me a perfect compromise between Verdi's individual (and, if you will, operatic) melodic style and liturgical tradition. The whole conception of the threefold invocation of the Lamb of God is as original as it is simple. The chorus repeats the phrases announced by the solo voices exactly, the sopranos, altos and tenors in unison, the bass an octave below. The orchestra (clarinets, bassoons and strings) doubles the voice parts. Then the soloists repeat their strain in a minor variation, but with no alteration of the melody, against a throbbing accompaniment of flute and clarinet, with the violas playing the melody a third above the mezzo-soprano. The chorus again sings the original major version harmonized and with a fuller accompaniment, the sopranos on this occasion taking the melody an octave above the altos. The third invocation of the soloists is an exact repetition of the opening but with a running three-part counterpoint in quavers for three flutes. The chorus again responds with another harmonized version, while the strings soar up into the ledger-lines. A brief coda ends this beautiful prayer for peace everlasting, the voices sinking quietly to low C, after which the violins scale the common chord up to C *in altissimo*.

The 'Lux aeterna' is set as a solo trio, and, no doubt, had Verdi not already set the 'Libera me,' which is not part of the Mass for the Dead, but a sequence of Responses to the prayer 'Non intres,' with which the Burial Service proper begins *after* the Mass, this would have been the final movement of the work and would have contained the reprise of the opening 'Requiem aeternam' which was in fact reserved for the 'Libera me.' As it is, Verdi has to find yet another musical setting for the words 'Requiem aeternam dona eis.' His invention does not fail to produce the most sombre of all the versions of this prayer, in which once again we may perceive a compromise between Gregorian plainsong and the Verdian style. It is announced by the bass soloist over a roll on two timpani and punctuated by solemn chords for brass and bassoons:

The whole movement has an air of solemn mystery, from which even the flickering *staccato* semiquavers of the piccolo [1] (accompanying 'lux aeterna luceat eis') detract nothing because imagination, and not an aping imitativeness, is at work. It might have been thought that after the Offertorium and the 'Agnus Dei' the sense of peace, which is the only consolation, could be carried no farther. Yet in the last pages of the 'Lux aeterna' the miracle is performed with the aid of string tremolos, the solemn brass chords of the example just quoted, and a cadenza for two flutes.

We awaken in the 'Libera me' to a world of urgent human terror, the world of the Leonoras and Amelias. It is the soprano soloist who leads here. She has had no independent music allotted to her up to this point. For the mezzo-soprano is the heroine of the *Requiem Mass* proper, and the soprano is employed only in the concerted pieces. But here she is alone, muttering her fearful prayer for deliverance from the pains of hell, and picturing to herself the horrors of 'that awful day':

---

[1] Those who like to trace 'influences' to their source may be interested to compare with this passage Brahms's use of the piccolo in his fourth Symphony, composed a dozen years later. Brahms, we know, had studied Verdi's score and admired it from the first.

After this dramatic scene come the reprises of the 'Dies irae' and of the 'Requiem aeternam,' which have already been fully discussed, and the movement ends with the 'Libera me' fugue.

And when all this has been said—at some expense, I fear, to the reader's patience—what has been said? We have done no more than pick out and prod over a few choice plums in the pudding, leaving as many no less rich behind. We can derive from such piecemeal sampling no more idea of the total mass, than we should have of the grand sweep and spring of a cathedral from seeing a bit of tracery, a broken corbel and a statue torn from its niche. Put back, then, the quotations into their context, and perceive that they are something more than happy tags like

'Out, out, brief candle!'; that they are part of a living, growing organism. Observe their growth under the creator's hand, and his art in holding the interest by sure strokes of contrast and by a vivid enhancement of the meaning of his text. Note the spread and expansion of the music as it grows to a climax, the just placing and proportion of those climaxes, and the skill with which the descent is made on the further side—as great a test in musical composition as in mountaineering. See, in a word, the immense design as a whole. And that is a thing that each must do for himself with the score and in the concert hall, reading and hearing it many times; for it cannot be communicated at second hand with pen on paper.

What may be added is a note on Verdi's style, simple here as everywhere. It is a vocal style allowing the greatest possible expansion to the voices. He puts them to no superhuman tasks, as does Beethoven in the Mass in D, but gives them every assistance from the orchestra. For it will be observed that in nearly every bar, where there is accompaniment at all, the voice part, solo or choral, is doubled by some instrument. In this way the vocal tone is reinforced, for the hearer does not distinguish between the voice and the supporting instrument, but is inclined to give all the credit to the singers, provided they are in tune and the performance is properly balanced. This is Verdi's general practice in all his works, but it is not to be deduced that, because it is a simple matter to write an instrumental part in unison or at the octave with the voice, composition with Verdi consisted of no more than dipping into his full treasury of tunes and picking out one that seemed apt to the occasion. In his early works it did sometimes amount to little more than that, but by the time he had reached maturity he had developed, and he continued to develop during the rest of his life, a very keen and subtle ear for orchestral colour, and although the texture of his music is rarely complex and is always translucent, it has the sureness of effect that only comes when an artist is completely the master of his material and knows exactly what he wants to do and how to do it.

It is an incidental merit of the *Requiem* that it brings out Verdi's wide resourcefulness and his self-restraint. He had never written in any of his operas choral music that suggests a capacity for composing the great choral movements of the Mass, because in the theatre such music, direct though it is, would be out of place. But, when the occasion arose for drawing upon this unsuspected ability, it was there ready to his hand.

We have discussed the design of the *Requiem* and its imaginative power, and we have touched upon some of its details. But what of its spiritual content, the ultimate criterion of a work of art aspiring to greatness, whether 'religious' or not? Its appeal, it must be admitted, is, like all Verdi's music, direct to the emotions, which are stirred by the exploitation of the beauty of the human voice. It has no great intellectual pretensions and never attempts the ineffable, though it comes near to expressing it by the sheer simplicity of its beauty in such movements as the 'Sanctus.' But if it never attains such transcendental heights, such mystical expression of the highest human thought, as is reached in Beethoven's 'Dona nobis pacem' or the 'Seid umschlungen, Millionen' in the ninth Symphony, neither is there that sense of strain, of an endeavour to include what is beyond the limits of human art, that we feel when confronted with certain works of Beethoven and Michelangelo. But there is no need to place artistic masterpieces in order of merit, giving them so many marks each as if they were examination papers with a prize for the best boy. No work of art is perfect or all-inclusive; if it were, the artist's occupation would be gone. Let us then set aside comparisons, rejoice that Verdi added in the *Requiem Mass* one more masterpiece to the sum of human achievement, and leave it at that.

The *Requiem* was performed for the first time in St Mark's Church at Milan on 22nd May 1874 under Verdi's direction. Stolz, Waldmann, Capponi and Maini were the soloists, and the chorus and orchestra were specially selected for the occasion. The work made so deep an impression, and so many people were disappointed of hearing it, that three further performances were given immediately at the Scala. Here it was received with all the fervour of acclamation of which an Italian audience is capable. The demands for repeats and the outbursts of applause in the middle of movements must have reduced it to the level of an ordinary operatic performance in that theatre. But little as such conduct may appeal to our more phlegmatic tastes in these matters—and one still finds it disconcerting to hear an Italian audience yelling and clapping and whistling whenever a tenor gets a good high note off his chest, just as if he had scored the winning goal for the home side—allowance must be made for the difference of temperament that it argues.

The Mass was, indeed, so successful in Italy, that Verdi and Ricordi had to quench the enthusiasm of local choral conductors who, without asking leave, attempted to perform it with a brass band here and a couple of pianofortes there, in default of the proper orchestral resources. Verdi certainly did not regard the work as designed, like the projected Rossini Requiem, for a single occasion or to be revived only at rare intervals to celebrate the anniversary of Manzoni. He toured Europe to conduct it in Paris, London and Vienna. But he would not hear of a proposal made by Gye, the director at Covent Garden, that he should kill two birds with one stone and combine it with a performance of *Aida*! The London performances, three in all, were given in the more respectable surroundings of the Albert Hall, with Stainer at the organ and a choir of 1,200 trained by Barnby, just a year after the first performance in Milan. The critics were divided in their opinions upon the work, the *Daily Telegraph* enthusiastic, the *Morning Post* shocked into derision and *The Times* rather non-committal but, at least, allowing the sincerity of the work. The public, on the whole, was surprisingly enthusiastic, though some shook their heads at this strange way of writing sacred music.

Paris, which was visited on the way to London, was more whole-hearted in its acceptance of the *Requiem*. The four performances originally planned were doubled in response to the public demand, and Verdi was made a Commander of the

Legion of Honour.   In Vienna, as we have already seen, opinion was less unanimous.   But Hans von Bülow's barking only had the effect of making Brahms send for the score. 'Bülow,' he rumbled after studying it, 'has made an ass of himself; Verdi's *Requiem* is a work of genius.'

CHAPTER XV

INTERMEZZO [1]

FOR the moment Verdi was exhausted—mentally by the labours of composition, physically by the European tour with the *Requiem Mass*. Sixty-two years old, he felt that the time had come to retire and enjoy in his country home the proceeds of his toil. His accounts, he put it to the Countess Maffei who was hinting at more work, were balanced, and his duty to the world was conscientiously done. He settled down at Sant' Agata with Giuseppina and his horses and his dogs. It seemed that for what remained to him of life he would subscribe to the philosophy of Candide and mind his garden. This did not mean just pottering round the estate and admiring the trees he had planted a dozen years ago, and then coming in to tell Peppina how many inches the ten *Magnolia grandiflora* had added to their original five-foot height. He went to market to buy his cattle; he supervised in person everything from the breaking-in of a colt to the sinking of a well; he improved, in the face of peasant prejudice, the management of his lands and the methods of farming. The winter he spent usually in Genoa, where there was little music and less 'society.'

Yet, however desired and well-occupied, retirement cannot be without a wrench that leaves an ache, and in the letter he wrote to Maria Waldmann, who was about to leave the stage on her marriage to Count Galeazzo Massari in 1876, we can catch the echo of Verdi's own regrets:

You will have been in Venice for some days, I suppose, concentrating upon your rehearsals for the opera season which will be your last.

---

[1] Intermezzo.—A dramatic entertainment of a light and pleasing character, introduced between the acts of a tragedy, comedy or opera, for the purpose of relieving the attention of the audience from the excessive strain demanded by a long and serious performance.—GROVE.

The last!—it is a sad word that closes a world of memories and comprises a life passed in agitation, happy or the reverse, but always dear to those who have the fibre of the artist. You are fortunate, however, in that you have found a great compensation in your change of fortune. That is not so with others for whom this word *last* means: 'All is over!'

But why should I retail to you, my dear Maria, these painful thoughts? I said the same thing to you the other evening in Paris.[1] . . . Forgive me, and, if I cannot write cheerfully about myself, tell me that you have happiness in abundance. You are young and beautiful, and at the pinnacle of your felicity. Write to me, then, not to give me news of *Aida* or the *Mass*, but to tell me about yourself. We pass the time here [Sant' Agata] quietly and, if not happily, well enough.

And, in spite of his often expressed lack of interest in the further fortunes of his operas, he kept his weather eye open for abuses. He was moved to righteous anger when *Don Carlo* was given 'in an indecent fashion' at Reggio with singers so incompetent that they had to cut much of their music, and at one performance presented an abbreviated version together with an act from *Les Huguenots* and an act from *Macbeth*. He was as alert as ever to see justice done to himself in the matter of royalties and the protection of his copyright. He rates Léon Escudier for not settling a small account with promptness. He grumbles to Ricordi about the delay in taking legal action to stop unauthorized performances of the *Requiem* and some of his letters to his publisher are sharp indeed:

GENOA, 10*th March* 1877.

It is the longstanding habit of Messrs Ricordi to embarrass me in their dealings with my business. The contracts are there, to each party his own share:

I write the operas.

The firm administers them.

And so Messrs Ricordi have not asked my authority (it was within their rights) to give *La forza del destino* at the Scala. But they should not have put upon me the disagreeable task of refusing a request from an old

---

[1] He was in Paris for the first performance of *Aida* at the Théâtre des Italiens.

friend, whom I love and respect, to perform the duet from *Aida* at a benefit concert in Ferrara.

His morbid aversion from the exploitation of his own per, sonality, as opposed to that of his works of art, is exhibited once more in his attitude towards a proposal to erect his statue at the Scala in 1881. He tried, in vain, to turn the project aside by offering to add his name to the list of subscribers to a statue of Bellini, guaranteeing to complete the sum required for it on condition that no statue of himself should be put up either then or in the future without his permission. His statue was unveiled on 25th October, and he writes grumpily to the Countess Maffei a few days later:

A thousand thanks for your note of the 25th October! But do you realize what the 25th October means at the Scala? It means that I am an old fogy (which is true enough) and a veteran put up among the other invalids! . . . I have protested against it and continue to protest.

And two years later we find him once more declining to be made a show of at the same theatre:

DEAR GIULIO [Ricordi],
' *Maestro* Verdi will come to Milan to be present at the rehearsals of *Don Carlo* [the revised version in four acts given at the Scala for the first time in January 1884], and will naturally, we may hope, attend the first performance, etc.' This paragraph in the *Corriere* lays me under an obligation to the public, making out that I shall come and perform the usual pirouettes and show my beautiful snout! I wrote yesterday to have this report denied before I come to Milan. . . . It is not possible, as you suggest, to produce the opera on the 1st, nor on the 2nd, nor—— I cannot fix the date. Do not tell me that the singers have studied the opera and know it. I don't believe it. Two things they certainly do not know: how to pronounce their words and how to keep in time. These qualities are essential for *Don Carlo* more than for any other opera of mine. Faccio [the conductor] can begin and carry on with the rehearsals, and I recommend and demand that he shall insist upon clear enunciation and strict tempo above all else. These are pedantries! But if an opera is made that way, in that way it must be performed, if there is to be any hope of success. As soon as I see the

above report contradicted, I will come to Milan. Let me repeat: *I will attend some rehearsals, especially of the new portions of the work.* Nothing else, nothing else! Absolutely, *nothing else*!!!

This mood of prickly exasperation seems to have been aroused in Verdi by anything connected with the Scala Theatre. His long-standing grievance against Merelli's slovenly productions still rankled in his mind. More than thirty years before he had stipulated that *Stiffelio* might be produced at any first-class theatre except the Scala, and in 1866 he had spoken of it as 'the opera house where nowadays they do not know how to perform an opera.' In spite of the reason for this prejudice, his attitude seems ungenerous towards the theatre that gave him his first opportunities and where he won his spurs with *Nabucco*.

We have already observed in Verdi a curious streak of perversity that led him at times to quarrel, as it were, with his own shadow. It is singularly at variance with the magnanimity he normally displayed in his relations with his fellow-men, and the genuine humility of his attitude towards any one whom he respected. That an artist, endowed with an abnormal sensibility, should not suffer fools gladly is not necessarily a sign of arrogance and spiritual pride, but rather a sense of values that is impatient of insincerity and the second-rate. We may say that Verdi's attitude, which amounted almost to an active hostility, towards his neighbours at Busseto was dictated by his desire to avoid social contacts involving waste of time in small talk, about which he was most certainly of Mr Escot's opinion.[1] And there was, of course, a perfectly valid artistic basis for his dislike of the Scala. Yet

---

[1] 'Ignorance and folly take refuge in that unmeaning gabble which it would be profanation to call language, and which even those whom long experience in "the dreary intercourse of daily life" has screwed up to such a pitch of stoical endurance that they can listen to it by the hour, have branded with the ignominious appellation of *small talk*. Small, indeed!—the absolute minimum of the infinitely little.'—PEACOCK, *Headlong Hall.*

his manner of expressing himself in these matters leaves an unpleasant impression. It is too much like a case of biting the hand that had fed him.

Now lack of generosity and gratitude is, in general, the last charge that can be levelled against Verdi. He never forgot his debt to Antonio Barezzi, and instances have already been given of his readiness to help others who might be handicapped by a poverty like that of his own boyhood. Tempting, therefore, though it may be to find some psychological explanation of these rather spiteful outbursts and to lay the blame upon some early-inflicted trauma in his soul, I think we must look elsewhere for a solution. For, were the psychological explanation as correct as it would be fashionable, one would expect to find a revulsion against those who had been most helpful to Verdi in his youth and a suppression of his sympathy with others similarly unfortunate.

Biographers are often inclined to forget that their subjects have bodies as well as minds, and that a chill on the liver may be as accountable for an ill-tempered and ill-judged action as any other cause. It is not made clear by the Italian biographers what precisely was the diagnosis of Verdi's frequent but not serious illnesses during his middle years, and it is possible that medical science in Italy had not reached the point of naming precisely the trouble from which he suffered. But from the symptoms and from the treatment prescribed, it is possible to be fairly certain that he was the victim of a chronic intestinal complaint, not serious enough to make him really ill, but sufficient to put a strain on his nervous system. This would amply account for the irritability that seems at odds with the poise and dignity of his character.

In the summer of 1879 there burst upon the placid surface of the waters that seemed to have closed for ever over Verdi's creative activity a bubble, and a most surprising and unexpected sort of bubble. It took the form of a protest to Giulio Ricordi about an article in his paper, the *Gazzetta musicale*:

I have read Dupré's article in your paper about our first meeting and the judgment pronounced by Jupiter Rossini[1], as Meyerbeer used to call him. But hold a moment! Here have I been for the past twenty years looking for a comic-opera libretto, and just at the moment when I think I have found it, you go and print an article that will put the public in a state of mind to damn my opera before it is even written, and prejudice my interests and your own. But have no fear. If by any chance, misfortune or disaster, and in the teeth of the Judgment of Great Jove, my miserable genius drives me to write this comic opera, have no fear, I repeat. I will ruin some other publisher!

The explosion in Signor Ricordi's office of this bubble produced in the publisher the most alarming physical and mental reactions. Beckmesser himself, lighting upon the new song in Sachs's hand, was not put into a greater state of perturbation than Signor Ricordi, torn between joy at the prospect of a new opera by Verdi and horror at the idea of the ruin he threatened to some rival house. To Verdi he wrote soothing words. What was the value of old, out-of-date opinions? The public takes no notice of judgments anticipatory or posticipatory. We can laugh at Jupiters, we who are Jupiters ourselves. He explains that the offending article, as offending articles will, got into print without having met his editorial eye. And he apologizes, in a postscript, for not having added a note to the article (which he would have done had he read it before it was printed) explaining that Jupiter had made a mistake, and that the proof of his error lay in the character of Fra Melitone, a novel type, comic yet not comic, characterized in most original music, unparalleled in any other opera, shedding an entirely new light upon the author of so many masterpieces, and so on. The distracted editor spread the posticipatory butter thick.

[1] Rossini was reported as saying: 'Verdi is a composer of a serious and melancholy disposition. His ideas are sombre and thoughtful and pour out of his natural disposition with abundance and spontaneity, and are on that very account most precious, and I rate them most highly. But I doubt whether he can write even a semi-serious opera like *Linda*, much less a comedy like *L'elisir d'amore*.' Which seems a very shrewd and just pronouncement upon the evidence at Rossini's disposal.

What, then, was this comic subject that Verdi had in mind? The answer to this question, hitherto inscrutable, can now be given with reasonable certainty. For among Verdi's papers at Sant' Agata Alessandro Luzio came upon, and published in *Carteggi Verdiani,* a memorandum in Verdi's hand headed 'Molière's Tartuffe.' It is a copy of a sketch for a scenario in French, anonymous and undated but, from the handwriting, judged to have been written about 1868–70. It opens with a sentence that makes its purpose sufficiently clear:

One may note in *L'Imposteur* that diversity of persons, that variety of character so propitious to those conflicts and contrasts in which music excels, because by its very nature this art can present them better than any other.

Alas, that nothing came of this grand project! that the monumental credulity of Orgon, the common sense of Cléante, the astuteness of Elmire and the great central rascality of Tartuffe should have remained unsung! We may assume that the idea was dropped, in the first instance, in default of a librettist capable of translating into a concise and pithy operatic form the wealth and symmetry of Molière's alexandrines, and, in the second, owing to the sudden commission for *Aida*. But that, when Verdi's mind had once more returned to it—for we know of no other comic subject to account for the letter that so amazed Ricordi—it should not have been submitted to Boito, the one man who could have made a successful job of it, must be accounted one of the major disasters in the history of music.

But I anticipate. When he had recovered from the first shock and his mental faculties were restored to him, Giulio Ricordi perceived that, since the bubble had obviously contained air, and since the presence of air argued the possibility of life some/where beneath the water, it was time to act and to act both with speed and caution. Within a couple of days he had Verdi seated at his dinner/table with Franco Faccio as the third of the party.

Ricordi had for some years been attempting to bring Verdi and

Boito together again, and in this design he was abetted and even anticipated by those two good women, Giuseppina and the Countess Maffei. The countess seems at an early stage to have taken under her wing the young composer-poet and his supposed accomplice in the scurrilous affair of the sullied altars of Italian music. Already in 1863 the countess was sending Verdi complimentary messages from the two young men, who had 'the most pleasant and grateful recollection of you.' Verdi's recollection of them was neither pleasant nor a cause for gratitude. He summed it up two years later in the letter to Piave which is quoted in Chapter XI (page 133).

Much had happened since those days. Faccio was already forgiven and had taken Mariani's place as Verdi's favourite conductor. Boito, the composer of *Mefistofele*, was not now to be ignored like Boito, the author of a youthful indiscretion. Verdi had done his best to ignore him. Boito was not included among the contributors to the Rossini *Requiem*, though it may be remarked that Verdi had no part in the selection of the composers. For, a few months before that project was set on foot, *Mefistofele* had been produced at the Scala in the spring of 1868 with resounding failure, and it may well have been considered that the style of this youthful admirer of Wagner would consort ill with that of Nini, Buzzola and Bazzini (of *Ronde des lutins* fame). Since that date *Mefistofele* had been revised—for Boito realized that the fiasco at Milan was not due entirely to the stupidity of the public and the malevolence of conservative critics—and in this new form was produced at Bologna in 1875 with a success that established its composer as the most important musician of the younger generation in Italy. His opera still holds its place in the repertory, though it has never met with more than a *succès d'estime* abroad.

Verdi still made no sign, and turned a deaf ear to the blandishments of Ricordi, who communicated to him Boito's determination, after the Milanese production of *Mefistofele*, to write no more, 'unless he were fortunate enough to be invited to provide a libretto for Verdi, in which case he would put all else aside.' As flattery had no effect, Ricordi tried, with as little success, the more-in-sorrow-than-in-anger tone. It was regrettable that a man of Verdi's quality should be blind to Boito's true character. He might have behaved foolishly, but he was a nervy and eccentric fellow and did not always appreciate what he was doing. At bottom he was loyal and frank and an enthusiastic admirer of Verdi, and so on.

However much Verdi might affect the deafness of a stone, the words dropped by kind friends, to which may be added certain hints from the beloved and tactful Giuseppina, wore their mark upon the stone. So, on that evening late in August 1879, when he sat down to dinner with Faccio and Ricordi, and the conversation had come round, not perhaps altogether fortuitously, to Shakespeare and, by an easy association of ideas, to Rossini's *Otello*, and the two conspirators had expressed their contempt for the librettist's wretched travesty of Shakespeare's drama and commented patronizingly upon the musical judgment of Jupiter himself (exception being made for the grand moment where the gondolier sings Dante's lines from the tale of Francesca da Rimini) —when, after all this careful leading up to the point, one of them mentioned, as the man who could write a really first-rate libretto, the name of Boito, there was neither a frosty silence to shrivel the tender shoot nor an explosion of wrath to shatter the whole happy gathering.

Verdi's reaction to this suggestion may rather be likened to that of an extremely wary old trout who has seen a particularly delicious-looking fly drop on the water just above his nose, but is much too wily not to connect the sudden appearance of the insect with certain vaguely discerned movements on the river bank. He went so far as to rise and have a closer look at the fly; but not a bite! In his own less involved words he made the position clear to Ricordi a few days after the dinner party:

You know the origins of this cup of chocolate [sc. *Otello*]. You invite me to dine with Faccio. You talk about *Otello*, you talk of Boito. The next day Faccio brings Boito to see me; three days later Boito brings me a sketch of *Otello*. I read it and like it. I tell him to write the poem; it will always come in handy for him or me or someone

242

else, etc. Now if you come with Boito, I shall be obliged to read the libretto. Either I find it absolutely perfect and you leave it with me—and there I am as good as landed. Or I like it well enough and suggest improvements which Boito accepts—and find myself even more securely hooked. Or, I don't like it, and it will be too difficult to tell him so to his face. No, no! You are in too great a hurry.

So the anglers—Ricordi with the rod, Faccio with the landing-net and Boito in the background appropriately holding an unnecessary gaff—had to exercise their patience. And, if it be asked why, failing to get their fish with the 'Chocolate Fancy,'[1] they did not try a change of fly—the '*Tartuffe* Humbug,'[1] for example—the answer is that you don't catch a very wary old trout with a fly that you have cast so badly that the fish has seen the hook and made every sign of betaking himself to another pool in water belonging to your rival. Besides, it was quite obvious that the 'Chocolate Fancy' was very tempting to the fish. He could not leave it alone and it was only a question of how long he could resist taking it.

In the meantime, just to show his independence and to test the genuineness of Boito's willingness to serve him truly, Verdi set the poet the task of putting *Simon Boccanegra* to rights. To his eternal honour, Boito gracefully, though not without some private grimaces, undertook this piece of hack-work. He could not turn a thoroughly bad libretto into a good one, but his revision of the text was the occasion of a thorough revision of the music, and so has secured for posterity some of the finest music Verdi ever composed. It still awaits appreciation in England.

But to return to our fishermen. After many nibbles—in January 1880 Verdi was discussing with a third party what sort of man Iago was—the fly disappeared, the line spun out from the whirring reel—and at that precise and particular and vital moment the 'nervy and eccentric' Boito must needs drop his gaff into the stream. The exact occasion of this *gaffe*, to give the word its

[1] The enthusiastic angler will search Messrs Farlow's admirable catalogue in vain; these lures have long been superseded by 'Inky Boy' and 'Missionary' (much liked by cannibals).

French form, was a banquet at Naples after the first performance oι *Mefistofele* at the San Carlo Theatre in the spring of 1884—they had been playing their fish some time!—at which Boito said, or, what is more important than what he actually did say, was reᵎ ported in the press to have said, that he had undertaken the libretto of *Otello* with some reluctance, but that the subject now proved so fascinating that he regretted being unable to compose the music for it himself. The splash of this *gaffe* upon the waters was followed by a vigorous tug at the line, but the hook held and it was not long before the fish, already as weary as the reader from his struggles, was safely in the creel.

Two things are evident. First, that the lure had not been improvised at short notice, but had been carefully prepared. Boito could not have produced a scenario of *Otello* that would satisfy Verdi at first sight, out of his hat. It must have come out of his head after long study. The second is that Verdi already knew his *Othello*,[1] and of this the evidence is curious.

In 1871 Wagner's *Lohengrin* was performed for the first time in Italy at Bologna under Mariani's direction. Verdi went to hear it and took with him a vocal score in which he made notes upon the music and its performance. These comments are terse and to the point—often just 'brutto' or 'bello,' according to Verdi's opinion of the music. Many of the comments, however, are more precise: 'Why slow it down?' 'Chorus out of tune' and, as in most performances of the opera, 'brutto il cigno'! At the end there is the following summingᵎup:

Impression mediocre. Music beautiful, when it is clear and there is thought in it. The action, like the words, moves too slowly. Hence boredom. Beautiful effects of instrumentation. Too many held notes, which makes for heaviness. Poor performance. Much *verve* but no poetry or finish. At the difficult moments always wretched.

These comments are characteristic of Verdi's attitude towards Wagner, which was at once independent and respectful. He was

[1] To avoid confusion, I use *Otello* to mean Verdi's (or Rossini's) opera and *Othello* for Shakespeare's tragedy; similarly, Otello is the character in the opera, Othello the hero of the play.

neither blinded by the German composer's novel splendour to the
weaknesses in his music nor prejudiced by those weaknesses
against his great qualities. There is no actual truth in the incident which forms the climax of Werfel's novel about Verdi.
Verdi did not go to Venice with the idea of calling upon Wagner,
and then hesitate until it was too late and the master was dead.
But there is a spiritual truth in this fiction. Verdi would have
liked to meet his great rival—on equal terms. Wagner, on his
side, showed no such inclination and, had there been a meeting,
such was his characteristic German egotism that we may be sure
that he would have treated Verdi only with condescension,
de haut en bas. Verdi's attitude is beautifully summed up in the
lines he wrote to Ricordi on receiving the news of Wagner's
death in February 1883:

Sad, sad, sad.
Wagner is dead.

When I read the news yesterday, I was, I must tell you, overcome with
grief. Let there be no mistake: a great personality has disappeared—
a name that will leave a very deep mark upon the history of art!

But the note which is of particular interest to us occurs against
a line of Lohengrin's in Act III, where the hero points out to
Elsa that her love is his compensation for all he has lost for her
sake. Verdi's comment is: 'misero, Otello in brutto,' which may
be rendered as 'wretched debasement of Othello.' The passage
he seems to have had in mind was probably, as Luzio suggests,
Othello's

But that I love the gentle Desdemona,
I would not my unhoused free condition
Put into circumscription and confine
For the sea's worth.

The parallel may not seem very close—it is rather clearer in the
Italian versions of the two texts—but it is just the sort of association that springs to the mind during a performance and which,
if jotted down, must not be given too much weight. But such
associations do not occur unless their maker knows his poet,

and it is obvious that Verdi must have studied *Othello* thoroughly. And, it may be remarked, an operatic composer does not read a drama without in some degree visualizing its potentialities for his own art. Neither the subject, therefore, nor the possible ways of treating it were wholly novel and unconsidered when Ricordi and Faccio directed the conversation to *Othello* across the dinner-table. All Verdi's show of reluctance and his wrigglings were but the vain struggles of an indolent desire for peace and quiet against the overmastering urge of the artist to create, and possibly the only useful ally of his indolence was the realization that the new task would demand more of his energy than anything he had so far undertaken. The palmy days had passed away when an opera, with tonic-and-dominant accompaniment, could be turned out in a few weeks.

CHAPTER XVI

'OTELLO'

OF all Shakespeare's later tragedies *Othello* is obviously the one most suitable for operatic treatment. Its plot is simple and clear-cut, and the handling of it singularly free from the complications of side issues like the Polish question in *Hamlet*, or the sub-plots not essential to, yet inseparable from, the main theme like the Gloucester-Edgar-Edmund complex in *King Lear*. The play as a whole has a readily apprehended form and the characters (even the apparently exceptional Iago) are unusually concrete in comparison with the more vaguely generalized figures in *King Lear* or *Macbeth*. Even the motives of these characters are, provided we distinguish motive from justification in the case of Iago, sharply defined and free from the air of philosophic doubt which is one of the chief fascinations of *Hamlet*. That doubt is also the major argument against any curtailment of that play—since we need all the facts placed before us if we are to form any reasonable judgment of our own—and, still more, against its translation into operatic terms, which would involve the adoption by the composer of some definite attitude towards Hamlet himself, and so do away with any mystery out of which to pluck the heart.

Othello could be so translated without essential loss and even with some gain to the clarity of certain details. But it was not therefore an easy task to perform as admirably as Boito did it. The very paucity of inessential material in the play, the character of Bianca being the only one of any importance that could be sacrificed, made the librettist's problem the more difficult. With remarkable skill Boito performed the major operation of cutting away the whole of Shakespeare's first act, and then proceeded to graft upon the second such material as was necessary to acquaint the audience with the facts of the situation.

The opera begins, therefore, with Otello's arrival in Cyprus, and the first act contains, besides an abbreviated version of the scene between Iago and Roderigo,[1] the drunken brawl in which Iago involves Cassio and Cassio's degradation by the enraged Otello. At this point, in place of the scene for Iago and Cassio which ends Shakespeare's act, Boito substituted a love-scene for Otello and Desdemona, based upon the Moor's defence before the doge in the first act of the play. In this manner the necessary exposition of the drama is presented in action. The audience is not conscious of being told what has happened before the curtain rose; it acquires that knowledge unconsciously while absorbed in what is happening before its eyes. The reader will appreciate the art with which this opening act is constructed, if he will compare it with, say, the beginning of *Il Trovatore*, where Ferrando informs the audience of the past history of the house of Luna under the ingenuous pretence of enlightening the chorus on the stage.

In order to give clarity to his exposition and, in particular, a sharper definition to Otello's character at his first appearance, Boito made a slight adjustment in the Shakespearian arrangement of the action. In the play Desdemona is on the stage already when Othello disembarks; in the opera her entry is reserved until she is 'raised up' by the clash of weapons and the dreadful bell. This involves the sacrifice of the lovely speech that follows Othello's greeting to his 'fair warrior.'[2] But Boito rightly considered that the important point to make at this moment of Otello's first appearance was not his tender love for Desdemona —that could be, and is, fully exposed in the love-duet at the end of the act—but his force of personality and commanding presence. Everything in the opening scene is designed to lead up to this magnificent entry which at once emphasizes Otello's reputation

[1] This scene includes the essence of the dialogue between these two in Shakespeare's Act I, scene iii.

[2] Boito was evidently struck by this expression, for, unable to put it into his Otello's mouth, he adapted it for Desdemona, whose first words, on her entrance, are 'O mio guerriero'—one more emphasis upon Otello's martial character.

as a great soldier and his dignity as a man. The effect is achieved by concentrating upon the storm and its dangers, and then upon the revulsion from fear to rejoicing when Otello's ship is seen to be safe in port. Otello has only a dozen bars to sing, but the triumphant ring of his 'Esultate' is quite sufficient to establish his position as a great man.

Having fixed this image of the warrior Otello in the minds of the audience, Verdi and his librettist proceed, after a brief interlude of choral rejoicing, to delineate the other principal actors in the drama, likewise with a few deft strokes. Iago was the character that intrigued Verdi most. At one time he even thought of naming the opera after him—partly, perhaps, out of a modest wish to avoid even the appearance of competing with Rossini. One may suppose that it was an attraction of opposites; that he, most honest of men, was fascinated by the spectacle of corruption and infamy revealed under a seeming-honest exterior. He argued much with Morelli, the painter, about Iago's physical appearance and dress, and finally decided:

If I had to act the part of Iago, I should make him long and lean, with thin lips, small eyes set, ape-like, too close to the nose, and a head with a receding brow and large development at the back. His manner would be abstracted, nonchalant, indifferent to everything, incredulous, smart in repartee, saying good and ill alike lightly, with the air of thinking about something else. So if someone should reproach him for a monstrous suggestion, he might retort: 'Really? . . . I did not see it in that light . . . let 's say no more of it !' A man like that might deceive everybody, even up to a point his own wife. A small, malignant fellow would put every one on his guard and would take nobody in !

It may, perhaps, be questioned whether Verdi had any very complete intellectual conception of what Shakespeare intended when he created Iago. That point about the possibility of Iago deceiving others, even his own wife, in spite of his villainous nature, seems to indicate that kind of prosaic attitude which discusses whether the plot will hold water, as though it were a saucepan or other household utensil, and not the imaginative creation of a poet. Fortunately, however, the degree of Verdi's intellectual appreciation is of very little real importance, for when it came to translating Iago into terms of music, his poetic intuition did not allow him to go astray and turn the Ancient into a ranting villain of melodrama. His Iago, no less than Shakespeare's, serves to expose the rottenness that may lie beneath the fair exterior of man's mind, and the danger that that rottenness holds for any soul that comes into contact with its secret corruption. The finer the soul, indeed, the greater the risk of the contagion—*corruptio optimi pessima*. That is the true theme of *Othello*—the revelation of the infamy of which man is capable, and the tragic burden that infamy may lay upon his soul—that, and not the *crime passionnel* of a jealous husband who murders his wife in a fit of temper, which is merely a theme for Grand Guignol. It is not a pleasant spectacle, and its beastliness probably accounts for the ill-success of the tragedy with the average audience, despite its wonderful acting quality and the unmatched music of its poetry. Othello never attracts the public like the 'sweet Prince' Hamlet (though *he* can lift the lids from some unsavoury stews, when he is permitted his full say) or the man-of-action Macbeth, whose fault, ambition, involves no entry into the dark arcana of sexual turpitude.

Once the nature of the theme is understood, the question of whether there are too many coincidences in the play—though I have never thought them so improbable as to affect belief in the action—and such matters as the handling of the handkerchief business will be seen to be as academic as the problem of the angels and the pin-point. And the 'credibility' of Iago is not in question at all, if by credibility one means belief in the possibility of such baseness as his going unsuspected. Nor would one suppose that any one in this autumn of 1939 could find that degree of baseness unbelievable, when there are set upon the thrones of great nations, who have unsuspectingly enslaved themselves, tyrants whose policy is dictated by the intellectual sadist's passion for the destruction of other people's happiness (which is the mainspring of

Iago's actions), and whose rottenness is spreading its corruption over all that is fairest and finest in our civilization.[1]

Boito, the composer of *Mefistofele*, has, perhaps inevitably, been accused of seeing Iago with the eye of Goethe and of endowing him with qualities borrowed from Faust's evil genius. It may be that he underlines in Iago the 'spirit that denies,' but that spirit is surely already implicit in Shakespeare's conception of the char-acter, which set the example of cynicism and intellectual mockery followed by Goethe's Mephistopheles. We need not, perhaps, lay too much stress upon the fact that, when he is unmasked, Iago is called a 'hellish villain' and a 'demi-devil.' These are metaphors natural in their context. But Iago does regard him-self as in league with the 'Divinity of Hell.' It is unfair, therefore, to complain of any emphasis laid upon his devilish character by Boito, especially as one imagines that Goethe used Iago quite consciously as his model.

The chief count in the criticism of Boito's treatment of Iago is the 'Credo' which he put into his mouth. This is certainly a more explicit confession of his faith than is to be found in Shake-speare's play. Yet this soliloquy, which has to do the duty of several in the tragedy and must therefore be more compact of information, surely deserves our praise for its conformity to the spirit of Shakespeare rather than condemnation for any incon-sistency with that spirit. It is, in fact, constructed with astonishing skill from ideas culled here and there from Shakespeare, the most characteristic being his shuddering disgust with the physical corruption of the flesh in death.

The musical characterization of Iago is a perpetual source of wonder and admiration. At his first appearance, in the scene with Roderigo ('Drown thyself! Drown cats and blind pup-pies') he has a free and supple recitative that reflects the play of

---

[1] To any one who objects that this is an irrelevant political tirade, I would answer that it is precisely this applicability of the theme of a drama to an entirely different set of circumstances in a different age, this imperishable truthfulness to the essential facts of human nature, that differentiates great poetic tragedy from ephemeral melodrama.

his emotions, real and simulated, with absolute fidelity. At the first mention of 'woman,' the word is given a sneering twist of a semiquaver triplet. Iago's dark and lustful envy of his general's happiness at once colours the music when he speaks of the black kisses of Otello's bloated lips, and his jealous fury at being passed over in favour of Cassio finds scornful expression in the setting of the lines:

> He, in good time, must his lieutenant be,
> And I—God bless the mark!—his Moorship's ancient.[1]

The shake at the end of this quotation should be noted, for it is a characteristic of Iago's music throughout the opera.[2] The ornament will be found occurring again and again, sometimes in the voice part and sometimes in the accompaniment, but always with a peculiarly sinister effect. His music is also full of *appoggiature* and *acciaccature* which, like the shakes, are used not as 'graces,' but as the vehicle of Iago's sinister nature. Often they are accompanied by sudden little dynamic explosions that seem to give warning of what is bottled up beneath the honest bluff manner. That manner and the nonchalant air, as Verdi puts it, of throwing

----

[1] 'Ancient,' is of course, ensign, the most junior commissioned rank in the army. Iago was Othello's honorary standard-bearer, and, for practical purposes, his junior staff-officer. Boito altered the rank of Cassio to captain.

[2] Cf. the setting of Iago's speech about jealousy in Act II ('It is the green-eyed monster'), which provides another typical example of Iago's music.

off his ideas casually as though his mind were engaged with something quite different is cleverly suggested in snatches of *scherzando*
melody such as:

This kind of effect recurs, in a more robust form, in the *brindisi*
('And let me the canakin clink!'), and, more delicately, as befits
a scene that deals with trifles light as air, in his chaffing of Cassio
about the handkerchief he has found in his room.

The *brindisi*, or drinking song, deserves a moment's attention, not
merely because it is a rattling good rollicking song with, at the
same time, a sinister undertone in its chromatic sequences, but
because it is such a good example of Verdi's way of using a
conventional form and clothing it in a new way so that the form
becomes almost unrecognizable. If the reader will compare
Iago's *brindisi* with Lady Macbeth's in the banquet scene, he will
note that both have a similar orchestral introduction; but whereas
in *Macbeth* that introduction is an extremely formal affair, like a
toastmaster's call for 'Silence, please, my lords, ladies and gentlemen,' in *Otello* the introduction is much more than a matter
of form. It is full of character, full, incidentally, of those in-
cisive *appoggiature* so constantly associated with Iago, and it is
welded neatly and without any visible junction into what has gone
before and into the beginning of Iago's song. With two more
examples of the characteristic Iago music—the one showing his
suave, insinuating tone, the other his evil exultation in the moment
of triumph—I will for the moment leave this wonderful creation

to the further study of the reader, in the hope that what has been said will give him a hint of what to look for:

The drinking-scene, the brawl and Cassio's disgrace provide a fine example of Verdi's mastery of dramatic ensemble, swift, full of action and variety, yet musically coherent as a whole. At Otello's entrance, when the uproar has reached its climax, it is worth while observing, as an instance of Boito's care for and thorough absorption in his original, that to the rather flat and common-place 'What is the matter here?' he has added an idea borrowed from the splendid line in Act I, scene ii:

Keep up your bright swords, for the dew will rust them.

The first act ends, after the clamour has subsided, with the most beautiful love duet Verdi ever wrote. Indeed, it is the only pure love duet in all his tragic operas, for nowhere else, at least, until we reach the very different world of *Falstaff*, are we presented with a love scene undisturbed by any dramatic conflict. Always hitherto there has been some distraction from happiness, some

danger threatening or some concealment or disguise on the one
part or the other. Here there is felicity unalloyed, and not the
first rapture of lovers' meeting, but the settled calm of a deep
mutual adoration. Yet this lyric duet, infinitely tender and as
gently radiant as the starlight that illumines the scene, serves
incidentally to inform the audience of the past history of the lovers.
It is a most skilful gilding of the expository pill, which nine out
of ten will swallow without knowing it. And they will also
absorb, as unconsciously, a good deal of knowledge about Otello
and Desdemona with the factual information concerning their
history.

Desdemona is the gentlest, most innocent and most pathetic of
Verdi's heroines, even as Otello is at once the noblest and most
guileless of his heroes. There had been hints, as we have observed,
of Desdemona in the suffering Amalia of *Simon Boccanegra*, but
Otello has no forerunner. There had been robust warriors
before, Manrico and Radamès; but he is so much more besides.
He has an eloquence inherited from his Shakespearian prototype.
Mr Wilson Knight observes in the poetry of *Othello* qualities
that distinguish it from other Shakespearian poetry:

'It holds a rich music all its own, and possesses a unique
solidity and precision of picturesque phrase or image, a peculiar
chastity and serenity of thought.'

To these peculiarities may be added others. The language of
Othello, especially in Othello's own mouth, is conspicuous for
its curious and exotic words that fill out the lines, as it were,
with cyclopean blocks of some precious marble: anthropophagi,
Ottomites, Promethean, the Propontic and the Hellespont,
Aleppo, Sagittary, chrysolite, mandragora. These are but a few
samples of this strange, romantic ornamentation.

Secondly, there are few plays in which Shakespeare so often
touches the secret springs of meaning that lie hidden within words.
We cannot, by a paraphrase, explain what is the meaning of

It is the cause, it is the cause, my soul!

This is the very ecstasy of poetry, all overtones, the fundamental note of sense unheard. It has no 'meaning,' yet it comprehends a world of emotional experience.

Lastly there is the dreadful contrast to all this, when Iago's poison has worked upon Othello's love and destroyed his dignity. Then the tongue that was capable of fashioning the loveliest images falls to a low and guttersnipe abuse, pouring out filthy words and fouler thoughts until the mounting rage brings it to incoherence. These terrible outbursts of obscenity would be intolerable and artistically indefensible, were they not at the very core of the poet's theme—the appalling corruption of the finest. 'There is no dignity in Othello's rage,' says Mr Wilson Knight; 'there is not meant to be.' All the virtue has gone out of him and with it his power over words. His love for Desdemona killed, chaos is come again, and he can only rave of 'goats and monkeys,' of 'noses, ears, and lips,' or mutter that he will 'chop her into messes,' or sink to a mere ranting that sounds hollow beside the mighty tempest of King Lear's rage:

> Whip me, ye devils! . . .
> Blow me about in winds! Roast me in sulphur!
> Wash me in steep-down gulfs of liquid fire!

Yet a few moments later the devil is exorcized and Othello himself again. It is not for nothing that his final speech is the most jewelled of all—'the base Indian' and the 'pearl richer than all his tribe,' 'the Arabian trees' and their 'med'cinable gum,' and 'in Aleppo . . . a malignant and a turban'd Turk.' The tongue has regained its mastery of silver speech, and, though Desdemona cannot be recalled, Othello, no longer ugly or absurd, can die with dignity upon a kiss.

Not all of these poetic qualities can be translated into music. An exotic style will not be the equivalent of a use of exotic words in poetry, where the point lies in the sudden introduction of the strange word among ordinary ones. No tom-tom rhythm will achieve the same kind of effect as

> Drop tears as fast as the Arabian trees
> Their med'cinable gum.

Such images cannot even be safely translated into another language, so much do they depend upon the associations and idiosyncrasies of the original. Boito very wisely did not attempt to preserve this aspect of the *Othello* poetry in his libretto, and, with equal prudence, he refrained from translating some of Shakespeare's most beautiful lines. Among them goes by the board, besides the famous 'But yet the pity of it, Iago! O Iago, the pity of it, Iago!' what is, I think, the most poignant and tear-compelling passage in the whole of Shakespeare:

> O thou weed,
> Who art so lovely fair and smell'st so sweet
> That the sense aches at thee, would thou hadst ne'er been born.

It is precisely here that music comes into its own, taking over the expression of intense feeling and substituting for the poetic overtones its own even more suggestive power. The equivalence of Verdi's music and Shakespeare's verse is not susceptible of proof, but he must be very unimpressionable who comes away from a performance of *Otello* without an aching sense of the deep pity of it.

In the music of Otello and Desdemona Verdi has caught the peculiar fragrance, that 'chastity and serenity of thought' (to use Mr Wilson Knight's phrase) which characterizes the poetry of *Othello*. The love-duet is almost wholly free from any suggestion of physical eroticism, and when at the end Otello and Desdemona fall into each other's arms to music that is to add the poignancy of an echoed thought to the climax of the tragedy, the passion is dissolved in a serene tenderness, and the music takes on the starlit radiance of the southern sky where Venus outshines all other planets.

It is on this note of secure happiness that the first act ends, and, one feels, had Shakespeare written a scene for Otello and Desdemona at this point, that is the scene he would have written. Verdi and Boito can be given no greater praise. It is the librettist who has always received the chief credit for the excellence of the scenario of the opera, and, in default of evidence to the contrary, there was no reason to doubt that to him the chief credit was due.

But the recent publication of Boito's letters to the composer about the libretto proves that Verdi had a greater hand in its making than had been suspected. He was the same Verdi who had worried over Ghislanzoni's verses for *Aida*, and happily Boito was as ready to rewrite as poor, willing Piave himself:

Just take your pen and write to me: 'Dear Boito, please change such and such verses, etc.,' and I will gladly alter them at once. I will work for you, I who do not know how to work for myself; for you live in the true and genuine realm of Art, but I dwell in a world of hallucination.

That Boito's willingness to submit himself to Verdi was fortunate is evident from this correspondence. He had originally brought Iago back to the stage as an unseen, sardonic observer of the love scene with a speech about bringing discord to this sweet harmony. Verdi would not have the serenity of his duet disturbed by this rather cheap dramatic device. The insertion of the charming madrigal sung while the peasants of Cyprus pay homage to their new governor's wife was suggested by Verdi, who wanted something to break up the succession of duets in the second act.[1] Verdi seems also to have been responsible for the ending of the third act, which was originally a formal quintet with chorus for Desdemona, Otello, Iago, Emilia and Roderigo, each of whom gave expression to his own feelings. After Otello had sworn that nothing would now restrain his avenging arm, the movement culminated with his injunction to the people to continue their rejoicings for the victory over the Turks! Whatever criticisms may be made on the present ending of the act, which Salvini is said to have deplored as too melodramatic and which contains in its big choral section the most formal movement in the whole

[1] I have never been able to agree with those critics who regard this little scene as one of the weak spots in *Otello*. Judged by absolute standards the music may be somewhat trivial, but in its context it produces exactly the required dramatic effect of contrast with the tragic action that is just being set in motion, and Desdemona's repetition of the last line of the simple melody (quoted later in this chapter) is the first of those poignant moments that stir us so deeply.

opera, it is certainly a great improvement upon the original idea.
Finally, Verdi was certainly responsible for the final form of the
last scene of the opera. His sketch with Boito's pencilled amend/
ments is one of the most interesting of the documents reproduced
in Luzio's *Carteggi Verdiani*. It is necessary to emphasize Verdi's
contribution to the success of the libretto of *Otello*, not in order to
belittle Boito's ability, which was far above the ordinary, but be/
cause previous writers have, in the absence of any evidence to the
contrary, been inclined to give him the whole of the credit.

The first act ended in a mood of happy serenity. The second
begins with a clear intimation of evil forces at work, intent upon
the destruction of that happiness:

The rhythmic figure (*a*) from the brief orchestral introduction
becomes the sinister background of the scene between Iago and
Cassio, and the starting/point for one of the themes of the 'Credo,'
as shown in (*b*) and (*c*) of the example just quoted. How mal/
leable and pliant under Verdi's experienced hand the material
has become! The figure differs little from that which served a

similar purpose in *La forza del destino*, but the theme of fate (quoted on p. 142) in that earlier opera never achieves the freedom of development attained by this figure associated with Iago. The *Forza* theme, indeed, differs from the *Otello* one inasmuch as it is more in the nature of a tune, and is therefore less apt for symphonic treatment. It would be difficult to get away from its four-square shape. But this *Otello* theme is nothing but a rhythmic figure, like the first four notes of the C minor Symphony, out of which anything or nothing may come according to the power of imagin-ation shown by the composer. It is the kind of theme that is commonly called pregnant—which only means that even genius cannot alter the law: *Ex nihilo nihil fit.*

The second act of the opera covers the ground of Shakespeare's third act to the end of its third (and penultimate) scene which ends with the great mutual oath-taking ('Now by yond marble heaven') that Verdi turned into the finest of his tenor-baritone duets. As, however, the act is played in one scene, it does not give us the same sense of the passage of time as is created by the changes of scene in the play. The elimination of such inessential matter as the clown scenes further compromises the time factor. In a reading or a performance of the play—always providing that the order of the scenes has not been meddled with in order to serve the vanity of the actor or the scenic artist—we should not be conscious of any precipitancy in Othello's credulousness. Indeed, Shakespeare is most careful to underline his unwillingness to believe Iago's insinuations. It is the one point in which Boito does anything like a serious injustice to his original that we cannot but feel that his Otello is too ready to believe the worst. The opera is caught on the horns of a dilemma: it cannot reconcile the continuous forward sweep towards the climax of the act, which in music must not be interrupted, with the contrary notion of a lapse of time. The scene for Desdemona and the chorus, to which allusion has already been made, does do something towards marking a gap in time. For it is in the nature of an intermezzo, relieving for a moment the growing tension of the drama only to draw it tighter than ever with its poignant ending:

Although on this major point Boito must be held at fault, he redeems himself a little in his handling of the manner in which Desdemona's handkerchief comes into Iago's possession. Shakespeare made Emilia a willing, though blind, accessary to the theft. In the opera Iago snatches it from his wife behind the backs of their master and mistress, and that Emilia should not in the circumstances do more than vainly resist Iago is psychologically natural and convincing. The threads of the intrigue are drawn together more tightly and the action is less confused.

Desdemona's pleading for Cassio in and out of season is held against her by some critics as a sign of witlessness. That she is not the most tactful of Shakespeare's heroines may be granted; she is not endowed with that feminine intuition which, being a safeguard against making Desdemona's mistakes, is more appropriate to the heroines of comedy. But Desdemona's silliness—let us admit her fault—is surely one of the elements that endears her to us in the tragedy, however much it might exasperate in real life. Her fault is a human one, and it lends her a pathos that we never feel to the same degree in the presence of the upright Cordelia who, unlike Desdemona, cannot tell even the whitest of lies. Verdi does not dissemble this lack of intuition, and an ingenuous note comes into the music at the points where Desdemona makes her ill-timed pleas for Cassio:

Tu di me ti fai gio - co

There is something quite different here from the sweetness that pervades her music when she is distressed for Otello's distemper or later is pleading her own cause, a sweetness so fragrant that the sense aches at it. In this very scene, after Otello has thrown the handker-chief to the ground, there is an example of this type of melody which is, I think, clearly differentiated from those just quoted:

Dam - mi__ la dol - ce e
lie - ta__ pa - ro - la del__ per do - no

This is surely the true musical presentation of that candent innocence that, in the play, makes Othello exclaim:

> Look where she comes.
> If she be false, O, then heaven mocks itself.

After Desdemona's exit the action moves swiftly, indeed, too swiftly to convince. Otello almost at once declaims his farewell to arms in a magnificently pompous *arioso* introduced by a recitative that sends a cold shiver down one's back, so surely do the orchestration and the chromaticism of the music (at 'I found not Cassio's kisses on her lips') portray the sense of the ground sliding away from under his feet. To the noble poetry of the *arioso* there succeeds the first of those outbursts of undignified rage. Otello does not yet lose all control of his tongue, though he does of his hands and, as in Shakespeare, half throttles Iago. Then follows the narration by Iago of Cassio's dream, in which the suave hypocrisy of the villain finds its supreme expression.

The wedding of words to music, about which Verdi had often

been careless even so late as in *Aida*, attains in *Otello* the highest standard of exactness. And nowhere is this excellence so con-spicuous as in this narration of Iago's, which is so laid out for the voice that if the singer is faithful to his text he cannot fail to produce the precise effect intended down to the most minute nuance of vocal colour. Observe in the following passage the emphasis given by accent or length of note to each operative word in the first two lines, 'blando,' 'angoscia,' 'imago,' rising to the climax on 'baciando.' Then the drop to speech on the paren-thetic 'ei disse poscia' and the final turn of the screw on the monotoned line in which the emphasis falls naturally upon the word that will sound most painfully in Otello's ear, 'Moro' (the Moor):

-ma-go qua si ba - cian - do

sempre sotto voce, cupo

Ei dis-se po-scia: Il rio de - sti - no im-

Flute

Flt. & Strings tacent

Clar. Fag. Hrn.

-pre - co che al Mo - ro ti do - no

Otello's reason, already shaken in its seat, topples for a moment and, as in the play, he howls for blood. It is the first of those 'ugly' moments to which reference was made in the discussion of Shakespeare's poetry in *Othello*. This ugliness, which consists in the revelation of the beastliness that lies hidden in each human soul, however noble, finds its echo in the music. To ears accus‐ tomed to all that has happened since Strauss wrote *Ein Heldenleben*, Verdi's music may sound little more than merely strident. It may seem no more than a recrudescence of that blatant vulgarity in writing for the brass which mars a great deal of his earlier work, and of which a conspicuous example has been noted in the finale of Act II in *Don Carlo*. But in *Otello* this note of ugly brassiness occurs only at those moments where Otello loses control of him‐ self, at those moments where in the play he raves about 'goats and monkeys,' and of 'noses, ears, and lips.' We do not find this particular kind of brass writing connected with Iago, for instance, though these instruments are freely used in the 'Credo' and else‐ where to enhance the terror his character inspires. Still less is it heard in those passages, like the 'Farewell to arms,' where Otello is his noble self, while, as though to point the contrast, it is precisely the brass used in the most mellow and nobly sonorous way that introduces his final monologue—that passage which, both as poetry and music, reassures us that man's soul can be, in spite of evil, unconquerable. I believe, therefore, that this note of blatancy, which now and again offends the ear in *Otello*, is a quite deliberate musical translation of the corresponding note of ugliness in Shakespeare's poetry.

Reference has already been made to the duet with which the act ends, and at this point I wish only to draw attention to one aspect of it—its strong rhythmic bass (*see* quotation on p. 163). This kind of *canto fermo* had been much used by Verdi in the past, but in *Otello*, where the melody of the vocal line is more than ever broken up into short phrases instead of being given the continuity of a self‐contained 'tune,' this characteristic becomes of first‐rate importance. It serves to bind together the vocal and instrumental phrases which make up the melodic line. In this particular instance of the duet, the *canto fermo* happens also to be the main melody, but elsewhere it takes the form of an *ostinato* figure, as for instance in the immensely impressive opening of the finale of Act III (nine bars before letter K in the score) and again later in the same scene (at letter M in the score). The figure, associated with Iago, that dominates the opening of the second act and serves as accompaniment to the scene with Cassio is another example of this use of *ostinato*. This device of creating dramatic excite⁄ment by the insistent repetition of a phrase, usually in combination with a cumulative increase in dynamic power, became one of the mainstays of Puccini's operatic style. The physical torture of Cavaradossi and the mental torture of Tosca, the brooding of the jealous husband over the dark waters of the Seine in *Il Tabarro*, the ravings of Suor Angelica, and the death of Liù in *Turandot* provide various examples of Puccini's effective use of this device, which never quite degenerates with him into a mere trick or mannerism.

Boito's third act compresses into one continuous action the last scene of Act III and the first two of Act IV in Shakespeare's play. In order to do this the two scenes between Othello and Desdemona in Acts III and IV are run into one, the demand for the handkerchief being followed by an abbreviated version of the most dreadful scene in the play, which ends with those lines of icy hatred:

> I cry you mercy, then;
> I took you for that cunning whore of Venice
> That married with Othello.

Emilia is not present during this scene in the opera, and so one of the improbabilities of Shakespeare's play—her silence about the handkerchief—is eliminated. Othello's speech, 'Had it pleased heaven to try me with affliction,' is used as a soliloquy after Desdemona's exit and at its end Otello becomes incoherent ('Handkerchief—confessions—handkerchief') without the incite⁄ment of Iago's 'lie with her.' But he does not fall into a fit— that is reserved for the end of the act—and the business of showing Cassio in possession of the handkerchief follows (without Bianca's help) in a duet between Iago and Cassio while Otello stands tortured behind the tapestry.

A brief but horrible scene in which Otello and Iago settle the fates of Desdemona and Cassio leads straight to the finale where Otello receives Lodovico and the other emissaries from Venice, learns that Cassio is to succeed him and in a rage strikes Desdemona to the ground.

It is an act of terrible violence, mental and physical, relieved by the *scherzando* interlude for Iago and Cassio and the splendour of the grand finale. Fair and foul are brought into deadly conflict, and in this conflict the composer finds an unsurpassed opportunity for tragic pathos and irony. The prelude to the act warns us of what is coming. The mood of it is plain enough, even if we do not at once recognize as the melody of Iago's warning against the 'green-eyed monster, jealousy,' the sinister theme which steals up from the bass and is treated in imitation by the higher strings and then is thundered out by the brass. After a brief colloquy between Otello, Iago and the Herald who announces the arrival of the Venetian ambassador, Desdemona's entrance is accompanied by a charming instrumental theme which is used in the manner of a *ritornello*—if that term does not suggest too stiff a formalism—during the subsequent scene:

This graceful figure never appears in the voice parts, though the turn at the end is an important feature in the fencing match between innocence and irony, between fair and foul. This duet, if the term may be applied to a movement in which the voices are never heard together, provides, with Otello's soliloquy that follows it ('Dio mi potevi scagliar'), a supreme example of that pliancy and easy malleability which we have already noted as one of the characteristics of *Otello*. Consider the first two phrases of this duet:

Verdi

Allegro moderato

Here is melody of the loveliest quality. But there is no rigidity as there is in the melodies of *Il Trovatore*. This *Otello* melody can be, and is, developed symphonically. The turn at the end may fall on different beats of the bar or even be extracted and modified for use as an *ostinato* accompaniment for a few bars (*see* after letter D in the score).

When Otello's rage grows and insinuation gives place to plain accusation, something more heroic is needed than this gentle strain. Desdemona pleads her case and sheds at Otello's feet the first tears he has caused her to this tragic melody in the grand style:

Andante mosso

But it is the first, more gentle theme that gives the last touch of poignancy to this painful scene, when Otello once more takes Desdemona's hand and craves her pardon for his error in mistaking her for his own wife. This is the very refinement of cruelty to turn against Desdemona her own melody, her own sweetness and chastity of utterance. And it is a perfect translation of Shakespeare's tragic idea.

The monologue 'Dio mi potevi scagliar' ('Had it pleased heav'n to try me with affliction') is an even more remarkable musical composition. Resolved into its elements it consists of a descending scale against which Otello declaims his thought upon two notes only, and those the tonic and dominant of the key, until in the last bar his voice rises—and the effect of the modulation is quite astonishing in its pathos—a major third instead of falling a fourth. There are all manner of 'imponderables'—of tonality and rhythm and part-writing—which combine to turn a monotone and a descending scale into the most tragic imaginable expression of disillusionment and of that utter emptiness of the human soul after it has given way to uncontrolled anger. There is first the tonality, the rare and remote key of A flat minor: when there are more than four flats in the signature, one may be certain that Verdi means tragic business. Then there is the rhythm of the descending scale which proceeds steadily enough, indeed, but has each note prefaced by a sharply accented triplet of semiquavers on the off beat. Add to this a syncopated accompaniment in the bass and introduce the whole by a double-dotted descending chromatic scale from dominant to tonic and you have this complex piece of simplicity:[1]

---

[1] I have quoted only the second and third verses. The first verse is identical with the second, except that it has not the syncopated figure for the bassoon and violoncello. The bassoon doubles the violoncello part throughout and the horn that of the contrabass, except during the descending chromatic passage at the beginning of each verse. The oboe is added to the violins at two points in the last verse, giving an added poignancy to the heavy mood.

It will be observed from this and other examples quoted—for instance, the excerpt from Iago's narration of Cassio's dream—that in *Otello* Verdi had found a solution of the fundamental problem of opera, namely the fusion of dramatic poetry and music, as complete and satisfying for the Italian language as was Wagner's for the German. And, although he had reached his solution by a very different approach, the result is not in its essentials very different. If the reader will turn up Pogner's address to the musicians' guild in the first act of *Die Meistersinger*, he will find that Wagner's procedure closely resembles Verdi's, especially in the use of a reiterated figure to hold the composition together. This resemblance is not to be taken as proof that Verdi was under Wagner's influence, for which there is no real evidence. It is quite possible for two independent minds to arrive at similar answers to a scientific or artistic question without drawing upon anything more than the sources of knowledge common to both of them. And even if we suppose that Verdi was more closely acquainted with the later Wagnerian operas than the available evidence suggests,[1] it would not materially affect his claim to independence. Indeed, I would say that Verdi's independence of Wagner would be more remarkable, if we supposed that he had made a close study of the Bayreuth operas, than it is if we accept the notion that no such liaison existed. For Wagner's personality was immensely powerful and was apt to dominate those who came into contact with it, usually with disastrous results. It is, on the whole, easier to believe in the composition of a prelude to the last act of an opera with cor anglais *obbligato* independently of any knowledge of *Tristan and Isolde*, than to credit the possibility of the cor anglais solo in *Otello* having been suggested by the Wagnerian precedent. So utterly dissimilar is poor Barbara's song from the shepherd's plaintive ditty.

Further examples of Verdi's masterly handling of recitative are afforded in the opening part of the final scene of the third act, both in the dialogue with Iago and, even more conspicuously, in the cruel asides to Desdemona which Otello inserts into his reading of the doge's decree. The opening of this finale is extraordinarily effective. The trumpets announcing the arrival of the ambassadors playing their fanfares at various distances behind the scene

---

[1] Verdi was no student of scores; he was of the opinion that operas are meant to be heard in the theatre, not read in the study. I know of no evidence that he ever heard *Tristan, Meistersinger* or *The Ring*. At the same time he had, unlike some of his contemporaries, the greatest respect for Wagner's genius. Indeed, his frank and generous acknowledgment of Wagner's greatness and the entire absence of any taint of envy or spite in his criticisms are among the most attractive aspects of Verdi's character, even as Wagner's petty malice towards those who might be regarded as his rivals was one of his less admirable traits.

and answering each other's calls across its vacant space after the manner of the brass in the 'Tuba mirum,' would in any case serve to awaken expectancy and excitement. But as a background to the arrangement of murder in quiet, cold tones, they take on the semblance of some infernal cachinnation.

The finale proper begins after Otello has struck Desdemona to the ground—that action which has so offended those critics for whom a blow against a woman is the ultimate and unforgivable crime, far worse than any mental cruelty. It is the most, indeed, the only, formal and conventional musical movement in the opera, and as such it is, perhaps, somewhat out of key with the tragic mood of the work as a whole. We are suddenly transported for a while from a world of most carefully preserved dramatic truth back into the old romantic style of opera with principals and chorus giving vent to their emotions in a grand melody at the full power of their voices. The essentially lyrical Desdemona becomes for the nonce a dramatic soprano, soaring up to high A's above the choral clamour like any Leonora. But if it is conventional, this finale is also firstrate. Its only possible rival in Verdi's works is the somewhat similar finale in the council chamber in *Simon Boccanegra*. Nor is it psychologically untruthful. It has already been remarked that its present form was suggested by Verdi in preference to Boito's original sketch which was evidently far more conventional. For it is, at least, unusual for the leading tenor to be on the stage and take no part in a long, concerted movement occupying fortyfive pages in the vocal score. Otello, having flung Desdemona to the ground, sits silent, torn between shame and fury, while she gives way to her grief and the rest express their horror and astonishment, until his nerves will stand it no longer, and he screams for quiet and solitude—which is just how an exasperated man who has made an exhibition of himself in public would act. The crowd disperses and Otello, left alone, falls in a fit, while the people outside the palace, ignorant of the scandal, are still shouting for their governor and the Lion of Venice, and Iago spurns the fallen lion with his foot. A finale that ends in this way, not on a grand major chord for the assembled company, but in a dramatic action that empties the stage and leaves the hero senseless beneath the heel of his adversary, cannot be dismissed as merely conventional, for all that we have to apply that adjective to the musical style of the main part of it.

For their fourth act Verdi and Boito compressed the two scenes in Desdemona's bedroom (Act IV, sc. iii, and Act V, sc. ii) into one scene. To Shakespeare's 'Willow Song' they added an 'Ave Maria' for Desdemona, but otherwise, except that Emilia is not murdered by Iago, they kept closely to the original. The action at the very end is a little simplified, so that nothing is allowed to distract our attention from the central figure of the tragedy. For this ending Verdi was, as we have already noted, mainly responsible.

This scene is set to music that surpasses everything else Verdi ever wrote in depth of tragic feeling, in euphony and in the economy of the means employed. Desdemona's singing of the 'Willow Song' is, I suppose, the most affecting scene in all Shakespeare's plays. To have translated that scene, whose effect lies in its absolute simplicity, into the terms of nineteenth-century Italian operatic music without losing its freshness and innocence is an almost miraculous achievement. Here — and, indeed, throughout the act, in Otello's music no less than in Desdemona's — that note of chaste serenity which characterizes Shakespeare's poetry in *Othello* is most faithfully preserved.

The music of the scene between Desdemona and Emilia is made up of three brief figures, which are stated in the lovely prelude to which allusion has already been made. They consist of such abstruse and complex musical devices as an arpeggio for the cor anglais out of which the melody of the 'Willow Song' develops, a little rhythmic figure for three flutes that is like the sigh of a breaking heart, and three minim chords (tonic and dominant) low down in the *chalumeau* register of the clarinets that sound like a ghostly death knell. These three elements are marked (*a*), (*b*) and (*c*) in the following example:

To this material is added a lovely passage for the wood-wind, which is used as a *ritornello* to introduce each verse of the 'Willow Song':

During the scene the figure (*b*) announced by the flutes is developed symphonically and becomes an important feature in the music, especially at that most moving moment of all when Desdemona calls Emilia back to bid her a passionate farewell. The three clarinet chords may, I suppose, be regarded as an augmentation of the three quavers for the flutes, if analysis must be carried to extremes. But they have a life and a function of their own. They seem to express a dull foreboding, the awful numbness of fear at the heart. They reappear, fully scored and harmonized and reiterated a dozen times at the opening of Otello's final speech, 'Niun mi tema.'

Desdemona's farewell to Emilia is one of those strokes which only opera can bring off, because its effect depends upon a combination of musical pitch and dynamics with dramatic action. Desdemona says 'Good night' quietly on a low F sharp. Then, as Emilia goes to the door, the empty fifths, still played quietly, but with their ominous accentuation, bring back all Desdemona's fears. With passionate terror she cries out 'Ah! Emilia, farewell,' her voice rising to A sharp above the stave and descending again in pitch and loudness to its original F sharp. Again the procedure is simplicity itself, and the effect overwhelming.

The 'Ave Maria,' which follows, serves as a point of repose for our sorely wrung emotions. Its sweet serenity of mood is as admirable as the masterly flexibility of its declamation and the graceful counterpoint of its accompaniment for muted strings. It was a risky thing to attempt, for it might so easily have lapsed into a false and mawkish sentimentality. But Verdi's sincerity of purpose saves him from that sin. Then, when the prayer has vanished into thin air upon a long-held A flat in altissimo on the violins, the double basses, also muted, enter softly [1] upon the lowest open note of the four-stringed instrument, E♮. Otello is in the room, coldly murderous. This passage for the basses is a *locus classicus* not less honoured by writers on instrumentation than the introduction to the finale of Beethoven's ninth Symphony or the scherzo of the fifth. It is not, however, as a model for students, but as a signal example of Verdi's imaginative power that this passage most deserves our attention. Stanford is said to have called the double bass 'a dangerous rogue-elephant,' and dangerous it would be in unskilful hands. But no other means would serve so well to portray the terrifying stealth of Otello's entrance here, or reveal so truthfully the raw savagery of his mind poisoned to madness by Iago's venom. The long soliloquy of the basses is interrupted by a phrase for the violas which becomes of prime importance during the ensuing scene:

---

[1] The marking in the score is *pianissimo*, but most conductors demand a heavy *sforzando*, which is certainly effective and may possibly have the authority of tradition based upon the early performances.

This agitated staccato muttering that comes to a halt on a soft thud of the big drum, is like some horrible idea repeating itself over and over in the brain and, as the scene progresses, it becomes more insistent. The ominous minim for the drum is transferred to the brass, and then the semiquavers overwhelm these sinister pauses as Otello stifles his wife. Throughout the scene Otello acts calmly, without passion. He approaches the murder as a terrible and appalling duty to be performed, a solemn sacrifice to be made. Only at the moment of action does the brutality of the third act break in again. It is this air of a judicial sentence being duly carried out that so deeply shakes the spectator's soul, while preserving him from being merely shocked by the physical violence.

There follow quickly the re-entry of Emilia, the arrival of the other characters, the enlightenment of Otello and his noble peroration which makes amends for all the blindness and brutality of his actions. Here once more the declamation is so masterly, that perhaps the most moving moment of all is the line: 'Come sei pallida, e stanca, e muta, e bella' (the equivalent of Shakespeare's 'Cold, cold, my girl'), which is set unaccompanied to phrases that have no very distinctive melodic form, and which yet wring tears from us every time we hear them. So the journey's end is reached, and Otello dies upon a kiss to the music first heard at the end of the love duet in Act I.

Something must be said, though it can be but little, about the orchestration of *Otello*, which Stanford used to hold up as a model to his pupils—and, especially, as a model of what to leave out. Some indication has, I hope, been given in the musical quotations in this chapter of the economy of means Verdi used. The scoring of Otello's 'Dio mi potevi scagliar' and of the opening of the last act are notable examples of this economy, which, since it never produces a sense of bareness, argues an extraordinary sureness of touch and an exact knowledge of how best to achieve a given effect. Having got what he wants, Verdi never spoils it by a superfluous note or a thickening of the texture. His scoring has, at its best, a translucence only surpassed by Mozart's. But economy does not mean parsimony. No expense is spared to get the colour exactly right and, if pure ground lapis alone will serve, pure ground lapis it must be and not any old blue out of a three-penny tube. The score of *Otello* contains many special instruments and effects, of which the cor anglais in the last act is the most conspicuous example. It is not used earlier in the score at all, not even in order to give the player something to do in the *tutti*, but its sad tone colours the whole of the fourth act. Then for accompaniment to the madrigal sung to Desdemona he uses two *cornamuse*[1] (Italian bagpipes), mandolines[2] and guitars. And I wonder how many of all the people who have heard *Otello* know that during the whole of the first scene up to the entrance of Iago and Roderigo, fifty-three pages in the full score, there is a

---

[1] He allows the substitution of two oboes for this strange instrument, which, I imagine, is rarely used in performances of the opera.

[2] In the stage direction Verdi implies that the mandoline represents the 'guzla (una specie di mandola)' on which some of the singers accompany themselves. Verdi's theoretical knowledge of curious instruments was evidently less exact than his practical knowledge of the normal components of the orchestra. For the guzla is a one-stringed instrument played with a bow.

pedal point for the organ on the notes C, C♯ and B. This discord played on the low notes of the pedal organ is, of course, not intended to be heard as an individual voice; it is a back-ground to sounds of the tempest and dies away as the storm subsides.

Of the felicitous touches in the score, which might be cited from almost every bar, it is impossible to speak here. But, since the instrument itself is of the crudest, and had been used in the not very distant past of *Aida* in the vulgar thumping style, it is worth calling attention to the subtle use made of the big drum. An instance has been quoted from the passage accompanying Otello's entry in the last act, and another will be found at the words 'Otello fù' in his final speech, where the drum is doubled by a *pizzicato* note on the basses. This tragic use, as a note of sombre colour, of an instrument generally employed rhythmically for stirring marches, is not, perhaps, strictly original, for precedents might be quoted from the ninth Symphony (where it is in the transition stage from the military to the tragic) and from the *Marche au Supplice* in Berlioz's *Symphonie fantastique*. But Verdi must have the credit for his imaginative extension of this instru-ment's powers of expression, of which other instances are the 'Mors stupebit' in the *Requiem* and the closely parallel passage at the end of Iago's 'Credo.'

Some critics have been shocked that Verdi should have inserted into this tragedy, for its production in Paris in 1894, a con-ventional ballet to be performed in Act III for the entertainment of the Venetian ambassador.[1] But this compliance with the demands of the Paris Opéra is surely all of a piece with Verdi's attitude towards his art, which was primarily that of a craftsman

[1]This ballet music, which is printed at the end of the miniature full score of the opera, is a suite of 'characteristic' dances. As the last of Verdi's compositions for the theatre they deserve attention, especially for their delightful scoring. According to our notions of propriety they are, perhaps, out of place in *Otello*, but they might well be used for an independent ballet, now that this form of entertainment is so popular and appropriate music for it so difficult to find.

whose duty is to supply his employer with the kind of article he
has ordered. It was, perhaps, an out-of-date point of view to take
in the latter years of the nineteenth century, and it is precisely at
the opposite pole to the spiritual pride of the artist who must create
according to his own unhampered design or not at all. That
opposite point of view found its supreme expression at Bayreuth.
It is pointless to argue which of the two is the better way. Let it
suffice that between them they produced the two great tragic
masterpieces of nineteenth-century music—*Tristan* and *Otello*.

CHAPTER XVII

'FALSTAFF'

At the beginning of November 1886 Verdi announced the completion of *Otello* to his librettist:

> Dear Boito,
> It is finished.
> Let us drink to ourselves . . . (and to *him*!)
> Addio,
>
> G. Verdi.

Six weeks later he parted reluctantly with the last act to the copyist, Garignani. 'Poor Otello!' he exclaimed, 'he will return here no more.' For seven years he had lived in close communion with these characters, and they had become like children to a parent. Now they were grown up and must go into the world and make their own way. Later, amid all the plaudits of the opera's triumphant production at the Scala, he sighed for their company:

> I loved my solitude in the company of Otello and Desdemona! Now the public, always eager for novelty, has robbed me of them, and I have only the memory of our secret conversation, our cherished intimacy.

The first performance on 5th February 1887 was, indeed, a most notable occasion. Representative musicians from all parts of Europe came to Milan, as a few years earlier they had gone to Bayreuth to hear *Parsifal*. They can hardly have failed to imagine that on this occasion, too, they were witnessing the final work of an ageing composer. Verdi himself proclaimed it to be the 'last shot' in his locker. It was not surprising, therefore, that *Otello* was most favourably received. But the enthusiasm was more than respectful and affectionate; it was whole-hearted. It swept away the doubts, secretly harboured by Verdi up to the last moment, about the success and worth of all his effort—doubts that made him insist on the right to withdraw the opera even at the very last moment. It is a little difficult to understand, at this time of day, how new and daring *Otello* must have seemed to that first audience. We can see how everything in the score is im/ plicit in the composer of *Il Trovatore, La Traviata* and *Aida*, but the critics who wrote of the first performance found in it hardly a trace of the Verdi they knew.

The performance was conducted by Franco Faccio and the singers included Mme Pantaleoni (Desdemona), Tamagno (Otello) and Maurel (Iago). The tenor and the baritone became especially associated with the parts they created and Maurel's Iago remained, by common consent, one of the greatest operatic performances of his time, comparable with those of the de Reszkes in Wagner. About Tamagno opinions vary. He pos/ sessed a voice of unusual power, but he was not endowed with a similar measure of intelligence or musicianship, and he had to be carefully and arduously coached.

In spite of its initial success, *Otello* did not travel abroad quickly. But that was due to the difficulty of doing it full justice both in casting and in the details of performance. It reached London in 1889, and Verdi was particularly anxious about its reception in Shakespeare's country. All his misgivings about the 'Credo' returned and he chaffingly put the chief responsibility for it upon Boito. To Faccio, who conducted the performances, he wrote after hearing of its success:

By telegraph and from Muzio accounts have reached me of *Otello* in London. You confirm these accounts and give me great pleasure, although at my age and in the present condition of our music a success is nothing to shout about. You talk of the 'triumph of Italian art'! You are mistaken! The young Italian composers are not good patriots. If the Germans springing from Bach have arrived at Wagner, that is well. But if we, the descendants of Palestrina, imitate Wagner, we commit a musical crime and produce works that are futile, not to say harmful.

I understand that Boito has been highly praised, and that gives me the greatest pleasure. Praise given to *Otello* in Shakespeare's own country is valuable indeed.

Among the young Italian composers who had come under Verdi's notice lately was Giacomo Puccini, of whom he wrote to Arrivabene in June 1884:

I have heard the composer Puccini well spoken of. . . . He follows modern tendencies, which is natural, but he remains attached to melody which is above passing fashions. It appears to me, however, that the symphonic element predominates in him. There is nothing amiss in that, but here it is especially necessary to go cautiously. Opera is opera; symphony is symphony. And I do not believe that it is good to introduce bits of symphony into an opera simply for the fun of making the orchestra dance.

This is a remarkably perspicacious judgment upon a composer who was at the very beginning of his career. Puccini's *Le Villi*, his first and now almost forgotten opera, had been produced a few weeks before this letter was written, partly through the influence of Boito, who no doubt drew Verdi's attention to the young man. And apart from the insight, how generous and tolerant are the old man's words!

Verdi retired to Sant' Agata and devoted himself to his hobby, the cultivation of his estates. This time it really seemed that his career as a composer was at an end. He would remain the venerable figure-head of Italian music, to be celebrated in face of his own opposition on the jubilee of his first opera or to lend his support, more willingly, to the celebration of other masters. Much as he disliked such festivities, he permitted Joachim to number him among the patrons of the Beethoven centenary celebrations at Bonn: 'Where Beethoven is concerned, we must all do reverence!' And when Rossini's centenary came round in 1892, Verdi even took an active part in the proceedings and conducted the prayer from *Mosè*.

By that time the new cat was out of the bag. Once more there was a dinner party and an indiscretion, this time calculated, on Boito's part. The poet gave the toast, not of the aged guest of honour, but of 'Pot-belly'—an allusion promptly explained by Ricordi, who called out: 'Falstaff!'

This was in November 1890. The earliest mention of *Falstaff* in Verdi's correspondence occurs rather more than a year before, by which time it appears that the scheme of the opera had already been thoroughly discussed and settled. The manuscript of the text contains comparatively few emendations, from which fact Luzio deduces a very thorough preliminary survey of the ground by Verdi and Boito.[1] Even the new correspondence published in *Carteggi Verdiani* throws no light upon the origins of the new project. But it is, perhaps, not stretching imagination far to suggest that one spur to Verdi's intent was the desire to avenge once and for all the defeat of long ago, the disastrous *Un giorno di regno*, and to prove in the teeth of all the pronouncements, even of Great Jupiter Rossini himself, that he, Giuseppe Verdi, was capable of composing a comic opera. If there was a touch almost of quixotry in the venture, there was also a large measure of trepidation.

Do you realize [he wrote to Boito in July 1889], when you are drawing your portrait of Falstaff, the enormous number of my years? I know that in reply you will exaggerate the state of my health, saying it is robust and of the best. . . . That may be; none the less you will agree with me that it may be thought very rash of me to undertake such a task. Suppose I find the strain too great and cannot finish the music? Then your time and labour would have been wasted to no purpose. For all the wealth in the world I would not have that happen. Such an idea is intolerable, all the more so if, in writing *Falstaff*, you should find your mind distracted from *Nerone* (I will not contemplate the possibility of your giving it up) or its production delayed. I should be blamed for the postponement, and the lightnings of the public's anger would fall upon my head!

Verdi may be absolved of guilt in causing the delay in the

---

[1] It is not true that Verdi accepted the libretto as it stood without changing a word, but the alterations amounted only to minor verbal adjustments and the excision of superfluous lines.

long process through which Boito's *Nerone* went, a process which was not complete even when he died in 1918—unless we suppose that his contact with a far greater artist set up for Boito, always a man of the highest aspirations, a standard of excellence to which he felt he could not attain, but towards which, like the young man in Longfellow's poem, he struggled to the end of his life.

Verdi also felt that he could not end his career more triumphantly than with *Otello*—an argument of which Boito acknowledged the weight. But, he countered, it was valid for his contemporaries only, not for history, which assesses the whole worth of a man.

It is rare, indeed [he continues], for an artist's life to end with a worldly victory. Such a victory is *Otello*. All the other arguments about age, strength, your exhaustion or mine, etc., have no validity and present no obstacles to a new work. . . . I do not think that you would find the composition of a comic opera fatiguing. Tragedy makes its author genuinely suffer. His mind undergoes a painful experience and his nerves are unhealthily strung up. But the jests and laughter of comedy exhilarate both mind and body. . . . You have longed for a good subject for a comic opera all your life, which proves that you have a natural bent for the noble art of comedy. Instinct is a good guide. There is only one way of ending your career better than with *Otello*, that is to end it with *Falstaff*.

The *Merry Wives of Windsor* presented Boito with a very different and, on the whole, a less difficult task than *Othello*. In the one he was confronted with a poetic masterpiece whose form must be carefully handled if it was not to be distorted and ruined; in the other he was faced with a farce bearing every indication of having been hurriedly put together and consisting of a number of repetitive episodes loosely strung together round the paunch of Sir John Falstaff. And it is round his borrowed paunch that they are strung, for of the personality that makes the Falstaff of *King Henry IV* one of the great comic figures in our literature there is hardly a trace—only a fat man in a series of funny situations. The comedy is said to have been the result of a command from Queen Elizabeth to exhibit the fat knight in love—which is precisely what Shakespeare failed to do. Falstaff makes no pretence of being in love with either of the merry wives.

This is no occasion, then, for pulling long faces or talking of the iniquity of tampering with Shakespeare's text, as though it had the sanction of divine inspiration. Boito's first task was to reduce to a manageable form the sprawling, shapeless mass, to cut away the loose ends and irrelevant side-issues, and to rehabilitate Sir John Falstaff as a man of character. This task he carried out with the greatest skill, and no one who reads his libretto without prejudice can fail to acknowledge that, on its own merits as a comedy, it is a great improvement upon the original.

There were hardly any superfluous characters in *Othello*, who could be dispensed with; there are nine in *The Merry Wives*. Shallow, Slender, Evans and Caius could be rolled into one —their complaints against Falstaff and his minions, and the pretensions of two of them to Anne Page's hand, being concentrated in the person of Doctor Caius. Then Master Page was of no real use to the plot, so he could go; and to tighten up the unities his daughter Anne became Nannetta Ford. And, last major excision, the whole incident of Falstaff's disguise as Mother Prat, the fat woman of Brentford, which is but a weak repetition of the buck-basket episode, could be cut out bodily. Among the lesser figures Nym disappears—what is essential in his part being taken over by Bardolph—together with Rugby, Simple and William Page. Robin, the boy, remains as a *persona muta*.

With these characters and the by-plots in which they figure Boito rejected all those topical allusions that make *The Merry Wives* such a mine for the historical annotator of Shakespeare's text. Gone are the references to deer-stealing and the Lucy arms, to the idiosyncrasies of Ben Jonson and to the court of Queen Elizabeth. Out went 'cosen Garmombles' and the 'Duke de Jaminie,' and the curious affair of the post-horses of Maidenhead, Reading and Colnbrook. And, it must be confessed, with all these superfluities and obscurities, went also much that gives the play its immortal quality—the tang of English character and of the English countryside that makes Shakespeare's hand unmistakable, for instance, in the opening scene for Shallow and in the salt humour of Mrs Quickly's speech.

The gains are greater, and not only in form and concentration. It would have been futile to concentrate upon a figure that was nothing more than a padded belly. By a piece of patient recension Boito has substituted for the dummy the real Shakespearian Falstaff of the histories in all his grand unscrupulousness and geniality. Bardolph refusing to play pander substitutes for Nym's original Jonsonian excuse of his 'humour' that of his own 'honour,' and so provides the cue for the insertion of the great speech upon that topic from *Henry IV*, Part I. Even more ingenious is the invention of a repetitive objurgation of the world's vileness in the very manner of the 'plague of all cowards' speech in the same play, which serves to strengthen the scene of Falstaff's discomfiture after his ducking in the Thames. To this is added an excerpt from another of his *bravura* pieces—the speech on the effects of wine from the second part of *Henry IV*; and among other borrowings from the historical play may be mentioned the description of Bardolph's nose. In this way Boito reconstructed as far as was possible within the framework of the Shakespearian farce the great figure of the true Falstaff.

The resultant libretto consists of three acts, each containing two scenes. The location alternates between the Garter Inn and Ford's house (and garden) until at the end we reach the mock fairyland of Windsor Forest with Herne the Hunter's oak as the central feature. As an example of dramatic form the libretto is without superior. The action is swift, compact—indeed, an astonishing amount is compressed into a small space—and convincing, and it moves to its climaxes with an appearance of a natural ease that conceals a great skill in its handling.

Falstaff was composed slowly and methodically. Verdi worked at it for two hours, neither more nor less, each day. He had read somewhere a warning against the dangers of overwork to elderly people. Always timorous about the state of his health, he was determined to run no risks. His hypochondria did not grow less with the passing years. A visit to Montecatini, the spa in the

Tuscan hills above Lucca, to take the waters, remained an annual fixture in the routine of his life.

Verdi enjoyed himself enormously in spite of his misgivings. He was, he said, composing *Falstaff* for the fun of the thing. He even suggested that it might never be given to the public. But that was only a saving clause to cover the risk of the work not turning out to his satisfaction. Nothing could be wider of the mark than the idea of Verdi writing an opera as an intellectual exercise, for his private amusement, or in order to create a work of art without regard to a possible audience. When he composed he had one eye always on the box-office, and not upon the stars or Mount Parnassus or a vague future in which he would find his reward. Those are, more often than not, the objects of the conscious gaze of minor and usually unsuccessful artists. As in everything that concerns artistic creation, there are exceptions. But if a refutation of the slogan 'Art for Art's sake' is ever needed, it may be found in the operas of Verdi.

We may suspect, too, a mischievous delight in mystification for its own sake, to tease his friends and bamboozle the press. Even as late as January 1891, and even to so close an associate as Giulio Ricordi, Verdi persisted in his coy refusal to come to terms about *Falstaff*:

To come to *Falstaff*, all projects for the future seem to me folly, absolute folly! I will expound myself. I am engaged on writing *Falstaff* to pass the time, without any preconceived ideas or plans; I repeat, *to pass the time*! Nothing else. All this talk, these proposals, however vague, and this splitting of words will end by involving me in obligations that I absolutely will not assume. I tell you again: *I am writing to pass the time*. I tell you the music is only about half finished, by which I mean half sketched. There remains the greater part of the work: the concerting of the parts, revisions and adjustments, besides the instrumentation, which will be most exhausting. In fine, to put it in a word, the whole of 1891 will not suffice to finish it. So why make plans and accept terms, however loosely worded? Besides, if I felt myself in any way, even in the slightest degree, tied, I should no longer be *à mon aise* and could do nothing well. When I was a young man, in spite of ill health, I could work at my desk for ten or even twelve hours without a break! And many is the time I have set to work at four in the morning until four in the afternoon with nothing but a cup of coffee inside me. . . . I can no longer do that, alas! . . . To conclude, it would be best to say now and later to every one, to every one, that I cannot and will not make any promises about *Falstaff*. If it will be, it will be; and it will be what it will be!

Six months later to the same correspondent he wrote:

You are joking, my dear Giulio! . . . How? For six or seven months no one has given a thought to. *Falstaff* or to the Venerable Veteran of Sant' Agata. The theatres, too, have gone their way from failure to success (little enough of this!), and now you come and tell me that a subvention would be less badly needed [i.e. if *Falstaff* were to be produced]! It is inopportune to talk of *Falstaff*, which proceeds very slowly, and I am inclined to think that the vastness of the Scala might ruin the effect. In writing *Falstaff* I have thought neither of theatres nor of singers. I have written it to please myself, and I believe that it ought to be performed at Sant' Agata and not at the Scala.

I have already suggested that Verdi's protestations about writing to please himself without a thought for theatres or singers, by which he meant a particular theatre and individual singers, should not be taken too literally. In fact, a few days later Boito was writing to announce that he had discovered the right singer for Mrs Quickly. Verdi's misgivings about the effect of *Falstaff* in so large a theatre as the Scala, on the other hand, were real and well founded. *Falstaff* requires for its proper effect the intimacy of a small auditorium; it is almost chamber music.

It is usual to regard *Falstaff* as a kind of miraculous 'sport,' bearing little relation to any other opera of Verdi's. That its production by a composer in his eighth decade deserves the adjective will hardly be disputed, and not the least astonishing thing about it is the complete freedom of its musical style from the conventions of Italian *opera buffa*. Verdi's admiration for Rossini coupled with his total inexperience (apart from the unhappy experiment of fifty years before) of comic opera might reasonably have produced a work in the accepted and still popular style of *Il Barbiere di Siviglia* and *Don Pasquale*. But Verdi, by adapting the style he had developed for tragedy and carrying it to the extreme limit of which it was capable, produced a comic masterpiece as unique and original in its own way as *Die Meistersinger*. At the same time, once we get below the surface of its unique musical style, *Falstaff* is seen to be in the true succession of the *opera buffa*. Its roots may, indeed, be traced back to the old Italian Comedy, which, in fact, provided the original bare bones of Shakespeare's plot. Pistol, at least, among the characters has Latin blood in him and one of his collateral descendants may be found in the braggart Rodimarte in Alessandro Scarlatti's *Il trionfo d' onore*.

If we accept the description 'miraculous,' not as an easy catch-word but as an expression of the constant wonder and admiration that the music of *Falstaff* arouses in us, let us stop there and reject the 'sport.' For once we have recovered our breath, taken away by the speed and exhilaration of our experience, and come down to cold analysis, the score of *Falstaff* will be seen to be a perfectly logical development of the musical style of *Otello*. The material has become even more pliable, the themes even shorter, and the equipoise between voices and orchestra perfect. The melody is recognizably the melody of Verdi, but it comes now in brief snatches that elude the ear and make the listener wish to call the music to halt in its swift passage, that he may examine and appreciate to the full its fleeting beauty. For not only have the long melodies square-cut to an eight-bar pattern, that could be seized at once by the memory and carried away from the opera house, given way to a more subtle and, as it were, kaleidoscopic style, but the tunes no longer begin and end with an obvious signal; they tend to melt into one another and the distinction be-tween them and recitative has grown so faint that the music becomes a continuous *arioso*. The melodic ideas dissolve and reshape themselves in new forms with a swiftness that keeps even the most athletic brain for ever panting at their heels. For this reason it is that there is really nothing that can be lifted from *Falstaff* for performance in the concert hall, though baritones do occasionally show off their command of patter by singing 'Quand' ero paggio.'¹ And that very exception gives a measure of the diminutive scale of the component parts of the opera. It is all over in a few seconds. This little song is also typical of the work as a whole, which is so brief that the time it takes to perform is less than that of the third act of *Die Meistersinger*. Beside Wagner's immensely solid comedy, Verdi's is seen to be not merely swift and compact but also of the lightest imaginable specific gravity.

This nimbleness of thought makes quotation from *Falstaff* for the purpose of appreciation both difficult and unprofitable. For if one begins, where is one to stop? On every page there is something worth our attention, but to take a bar or two out of its context is to rob the quotation of its real effect, and any multiplication of such extracts carries with it the risk of laying too much emphasis on points of detail and so missing the larger beauty of the whole score. Bearing this danger in mind, I propose, however, to quote one or two salient themes which will show not only how keen was Verdi's sense of comic character, but also how he managed to compress the full expression of that sense into phrases of no more than half a dozen notes.

Here, then, is Falstaff, got up to kill, setting forth on his visit to Mrs Ford:

And here is the same gentleman ruefully cursing a wicked world that contains such horrors as dirty linen and cold water:

---

¹ This is another loan from *Henry IV*, Part I (Act II, sc. iv), where Falstaff says: 'When I was about thy years, Hal, I was not an eagle's talon in the waist; I could have crept into any alderman's thumb-ring!'

Mrs Quickly is touched off in a phrase that makes visible the exact movement and timing of her curtsy every time we think of it, as well as the suppressed laughter behind her hand:

And when she informs Sir John that Ford is away from home between two and three, she puts the words to a phrase so catching that it infects the whole score with its rhythm (*a*). It cannot be a mere coincidence that Mrs Ford's greeting to Falstaff when he enters in the second scene of Act II echoes this rhythm (*b*). With Sir John himself it becomes an obsession (*c*):

Another characteristic phrase of Quickly's is quoted both for its own comic sake, and because it may amuse the reader to trace

293

its previous incarnation an octave higher in the recitative to one
of Verdi's most famous arias written forty years earlier:

Po-ve-ra donna!   Po-ve-ra donna!

I have drawn attention to this recurrence—we need not argue
whether it is an unconscious reminiscence or a conscious parody
—also because it provides the clearest and most easily demonstrable
symbol of the essential unity of Verdi's music from first to last.
The musical material of *Falstaff*, reduced to its elements, is the
same as that which had served him for half a century. These
elements are the simple harmonic and melodic processes which
had furnished forth the popular operas of his middle age. Only
now, as we have seen, they have been dissolved, as it were, in
the alembic of the composer's maturing genius. They have lost
their sharp corners and square edges; they have split up into smaller
units; and they have acquired a new fertility, the capacity to
reproduce themselves in new forms. If they have lost something
of their old forcefulness and drive, they have also shed their
crudity. The most vulgar genius of the age had become the
most aristocratic.

Naturally the closest affinities to *Falstaff* will be found in *Otello*,
but it is astonishing how close those affinities prove on investiga-
tion to be. All the compositional methods, all the means of
expressing character and, with one exception, all the methods of
creating atmosphere and dramatic tension employed in *Falstaff*
have their precedents in *Otello*. But they are worn with a comic
difference. The parallel between Falstaff himself and Iago is
quite astounding, so little would a resemblance between the two
strike a casual listener. Yet the shakes, the appoggiaturas and the
sharply broken rhythms that served to portray the lean ugliness of
Iago's soul are used to portray the more venial villainy and the
paunchy chuckles of the fat knight. Falstaff's monologue on

honour was described by Stanford as the comic brother of Iago's creed, and in the following passage, which occurs at the moment of Falstaff's triumph after his interview with Quickly, most of the elements of the characteristic Iago music recur, but, like Bottom, translated:

Allegro sostenuto

It is, in part, the instrumentation that does the trick, just as it helps to translate the triumphant strutting of 'Va, vecchio John' into the dirge-like repetition of the passage after Sir John's ardour has been cooled in the Thames.

It would be, I suppose, difficult to find two pieces of music farther apart in emotional significance than Otello's monologue, 'Dio mi potevi scagliar,' and the fairy song of Nannetta Ford in the last act of *Falstaff*; yet the compositional process of the following passage, taken from what is in effect a choral *ritornello* to that song, is exactly the same, consisting of a decorated scale descending by thirds (in place of one descending diatonically) with a syncopated accompaniment:

This brings us to one particular—as apart from the novel and entirely successful handling of the comic idiom generally—in which *Falstaff* shows an entirely new advance. Magic and the supernatural had hitherto eluded Verdi's imagination. The devils of *Giovanna d'Arco*, the witches in *Macbeth*, even the ghost (if it is the ghost) of Charles V in *Don Carlo*, either evoked from him nothing more than a conventional type of music that seems to modern ears nearer to pantomime demonry than to tragic horror, or suggested to him an equally conventional use of the liturgical style. Ulrica's incantations are unlikely to arouse a sense of awe in the spectator; more probably they will make him smile. It is true that the scene of the visions in *Macbeth*—a part of the new music added during the revision of the opera in 1865 —is at least partially successful. But it is dignified rather than awe-inspiring. Perhaps a more genuine exception would be Lady Macbeth's sleep-walking scene, where Verdi does recreate out of the material of a conventional 'mad scene' that sense of the uncanny which pervades the original in Shakespeare. And there is another exception that shall be noted later. But in *Falstaff* there was no occasion for such serious horrors, only for a vision of fairyland and enough of spookiness to scare a credulous old man.

And here Verdi has gone one better than Shakespeare, supplying the touch of magic that transforms the farcical climax of the play into a scene of enchantment which need not fear comparison with the most imaginative visions of the fairy world. It is not improbable that, just as Boito 'read into' his Falstaff the character drawn in *Henry IV*, so Verdi translated from *A Midsummer Night's Dream* the poetry of the fairies. No other music captures so completely the freshness and innocence of that poetry as this scene in *Falstaff* and Mendelssohn's overture for that other play. It is amusing to think of the octogenarian meeting the boy of seventeen as an equal on this enchanted ground after a journey along such diverging paths, on which they had set out as contemporaries.

Verdi had, as the saying is, grown old gracefully, which means that he had not forgotten what it was like to be young, and, when that happens, age is to be numbered among the more beautiful manifestations of the human soul. In this instance it manifests itself in a tenderness of feeling that sheds a glow upon all the scenes in which Nannetta Ford appears. Her music, and Fenton's, runs like a silver thread through the rich tapestry of robust laughter. Like so much else in the opera, their music consists of short snatches of song rarely exceeding a page in duration. The most characteristic is the recurrent couplet[1] that gives poetic substance to their love-making, the most chaste and innocent in Verdi as in Shakespeare. And could the sweetness of Anne Page be more faithfully represented in music than by the following phrase with its fluttering accompaniment of flutes, which takes us back to fairyland again?

Besides this lyrical magic, there is also an element of comical

---

[1] See vocal score, p. 96 (Act I, sc. ii, after No. 31), 'Bocca baciata non perde ventura,' etc.

magic associated with the trick devised by the merry wives to frighten their suitor out of his five wits. It makes its appearance when Mrs Quickly delivers the message to Falstaff that bids him to a rendezvous at Herne's oak. The plotters, who are eaves-dropping according to comic convention, come forward as Falstaff leaves the stage and Mrs Ford takes up the tale '*con voce grossa*' in phrases [1] that have a note of eeriness sufficient to send a shiver down other backs than Mrs Page's, until it is dissolved in laughter at the description of the length of the sable hunter's horns. For the good old joke at the expense of cuckolds is fully exploited with *obbligato* for the appropriate instrument. This note of eeriness had rarely been sounded by Verdi before, and never so surely as in Otello's description of the magic power of the strawberry-spotted handkerchief, where the effect is pro-duced by similar means, chromaticism and a dark-coloured orchestration.[2]

[1] See vocal score, p. 319 (Act III, sc. ii, after No. 14), 'Quando il rintocco della mezza-notte,' etc.

[2] A hint of this feeling will be found in the first scene of *Il Trovatore,* and something more than a hint in the scene by the gibbet in *Un ballo in maschera.*

'Falstaff': The Concerted Music

Before we leave the magical, the reader's attention must be drawn to one other passage that merits the adjective in its metaphorical sense. At the end of the first scene in the third act, when the plotters have laid their various schemes for fooling Falstaff and marrying off Nannetta, when the victim of the hoax has gone upstairs to don his finery and his antlers, and when Mrs Quickly has trotted off to join her gossips, there follows a postlude for orchestra that is worthy to set beside the magical ending of the second act in *Die Meistersinger*. Here it is sunset, there moonrise; but its poetic purpose and enchantment are the same. It serves, too, to prepare us for the ensuing nocturne which opens with distant horn fanfares summoning the company to the revels, just as the shriller trumpets in *Otello* call the citizens of Cyprus to a more terrible spectacle.

It has already been noted that one of the characteristics of *Falstaff* is its swiftness of movement. This extraordinary nimbleness is most conspicuous in the concerted music. The chattering quartet of women in the first act is followed by a no less rapid and excited quartet of men and the scene ends with an octet for the two groups. Yet despite the complexity of dramatic motives—most of the characters have their individual point of view—the texture is singularly transparent. It would be idle to pretend that the audience can follow in detail the several threads of thought that are woven together, but the gist of it all is intelligible enough. The no less elaborate finale of the second act is even more lucid, because here the action explains what it is about, while the finale of Act III is as clear as the moonlight that illumines the scene.

This last finale falls into three parts: the teasing of Falstaff, the betrothal of Nannetta to Fenton and an epilogue in the form of a fugue. The first part contains the one weak passage in the opera, the pinching chorus of the fairies, which is somewhat jerky in rhythm and never quite comes off in performance, though the penitential antiphonals of Falstaff and the 'grown-ups' are richly humorous and include a pun as monstrous as the hero's own circumference, to which it refers:

> *Alice, Meg and Quickly.* Fallo pentito, Domine!
> *Falstaff.* Ma salvagli l' adomine!

Verdi

The second part is based upon one of those melodies which seems to tell us that the revels now are ended.[1] It also has an astonishingly English air about it, as though in the very contemplation of Windsor Forest Verdi had caught the accents of Purcell's countrymen and successors in the eighteenth century:

At the end comes a *vaudeville*. The singers line themselves up before the footlights, drop their characters and address the audience in their proper persons. 'Tutto nel mondo è burla,'

[1] The melody of 'Pace! pace! mio dolce tesoro!' in *Figaro* is another of this type that seems to signalize the resolution of the dramatic complex and the ending of the action.

they sing; 'l' uom è nato burlone'—which may be interpreted as
'All the world's a stage and men and women merely comedians.'
To the last Boito had his eye on Shakespearian ideas that could be
brought in. Verdi set it as a fugue in C major, the key generally
associated with Falstaff throughout the opera. Astonishing
though it may seem, this fugue has actually been criticized as a
piece of pedantry. It is certainly a marvel of technical skill. It
is not, however, as a learned *tour de force* that it affects most listeners,
but rather as the supreme musical expression of 'laughter holding
both his sides.'

Verdi's enormous enjoyment of the fun of writing *Falstaff* is
evident in almost every page of the score, but one suspects that,
along with the fugue, he enjoyed most the scene between Falstaff
and Ford in Act II. From Falstaff's unctuous salutation (with
which Ford mocks him in one of the most amusing passages in
the last finale) of the supposed 'Signor Fontana' (Master Brook)
to his triumphant exit in his courting finery this scene is a masterpiece of comedy. Nowhere does Verdi use themes as *Leitmotive*
in the Wagnerian sense, but into the score are woven melodic
fragments that have appeared already and, by awakening associations with their original context, produce an effect of quick and
pointed wit. Mrs Quickly's 'dalle due alle tre' is, as we have
noted, all-pervasive, and when Ford is left alone it is the phrase
to which Falstaff had boasted that he would make him a cuckold
that keeps running through his head and drives him to frenzy.
This monologue of Ford's is musically one of the finest things in
the opera, and it is remarkable for the skill with which Verdi
prevents its seriousness from overstepping the limits of comedy.

What fun Verdi had, too, with the orchestration! His mastery
of instrumental effect, like his feeling for the right setting of words
and for the balance of voice and accompaniment, had developed
even beyond the consummate skill of *Otello*. And he uses this
mastery with a gusto that is never allowed to degenerate into showing off for its own sake, still less to lapse into vulgarity. The
underlining of Falstaff's repeated 'No's' in the monologue on
honour with staccato chords emphasized by an *acciaccatura*, the

airy whiffling of the woodwind at 'What is in that word honour? Air,' and the great shake of the whole orchestra that accompanies his description of the effect of wine, are famous points in a score that has in almost every bar some happy touch of beauty or stroke of wit.

The swiftness of movement, the quick play of wit, the subtlety and restraint of the comedy, the aristocratic air of it all combine to make *Falstaff* one of the most difficult operas to appreciate, though its richness of humour and robust vitality save it from being merely recondite. The composer who had made the greatest popular reputation of his time ended by producing the musicians' opera; the romantic had turned pure classicist; and the master of theatrical effect said farewell to the theatre in strict fugue.

FINAL CHAPTER

Every Man desires to live long; but no Man would be old.

J. SWIFT.

THE rest is a tale of sunset glow and dying fires. The glow was magnificent while it lasted. *Falstaff*, produced at the Scala Theatre on 9th February 1893, brought Verdi the homage of the whole civilized world. Musicians from all parts of Europe and from America gathered in Milan, and the anticipatory excitement was not lessened by the fact that Verdi firmly refused to intervene with the management to waive the rule against admitting strangers to rehearsals. Telegrams of congratulation poured in from the great, among them one from King Humbert, who expressed his regret at being unable to witness 'this new manifestation of an inexhaustible genius.' Acting up to its name, *La Perseveranza* continued its indiscretions and published a rumour that Verdi was to be created a marquis. Verdi promptly begged a friend in the Ministry to use his good offices to avert so unwelcome an honour.

When *Falstaff* set out on its triumphal career through Italy, Verdi followed its fortunes with an eager interest and, indeed, pursued the conductor, Edoardo Mascheroni, with good-humoured sallies. He had borrowed from 'Farfarello,' as he affectionately called him, the cost of his fare from Rome to Genoa, and chaffed him, with mocking quotations of the laughter of the Merry Wives, about the prospect of losing his hundred lire. Verdi was persuaded to go to Rome for the first performance of the opera in the capital by Boito, who was anxious about its success. He was afraid that in a theatre with such strict academic traditions of elegance and sentimentality, William Shakespeare would be like a bull in a Dresden-china shop. He also feared,

303

contrariwise, that the full-blooded humour of *Falstaff* might be refined away. In the event, the Rome production was a complete success. King Humbert was present at the head of a brilliant audience, and after it was over 'Farfarello' and the orchestra serenaded the composer at his hotel with a selection of his music, including the overture from his first success, *Nabucco*.

If the old lion could roar with laughter, he could also still roar with anger in defence of his rights. When there was a question of making cuts in *Falstaff* at the Opéra-Comique, he showed his claws, not for the first time on this same account, and insisted either that the opera should be performed as written or that it should be withdrawn altogether. 'I make this formal demand of you,' he wrote to Ricordi, 'as the publisher and owner of the score. As my friend, I beg you to attend to this matter, for I am not disposed to endure what I regard as an artistic out-rage.' Needless to say the Opéra-Comique did as it was told, and Verdi actually graced the first performance with his presence.

Generally, the note was more genial, even when his scorn was aroused. His temper mellowed with age. There was more of irony than wrath in his astonished exclamations at the proposal to give *Otello* in Italian at the Paris Opéra. Writing in French to the director, he declared that he was unable to reconcile the idea of an Italian work with the Opéra ('your great National Theatre'). If they wanted to give *Otello*, they must give it in French; and he instructed Ricordi in the same sense. The Opéra, too, bowed to the imperious will, and was rewarded for its obedience with a simplified version of the finale to Act III, the original being too complicated for the Parisian chorus, and the ballet music to which reference has already been made. The Opéra wanted something to offset the attraction of the production of *Falstaff* at the Opéra-Comique, and both operas were given for the first time in Paris during the season of 1894.[1]

[1] There had been talk of producing *Otello* at the Opéra three years before, but Verdi objected that he 'did not see the right person' to sing the title-part. Marchesi had written to suggest that his wife's most famous pupil, Nellie Melba, who had lately made her brilliant début

The following extracts from the letter-book of this period are characteristic:

To the president of a committee for the celebration of the twentieth anniversary of the liberation of Rome:

In my youth I could never write music for poems, hymns, and so forth on some particular occasion, though I did write a cantata in 1861 or 62 for an exhibition in London—and wrote it badly!

Now my pen is dry, and I could not possibly write anything worthy of the high solemnity and of the really splendid poem by Carducci.

To a German publisher:

Never, never will I write my memoirs!

It is quite enough for the musical world that it should have had to put up with my music for all these years! Never will I condemn it to read my prose!

To Mascheroni, on various occasions:

I have had no letter from you from Vienna. The last was dated 12th May [1893] from Trieste. Since then I have had no news of *Falstaff*; and I am not sorry. From my own annoyance I can picture yours: all the wearisome gossip, the caprices and, you will add, the *villainies*! It is bad, very bad; but do not delude yourself. . . . The theatre is like that, and so it must be. . . .

We are born to suffer! And you believe that it is possible to be a composer or an orchestral conductor without having to eat your heart out every day, a bit at lunch, another helping at dinner—and always a little left over for to-morrow! . . .

'So that's that,' as the man said when he had murdered his father! Not that we have murdered anybody; at most, we have flayed the ears of the good public. . . . Anyhow, my compliments to every one, my—what can I say? Well, I shout to you all: Bravo! ladies; bravo! gentlemen, and to yourself: *ten points*!

---

as Gilda, should visit the composer in order to study the part of Desdemona with him. Verdi received the suggestion coldly and expressed his usual dislike of the discussion of his affairs by third parties. 'I do not like people talking of my concerns before the time has come. Oh! this publicity! I hate it.'

So ended the tour of *Falstaff*, which had not been without the squabblings and intrigues that seem inseparable from any operatic enterprise. Nor had it been, from the financial point of view, an overwhelming success, and in the letters to Mascheroni there is a reflection of Verdi's disappointment at the falling of the mercury in 'that infallible thermometer, the box-office.'

Other things increased the natural melancholy of old age, that sees in each farewell a final parting. Verdi was deeply distressed by that sorest affliction of the ageing—the loss, one by one, of his old friends. Emmanuele Muzio, his only pupil and his companion on his first visit to London in the dim past, had died shortly before the production of *Otello*. Faccio was struck down by mental disease during the composition of *Falstaff*, and his condition preoccupied Boito, who took him to Krafft-Ebing's sanatorium at Graz in the vain hope of a cure. The passing of mere acquaintances ('poor Catalani') or total strangers of eminence in the world (like Wagner or Delibes) moved Verdi to sorrow. Then, in November 1897, the closest and dearest of them all left him.

Giuseppina had been ailing for some time, but she herself thought her illness no worse than a cold, whose most annoying symptom was that it deprived her of enjoying the scent of the flowers Verdi brought her. He bore her death with courage, but in silence. He could not bring himself to speak of the partner of his whole working life, who had encouraged his youthful efforts and advised him about his business even before friendship ripened into love. She had watched over his health, borne with his waspish irritability which could make him an exacting companion when he was in the throes of composition, and, for all that these moments of exasperation sometimes made her wish that he might never write another opera, never failed to stimulate and support him in each new venture. She showed neither jealousy nor ill will towards the women, chief among them Teresa Stolz, who were on terms of intimate friendship with her husband, and the fact that she had no cause for jealousy does not detract from the virtue. At the same time she was no 'doormat,' no meek Egeria content to be the mute inspiration of her husband's muse; she was a woman of spirit and character and wit. The gracious sweetness of her mind and her sense of fun are the traits that most impress the reader of her letters.

It is not surprising that her death shattered the health of a man so sensitive to loss as Verdi. The almost undiminished vigour of his mind gave way under the shock to a pathetic senility. He wandered from room to room, complaining that 'Peppina' was gone. Yet, even so, though his heart became affected at this time, his physical strength carried him on through three more years of ebbing vitality.

There was, indeed, at first little outward change in his habits. He went, as usual, to Montecatini in the summer, and to Genoa for the winter. At Sant' Agata he still entertained his friends. Nor did he lose his interest in his music, and when in the spring of 1898 there was yet one more, the final, *première* in Paris, he even for a moment contemplated going to hear the performance.

The novelty consisted of three *Pezzi sacri* (*Sacred Pieces*) out of four which Verdi had composed over a number of years just before and after the composition of *Falstaff*. The pieces are *Ave Maria* for four voices *a cappella*, *Stabat Mater* for chorus and orchestra, *Laudi alla Vergine Maria* for four women's voices *a cappella* and *Te Deum* for double chorus and orchestra. It will be noticed that they vary widely in the resources required, and they are in no sense a suite intended for performance together. In fact, both in Paris and at Turin, where the first Italian perform/ ance was given under Arturo Toscanini, the *Ave Maria* was omitted.

The *Ave Maria*, indeed, is an experimental piece, the only one in Verdi's career, designed as an exercise in harmony. The *Gazzetta musicale* had published an anonymous contribution about an 'enigmatic scale' consisting of the notes C, D♭, E, F♯, G♯, A♯, B, with F♮ in descending. Boito drew Verdi's attention to this scale and suggested that he should use it for a setting of *Ave Maria* as a penance for the 'Credo' in *Otello*, to which Verdi retorted that in *that* crime Boito was the chief culprit

and that in expiation he had better 'compose a *Credo* in four parts
alla Palestrina and put it into a work . . . I dare not name'
[i.e. *Nerone*]. The resulting composition is chiefly interesting
as an experiment in harmony and as a proof of Verdi's unceasing
mental vigour which even so late in life could stimulate a purely
speculative experiment of this kind. The *Ave Maria* is not a
composition of any importance in itself, but it is an interesting
study in a kind of harmony which the young composers of the
day, notably Debussy, were just starting to explore.

The *Stabat Mater* is at once more normal and on a larger scale.
The medieval Latin sequence provides a dramatic text of the
kind that had stimulated Verdi's imagination in the *Dies irae*.
The setting is remarkable for its straightforward treatment of
the text, which is unextended by any repetitions of words of
phrases. The scoring has the characteristic clarity that has been
remarked already in Verdi's later works, and once more, at the
most tragic moment, it is by soft strokes on the big drum that the
note of awe and mystery is sounded.

The *Laudi alla Vergine Maria* is a setting of some verses
taken from the last canto of Dante's 'Paradiso.' It is,
again, small in scope, but it has a lyrical charm that should
have made it more popular than it seems to be with small
choirs. There have been few separate performances in recent
years.

The *Te Deum* is of the four pieces the most considerable, a
worthy successor to the *Requiem Mass* itself. It provides also the
simplest example of that independence of mind which, even in
the setting of this familiar canticle, never took anything for
granted, nor followed a tradition blindly. This *Te Deum* is
unique. Other composers have either set it as part of a 'Service,'
or they have used it to celebrate occasions of public rejoicing—
the crowning of kings, the triumph of armies, or the marriage of
princes. It would have been natural to follow this practice in
composing a *Te Deum* on a grander scale than would serve for
liturgical purposes, even though no particular event was to be
celebrated. But Verdi read his text and followed the precept of

that philosopher who bade us 'Respice finem.' So accustomed are
we to the jubilant idea of the canticle that probably not one in a
hundred has perceived that the kernel of its thought lies in the
prayer for deliverance from the wrath to come and the avowal
of trust in God's mercy with which it ends. It is upon this
aspect of the canticle that Verdi concentrated his imagination, and
he produced not a paean, but a prayer and a confession of faith.
It is, as might be expected, a dramatic setting, and its musical
reflection of the text is truthful and very moving; for instance,
in the sudden overclouding of the music, as with a terrible doubt,
at 'Let me never be confounded,' followed by the small voice of
hope and faith embodied in a single soprano whose threefold
'In te speravi,' punctuated by a high trumpet note, leads the work
to its brief climax.

The music is based upon two liturgical themes, the first of which
is announced *senza misura* (like the plainsong 'Pange lingua' at
the beginning of Holst's *Hymn of Jesus*) by the choral basses without
accompaniment. This differs in no way from Palestrina's procedure in composing the Mass, *Assumpta est Maria*, except that
he used one theme as the basis of the whole composition. But
Verdi, composing at a time long distant from the age of plainsong,
could not do other than translate his material into the terms of his
own contemporary musical language. Otherwise he would have
produced only an archaic imitation. It is extraordinarily interesting to see how, out of the opening chant, he develops a melody
so typically Verdian that one has to rub one's eyes to make sure
that the notes are those of the original theme:

Like all great composers, Verdi proves that an old method of composition can be turned to a new account by the use of imagination. The *Te Deum*, his last finished composition, is a masterpiece of great subtlety, whose genuine musical quality is, perhaps, somewhat obscured by the obvious and sometimes strepitous contrasts of dynamics which Verdi characteristically imposed upon it. It is not so 'great' a work as the *Requiem* in the sense that it is not so large, nor so immediately attractive in its melody, nor so compelling in obvious dramatic effect. Yet, as a musical composition, it ranks high among settings of the canticle.

Verdi once claimed that, though he was not a learned, he was a very experienced composer. The *Pezzi sacri* make it evident that this is too modest an estimate of his powers. Yet he was right in stressing the importance to himself of practical experience. With every work he composed, he discovered something new, discarded some weakness that had become apparent. In this way he developed a technique of using the very simple and straightforward material at his disposal for an astonishing variety of purposes. And, what is even more astonishing, the same kind of musical ideas proved in his hands to be so well suited to the most diverse contexts that, once we have got past the initial recognition of a resemblance, we wonder how any one could invent music more apt for each particular occasion.

It is convenient to mention here also two less important Sacred Pieces, which Verdi produced in 1880. These are an *Ave Maria* and a *Pater Noster*, neither of them the Latin prayers, but with Italian texts by Dante. The *Ave* is a soprano solo with string accompaniment, very much in the style of the prayers that occur in some of the operas, of which Desdemona's is the most beautiful example. It is not a type of 'sacred' music that accords with twentieth-century taste, but it is surprising that it has not occurred to many enterprising sopranos to sing this quite beautiful air on the concert platform. But then, perhaps it would be more surprising if the kind of soprano who could sing it well showed enterprise. The *Pater Noster* is set for five voices *a cappella*, and approaches more nearly to the liturgical style of the later *Pezzi sacri*.

All these sacred compositions may be regarded as Verdi's tribute to the spirit of Palestrina and his contemporaries. In writing them he was practising what he had preached so often in his letters, for instance, in this to Arrivabene in 1879:

All of us, composers, critics, the public, have done all that is possible to renounce our musical nationality. We have come to a good end; another step, and we shall be Germanized in this as in so much else. It is a consolation to see how there are springing up on every side quartet societies and orchestral societies, etc., to educate the public in the Great Art, as Filippi calls it. Yet to me there comes every now and then a very unhappy thought, and I say to myself, under my breath: 'But if we in Italy were to form vocal quartets to perform the works of Palestrina and Marcello and their contemporaries, would not that be Great Art?'

It would be Italian Art. . . . The other, no! But peace, no one pays any attention to me.

The decline in Verdi's health was slow, but inexorable. Only once during his last year of life was there a momentary flicker of creative energy. The assassination of King Humbert in 1900 shocked Verdi deeply, and he was so moved by the beauty of the prayer composed by the widowed Queen Elena, that he jotted down some notes for a musical setting of the words. A few scribbled staves, hardly decipherable, are all that survives of his last musical ideas.

The original Aida, writing to the original Amneris, now a duchess and lately become a grandmother, gives an account of him in Milan at the end of 1900:

Our beloved master is well, despite his eighty-seven years. He enjoys a good appetite, sleeps well, often goes out for drives, sometimes walks a little, but complains of his legs, saying he would take longer walks, but his legs are too weak. For the rest he is in good humour, likes company and every evening has a gathering of his most intimate friends at his lodgings. Later on, in March, he will leave for Genoa.

A few days later Verdi wrote to the duchess (Maria Waldmann) for the last time, a brief note complaining of his weariness and ebbing strength. His enforced inactivity irked him sorely. He saw neither March nor Genoa again. On 21st January he had a stroke and, after a week of unconscious struggle, he died early on the morning of 27th January.

In accordance with his will,[1] a remarkably business-like and lengthy document drawn up in his own hand in May 1900, he was buried beside Giuseppina in the oratory of the Home for Musicians in Milan, which he had founded in 1895, and of which Camillo Boito, the poet's brother, was the architect. He expressed the wish that the funeral should be as modest as possible, and that it should take place either at dawn or in the evening without bells or music. This wish was literally respected. But, as the oratory was not ready, and authority had to be obtained for his interment there, he was laid in a temporary resting-place. When, a month later, the bodies of Verdi and his wife were buried together in the place he had chosen, the whole of Milan, and indeed all Italy, insisted on paying a formal tribute to the greatest Italian artist of the age.

---

[1] The chief beneficiaries under the will were the Home for Musicians at Milan, and other charities at Busseto, Villanova, and Genoa, which received one-half of Verdi's fortune of seven million lire (roughly £280,000) and his cousin, Maria Carrara (Verdi), who had faithfully nursed him through his last three years and was appointed his residuary legatee.

SUPPLEMENT I

(See page 12)

THE early career of Giuseppina Strepponi has been thoroughly explored by Frank Walker.[1] She was born at Lodi on 8th September 1815, while her father was still a student at the Conservatorio in Milan, which she herself entered as a paying pupil in 1830, being granted exemption (unlike Verdi) from the regulation concerning age limit. Two years later her father died, leaving his widow and four children in poor circumstances. A benefit concert in Trieste, where the family had settled, provided for Giuseppina's fees for a year, after which she was given a scholarship and, on finishing her studies, won the first prize for *bel canto*. She made her public appearance in 1835 at Trieste in Rossini's *Matilde di Shabran*. She quickly established her reputation as one of the leading sopranos of the day, and was able to support her mother.

The calendar of her engagements compiled by Walker shows her touring the principal theatres of Italy as well as visiting Vienna, even as the stars of to-day revolve round the opera houses of the world, with benefit of aircraft.

Her roles included Norma, Lucia di Lammermoor, and Amina in *La Sonnambula*, which seems to have been her favourite, as she chose it for her benefit performances. Her career as a singer was, thus, a strenuous one and it was darkened by the birth of two illegitimate children, one of whom (Camillino) survived and was boarded out in Milan, and in 1849 was settled with a friend of Giuseppina's in Florence. After this Camillino disappears from view, and it would seem that he died in 1853 or 1854. Of the second child nothing is known, apart from its existence; it most probably died in infancy. The father of these children was for many years thought to be Merelli, the director of the Scala Theatre, but Frank Walker has proved—so far as proof in such a matter is possible—that Giuseppina's lover was the tenor Napoleone

[1] *The Man Verdi*, Dent, 1962.

Moriani, with whom she was singing at the material dates. Moriani was a married man and her association with him left a deep scar on Giuseppina's memory. She could not forgive herself for her infatuation with 'the despicable M——', as she called him in her letters. It is significant that, in later years, she destroyed all the evidence of her career as a singer. Walker considered that the existence of Camillino presented an obstacle in Giuseppina's mind to the idea of marriage with Verdi, and that only after her son's death did she feel free to take this obvious step and regularize the position.

SUPPLEMENT II

(See page 172)

THE story of Verdi's quarrel with Mariani is a sorry one, out of which neither Verdi nor his wife comes with credit. Mariani, the most distinguished Italian conductor of his day, was devoted to Verdi. He expressed that devotion in his letters with a humility and, indeed, obsequiousness that often verge on the ridiculous. At the time of the proposed commemoration of Rossini after his death in 1868, Mariani was chosen to conduct the Requiem Mass, to which, at Verdi's instigation, the leading Italian composers of the day were to contribute. Unfortunately, as so often happens with such affairs when organized by a committee, things went wrong. Verdi, who was not on the committee, saw his idealistic scheme falling to the ground through lack of energy and co-operation on the part of the various parties concerned. Verdi could never stand being thwarted, and in his frustration he visited his wrath on the unfortunate Mariani, the one man who was really blameless in the matter.

Mariani had arranged a commemoration of Rossini at Pesaro, the composer's birthplace, at which his *Stabat Mater* and Cherubini's *Requiem Mass* were performed. From Pesaro he wrote to

Verdi inviting him to attend the performances and, with characteristic humility, offering to vacate his own lodgings so that Verdi
should be made comfortable. In the same letter he suggested using
the choir he had assembled at Pesaro for the performance of the
composite *Requiem* in Bologna. Verdi seems to have been annoyed
by the rival commemoration of Rossini at Pesaro. To one
correspondent he wrote: 'It is an ill-arranged festival.' To
Mariani he replied on 19th August 1869, curtly declining his
invitation. He then launched into a series of complaints about the
Bologna project:

Do you mean to say that we've got to entreat you, in order to obtain
the chorus you have at Pesaro? First of all you should have understood
before now that my *ego* has vanished, that now I am nothing but a pen
to write as well as may be a few notes, and a hand to offer my obol for
the effectuation of this *National Celebration*. Next I'll tell you that
nobody should have to entreat or be entreated, because a duty is involved
that all the artists must and should perform.

I have never been able to discover whether the project of the Mass for
Rossini has had the good fortune to be approved by you. . . . A man,
a great artist, who marks an epoch, dies: one individual or another
invites his contemporaries to honour that man, and in him our art. . . .
What does it matter, then, that the composition lacks unity? What
does it matter that the vanity of this or that performer is not satisfied? . . .

If this solemn ceremony takes place, we shall indubitably have done
something good, artistic and patriotic. If it doesn't, we shall have
shown once more that we act only when our own interest and vanity are
rewarded.

With all this we may agree. But why was this lecture addressed
to Mariani, the one man who seems really to have worked
whole-heartedly in the cause of the Rossini Mass? Unless there
was more reason for suspecting Mariani's lukewarmness than appears
in the correspondence; unless, perhaps, Mariani had pointed out
the drawbacks of a composite work, we can only conclude that
Verdi was piqued by the evident success of the commemoration at
Pesaro and correspondingly annoyed by the evident obstacles to
the fulfilment of his own project. He then imagined that Mariani,

too, was in league against him. For that there is really no excu
But there had been reproachful letters to Mariani previously on
subject of his lack of decision, and of his breach of contract w
the Genoa Opera in order to conduct at Bologna. This lack
reliability in Mariani's character may have suggested to Verdi
idea that he was also not to be trusted in the matter of the Ross
Mass. But there is really no excuse for the tone of lofty scorn
which his rebuke is couched.

There is even less excuse for some of the later letters to Maria
which are incredibly offensive. Verdi wanted Mariani to cond
the first performance of *Aida* at Cairo. But by 1871 Mariani v
already so ill that he felt unable to undertake the journey. Ver
who was something of a hypochondriac, seems to have been una
(as is the way with hypochondriacs) to credit the validity
Mariani's excuse. He testily accused him in public of breaki
his word, from which it would appear that at some point Mariar
objection had been overborne. He certainly temporized, much
Verdi's annoyance, before coming to a final decision. That b
Verdi and his wife believed Mariani to be untrustworthy
evident from the indictment drawn up by Giuseppina in
letter-book. The heads of his offence include, besides
'*Mascherade* about going to Cairo to conduct *Aida*,' the Mass
Bologna, 'the generally unknown but not less infamous a
cowardly underhand dealings and lies concerning his old and n
mistresses, and the continual deception of la Stolz' and 'his sor
avarice when his vanity is not in question.' It is not an agreea
portrait, and we need not be surprised that the Verdis both regar
Mariani's action in conducting the performances of *Lohengrin*
Bologna, the first in Italy, as a deliberate defection to the ene
camp. Instead of directing *Aida* in Cairo, Mariani preferred
devote himself to Wagner—so they thought at Sant' Agata. T
this reading of the situation was mistaken is proved by Maria
letters at the time, in which his admiration for Wagner is sho
to be well this side of idolatry. He was, quite simply, the c
ductor engaged for the season at Bologna and *Lohengrin* was to
one of the works performed.

Supplements

SUPPLEMENT III

(See page 198)

SOME biographers have attributed Verdi's quarrel with Mariani to a jealous rivalry over the singer, Teresa Stolz. Others, suppressing inconvenient evidence, have blackened Mariani's character beyond his deserts. During the years before *Aida*, Stolz was Mariani's mistress and when the Verdis visited Genoa they occupied apartments in the Palazzo Sauli, where Mariani also had a flat. What more natural than that, as other musicians have done, Verdi should have fallen in love with the singer who did him so much credit and that there should be quarrels with the jealous conductor, who turned against his friend in a fit of pique when deserted by his mistress, and to spite him became an ardent Wagnerite? The scandal was ventilated in a 'news story' published in 1875 in the Florentine *Rivista Indipendente*, which surpassed in scurrility and offensiveness even the salacious efforts of the gossip writers of to-day. The 'exposure' was introduced by a hypocritical paragraph about telling the public 'the truth without passion or prejudice.'

The true facts of the relationship between Verdi, Teresa Stolz and Mariani are not so simple or so romantic as the scandalmongers suggested. The singer was Mariani's mistress and Mariani had promised to marry her. On this understanding Stolz entrusted to him a large part of her savings, but Mariani, who seems to have been incapable of decisive action, kept on putting off the marriage. Moreover, he was at the same time carrying on a love affair with a married woman, the Marchesa Teresa Pallavicino Negrotto, a member of the Sauli family from whom the Palazzo Sauli was rented. The Verdis were, both of them, fully aware of Mariani's behaviour and seem to have persuaded the singer to break off relations with him. After some difficulty she got her money back.

To a man of Verdi's probity Mariani's conduct was unforgivable. Since the coolness between them at the time of the project

317

for the Rossini *Requiem* there had been a reconciliation, but their relations were never again on the old familiar footing. As we have seen, Mariani's refusal to go to Cairo to conduct *Aida* caused offence, for Verdi refused to believe in the validity of Mariani's excuse—the bad state of his health. Now came a final breach. The Verdis moved to other quarters when they were in Genoa. There was an unhappy final encounter at Bologna in 1871, whither Verdi went to hear a performance of *Lohengrin* under Mariani's direction. By a mischance the conductor was at the station, meeting someone else, when Verdi arrived. He was quite brutally snubbed when he humbly offered to help Verdi with his luggage, and there was further offence when, through no fault of Mariani's, Verdi's presence in the theatre inevitably became known, much to his annoyance. Mariani was evidently put out by his unfortunate encounter with Verdi earlier in the day, and the singers had an attack of nerves caused by the presence of the *maestro*. These facts should be taken into account when considering Verdi's annotations in his score, some of which are quoted in Chapter XV, p. 245.[1] Mariani was already mortally ill with cancer, from which he died two years later, in 1873. Even then Verdi did not relent. He sent a formal message of condolence, but did not attend the funeral. His only comment was: 'What a loss to Art!'

Verdi cannot be acquitted of insensitiveness and even downright cruelty in his treatment of Mariani, though there were faults on his side too. At least Mariani can be acquitted of transferring his enthusiasm from Verdi to Wagner out of jealous pique on account of Teresa Stolz. It was simply a matter of commercial rivalry between the publishing firms of Ricordi and Lucca, the latter being Wagner's Italian agent and the instigator of the production of *Lohengrin* at Bologna.

Moreover, up to the time of the production of *Aida* there was not a jot of evidence that Verdi took any special interest in Teresa Stolz. A few years later there is *some* evidence of an attachment. This is not contained in any communications between them. The

[1] Mariani's own account of these incidents is quoted in Walker's *The Man Verdi*, pp. 381–2.

singer's letters to Verdi are full of affection, but it is the affection of mutual friendship and admiration, not of passionate love. Verdi's to her are no more than brief, exclamatory notes, for instance:

Content! Happy, most happy! I'll write on Monday and tell you many, many things. Farewell, farewell, and always farewell!

This might, if other evidence existed, be interpreted as amorous ecstasy, were it not, as Frank Walker observes, exactly in the same enigmatic style as the notes he wrote to society ladies in Milan in the very early years. Moreover—a point that cannot be made in translation—he never used in his letters to Stolz the intimate *tu* (thou) but always the plural *voi*, except in one note written after Giuseppina's death. Stolz addressed him even more formally in the third person, *lei*.

The evidence adduced by Walker to suggest that there was something more than friendship between the composer and the singer consists of a few draft letters and diary notes in Giuseppina's letter-book, the more significant of which were suppressed or lightly skated over by Luzio and other Italian writers. From these it is clear that Giuseppina at least thought she had cause to resent her husband's relations with Teresa Stolz, with whom she none the less carried on a most amicable correspondence. On 21st April 1876, when all three were in Paris for the first performance of *Aida* at the Opera, Giuseppina drafted a letter to Verdi beginning:

' It didn't seem to me a fitting day for you to pay a call on a lady who is neither your daughter, your sister, nor your wife!' The observation escaped me and I perceived at once that you were annoyed. . . . as she's not ill and there's no performance, it seemed to me you could spend twenty-four hours without seeing the said lady . . .

She goes on to protest that she had never failed in courtesy and friendliness to the lady in question, and in effect demands to know whether 'the febrile periods of assiduity' that had occurred since 1872 have any serious meaning. 'If there's nothing in it,' she continues, 'be more calm in your attentions. . . . Think sometimes that I, your wife, despising past rumours, am living at this very moment *à trois*, and that I have the right to ask, if not for your caresses, at least for your consideration. Is that too much?'[1]

We do not know what reply she received to this protest. We do know that six months later, in October, Giuseppina drafted another letter (Frank Walker suggests that it was written from her sister's house at Cremona) beginning:

Since fate has willed that that which was my whole happiness should now be irreparably lost . . .

Teresa Stolz was staying at Sant' Agata at this time, and it looks as if the strain of a real *ménage à trois* had been too much for Giuseppina. Yet there was no irreparable breach between them. After a year or more of acute unhappiness the cloud seems to have lifted. Possibly Verdi's infatuation for the singer—for such there must have been, whether she became his mistress or not—passed away. The idyllic atmosphere returned to Sant' Agata and the two women remained, if one may judge from their correspondence, firm friends.

It is an old story, from which Verdi does not emerge with credit. He could be ruthless and tyrannical in his relations with his wife and his domestic servants, even as he could be unforgiving to those who offended him and implacable in defence of his rights. This is a dark and unpleasant facet of a character whose other aspects shine bright with personal probity, with generosity of feeling, with humility in the presence of those he respected and with integrity in his own artistic creation.

[1] See *The Man Verdi*, pp. 431–2.

APPENDICES

APPENDIX A

CALENDAR

(Figures in brackets denote the age reached by the person mentioned during the year in question.)

Year	Age	Life	Contemporary Musicians
1813		Giuseppe Fortunino Francesco Verdi born, Oct. 10, at Le Roncole, near Busseto, in the Duchy of Parma, son of Carlo Verdi, a poor innkeeper and grocer.	Dargomizhsky born, Feb. 2/14; Grétry (72) dies, Sept. 24; Macfarren born, March 2; Petrella born, Dec. 1; Wagner born, May 22.

Asioli aged 44; Auber 31; Baini 38; Balfe 5; Basily 47; Beethoven 43; Bellini 12; Benelli 42; Berlioz 10; Boïeldieu 38; Cambini 67; Carafa 26; Cherubini 53; Chopin 4; Clementi 61; Coccia 31; Coppola 20; Donizetti 16; Field 31; Fioravanti 49; Generali 30; Glinka 10; Gossec 79; Halévy 14; Hérold 22; Hummel 35; Jannaconi 72; Lesueur 53; Liszt 2; Marschner 18; Mayr 50; Méhul 50; Mendelssohn 4; Mercadante 18; Meyerbeer 22; Morlacchi 29; Nicolai 3; Pacini 17; Paer 42; Paisiello 72; Raimondi 27;

Verdi

Year	Age	Life	Contemporary Musicians
			Ricci (F.) 4; Ricci (L.) 8; Rossi 3; Rossini 21; Salieri 63; Schubert 16; Schumann 3; Spohr 29; Spontini 39; Tadolini *c.* 28; Vaccai 23; Viotti 60; Weber 27; Zingarelli 61.
1814	1	Italy invaded by Russian and Austrian troops. V.'s mother takes refuge in the church at Le Roncole with her baby and hides in the belfry.	
1815	2		Heller born, May 15.
1816	3		Jannaconi (75) dies, March 16; Paisiello (75) dies, June 5.
1817	4		Gade born, Feb. 22; Mabellini born, April 2; Méhul (54) dies, Oct. 18; Pedrotti born, Nov. 12.
1818	5		Bazzini born, March 11; Gounod born, June 17.
1819	6	Shows a great liking for the barrel organ he hears in the village streets and listens eagerly to travelling musicians who visit his father's inn.	Offenbach born, June 21.
1820	7	Becomes a chorister at the local church. The resident organist teaches him his instrument and an old spinet presented him by a priest.	Serov born, Jan. 11/23; Vieuxtemps born, Feb. 20.
1821	8		
1822	9	Makes rapid progress.	Franck born, Dec. 10; Raff born, May 27.
1823	10	Deputizes for his master at the church and is later ap-	Lalo born, Jan. 27; Reyer born, Dec. 1.

Year	Age	Life	Contemporary Musicians
		pointed organist; but his father sends him to Busseto for some kind of general education. He lodges there with the cobbler Pugnatta, a friend of his father's.	
1824	11	Walks to Le Roncole once or twice a week to carry out his organist's duties.	Bruckner born, Sept. 4; Cornelius born, Dec. 24; Smetana born, March 2; Viotti (71) dies, March 3.
1825	12	School at Busseto continued. His organist's salary at Le Roncole is increased.	Cambini (79) dies; Salieri (75) dies, May 7; Strauss (J. ii) born, Oct. 25.
1826	13	Antonio Barezzi, a merchant at Busseto and a friend of his father's, takes V. into his business. Barezzi is president of the Philharmonic Society, whose rehearsals, under Provesi (63), the cathedral organist, are held at his house. V. learns much from listening to them.	Weber (40) dies, June 4/5.
1827	14	Copies scores from the library of the Busseto Philharmonic Society. Provesi (64) offers to give him lessons, and he is allowed to practise on the piano of Barezzi's daughter Margherita (13).	Beethoven (57) dies, March 26.
1828	15	Overture by V. performed by the Busseto Philharmonic Society, Easter. He composes marches for military band, in which he plays the bass drum.	Cagnoni born, Feb. 8; Schubert (31) dies, Nov. 19.
1829	16	Provesi (66), too old to	Gossec (95) dies, Feb. 16.

Year	Age	Life	Contemporary Musicians

conduct the Philharmonic Society unaided, engages V. to assist him. He composes for the Society and produces a *sinfonia*.

1830 17 More orchestral music composed.

Benelli (59) dies, Aug. 16; Goldmark born, May 18; Rubinstein born, Nov. 16/28.

1831 18 Barezzi proposes sending V. to Milan with a scholarship from the Monte di Pietà e d' Abbondanza di Busseto, supplemented by an allowance of his own.

Marchetti born, Feb. 26.

1832 19 V. is examined for admittance at the Conservatorio, but is rejected as over age. Rolla, the conductor at the Teatro alla Scala, advises him to seek instruction from Lavigna, the *maestro al cembalo* at that theatre. While studying under Lavigna, V. hears many operas at the Scala and composes piano pieces, overtures, cantatas, etc.

Asioli (63) dies, May 18; Clementi (80) dies, March 10; Generali(49)dies, Nov. 3.

1833 20 Having deputized as conductor at a performance of Haydn's *Creation* by the Philharmonic Society in Milan, he is engaged to compose an opera for that organization. Marches for the religious processions at Busseto composed. On the death of Provesi (70) there,

Brahms born, May 7; Hérold (42) dies, Jan. 19.

324

Year	Age	Life	Contemporary Musicians
		V. hopes to succeed to Provesi's appointments.	
1834	21	The ecclesiastical council appoints a mediocre musician, Giovanni Ferrari, as organist in opposition to the Philharmonic Society, who give V. an allowance of 300 lire for three years. Returns to Busseto and lives at Barezzi's house again. Composition of the opera for Milan progresses and he still writes marches for the town band.	Boïeldieu (59) dies, Oct. 8; Borodin born, Oct. 30/Nov. 12; Ponchielli born, Sept. 1.
1835	22	The cathedral having banned V.'s music, it is performed at other churches and draws so many people that the cathedral gradually becomes deserted.	Bellini (34) dies, Sept. 24; Cui born, Jan. 6/18; Saint-Saëns born, Oct. 9.
1836	23	Marriage to Margherita Barezzi (18). Friendship with Temistocle Solera, with whom he puts the opera, *Oberto, Conte di San Bonifacio*, into shape; but the Teatro Filodrammatico is now unable to produce it.	Balakirev born, Dec. 31 (O.S.).
1837	24	Massini, the former *maestro* of the Società, recommends *Oberto* to the Teatro alla Scala. Birth of a son, Icilio.	Field (55) dies, Jan. 11; Fioravanti (73) dies, June 16; Lesueur (77) dies, Oct. 6; Zingarelli (85) dies, May 5.
1838	25	Having fulfilled his three years' engagement at Busseto, V. moves to Milan with his family and takes the finished opera with him.	Bizet born, Oct. 25; Bruch born, Jan. 6.

Year	*Age*	*Life*	*Contemporary Musicians*

The Scala accepts *Oberto.*
6 Romances for voice and
piano composed. His in-
fant daughter, Virginia, dies
at Busseto.

1839 26 *Oberto* produced at the   Mussorgsky born, March
Scala, Nov. 17, with a   9/21; Paer (68) dies, May 3.
moderate but lasting suc-
cess. The publisher Gio-
vanni Ricordi (54) makes
V. an offer for the score.
Bartolomeo Merelli, the
director of the Scala and
manager of the Imperial
Opera in Vienna, enters
into an agreement with V.
for the production of three
operas. Songs for bass,
L' esule and *La seduzione,*
and a *Notturno* for soprano,
tenor, bass and flute composed. Death of Icilio, V.'s
son, at Milan.

1840 27 Opera, *Il proscritto,* con-   Faccio born, March 8; Götz
sidered, but deferred when   born, Dec. 17; Svendsen
Merelli suddenly asks him for   born, Sept. 3; Tchaikovsky
a comic opera that is urgently   born, April 25/May 7.
required. A libretto pre-
viously set by Gyrowetz
(77), *Il finto Stanislao,* is
chosen and renamed *Un
giorno di regno.* His wife
dies, June 18. In spite of
these successive losses, V. is
obliged to proceed with his
comic opera. Production of
Un giorno di regno, Sept. 5.
It is a complete failure. V.

Year	Age	Life	Contemporary Musicians
		decides to give up composition and asks Merelli to release him from his contract.	
1841	28	Merelli shows V. the libretto of Solera's *Nabucodonosor* (*Nabucco*), and he is impressed in spite of his determination never to compose again. At Merelli's urgent request he agrees at least to take it home with him. *Nabucco* finished, autumn.	Chabrier born, Jan. 18; Dvořák born, Sept. 8; Morlacchi (57) dies, Oct. 28; Pedrell born, Feb. 19.
1842	29	Production of *Nabucco* at the Scala, March 9. It has an immense success in spite of a production patched up from old stock scenery and costumes. Giuseppina Strepponi (27) is in the cast. The management decides to commission the *opera d'obbligo* for the following season from V. and hands him a contract with a blank space left for the fee, to be inserted by himself. Strepponi advises him to ask the fee received by Bellini for *Norma*. The work chosen is *I Lombardi alla prima crociata,* Solera's libretto being based on a poem of the same name by Tommaso Grossi (51).	Boito born, Feb. 24; Cherubini (82) dies, March 15; Massenet born, May 12; Sullivan born, May 13.
1843	30	Production of *I Lombardi* prohibited by the Archbishop of Milan on account of the religious ceremonies to be staged; but the chief of	Grieg born, June 15; Sgambati born, May 28.

Year	Age	Life	Contemporary Musicians
		police, Torresani, allows it after a few trifling altera- tions. The opera produced at the Scala, Feb. 11. It has a great success, and the chorus, 'O mia patria,' provokes a patriotic demonstration against Austria. Opera, *Ernani*, composed for Venice to a libretto by Francesco Maria Piave based on Victor Hugo's (41) drama, *Hernani*.	
1844	31	Production of *Ernani* at the Teatro La Fenice, Venice, March 9. It has an enormous success and is produced in fourteen other Italian cities during the year. Opera, *I due Foscari*, produced at the Tea- tro Argentina in Rome, Nov. 3, with moderate success.	Baini (69) dies, May 21; Rimsky - Korsakov born, March 6/18.
1845	32	Opera, *Giovanna d'Arco*, set to Solera's libretto based on Schiller's *Jungfrau von Or- leans*, produced at the Scala in Milan, Feb. 15. Opera, *Alzira*, to a libretto by Cammarano based on Vol- taire's *Alzire*, produced without success at the Teatro San Carlo in Naples, Aug. 12. 6 Romances (2nd set) for voice and piano.	Fauré born, May 13; Mayr (82) dies, Dec. 2.
1846	33	Visit to Paris, Jan., for the production of *Ernani* at the Théâtre Italien under the title of *Il proscritto*. The new version contains some altera-	Weigl (80) dies, Feb. 3.

Year	Age	Life	Contemporary Musicians

tions exacted by Victor Hugo (44) who has taken exception to what he considered the mutilation of his drama. Production of the opera, *Attila*, at the Teatro La Fenice in Venice.

1847   34   Meeting with Andrea Maffei, who provides him with the libretto of *I Masnadieri*, after Schiller's *Die Räuber*, for an opera commissioned by Benjamin Lumley (36) in London. Visit to Florence, where the opera, *Macbeth*, based on Shakespeare by Piave, is to be produced. *Macbeth* produced at the Teatro della Pergola in Florence, March 14. Visit to London, where *I Masnadieri* is produced at Her Majesty's Theatre, July 22. Jenny Lind (27) and Lablache (53) are in the cast. It has only three performances, the third conducted by Balfe (40), and V., disappointed, leaves for Paris. A French adaptation of *I Lombardi*, entitled *Jérusalem*, produced at the Opéra, Nov. 26, with some new music added to it. Louis-Philippe (70) has two acts performed at the Tuileries and creates V. a Chevalier of the Legion of Honour.

Mackenzie born, Aug. 22; Mendelssohn (38) dies, Nov. 4.

Year	Age	Life	Contemporary Musicians
1848	35	On the outbreak of the Revolution, V. returns to Milan, March, but soon returns to Paris to compose *La battaglia di Legnano* for Rome. He goes to Trieste, autumn, where *Il Corsaro*, set to a libretto based by Piave on Byron's *The Corsair*, is produced, Oct. 25, without success. Departure for Rome, late Oct. War hymn, *Suona la tromba*, composed.	Donizetti (51) dies, April 8; Duparc born, Jan. 21; Mancinelli born, Feb. 5; Parry born, Feb. 27; Vaccai (58) dies, Aug. 5.
1849	36	Production of *La battaglia di Legnano* at the Teatro Argentina in Rome. The patriotic subject of Cammarano's libretto is greatly to the taste of a public living in an atmosphere of revolution. Cammarano provides V. with another libretto, *Luisa Miller*, based on Schiller's *Kabale und Liebe*. Departure for Paris, Feb., with Giuseppina Strepponi (34), whose friendship with him has now grown into a lasting intimacy. Cholera having broken out in Paris, he returns to Italy, going first to Rome and then to Naples, where *Luisa Miller* is produced, after many difficulties, Dec. 8. V. moves to the villa and estate of Sant' Agata near Busseto,	Chopin (40) dies, Oct. 17; Nicolai (39) dies, May 11.

Year	Age	Life	Contemporary Musicians
		which he had acquired in the previous year.	
1850	37	Spending his time between Busseto and Venice, V. composes the opera, *Stiffelio*, to a libretto by Piave, who also writes that of *La Maledizione* (*Rigoletto*), based on Victor Hugo's (48) *Le Roi s'amuse* and commissioned by the Teatro La Fenice. Production of *Stiffelio* at the Teatro Grande, Trieste, without success. The Austrian Government prohibits *La Maledizione* on account of alleged republican tendencies. After modifications in the plot and the change of the title to *Rigoletto, Buffone di Corte*, the production of the opera is allowed. V. retires to Busseto and completes the opera in forty days.	Basily (84) dies, March 25; Scontrino born, May 17.
1851	38	Production of *Rigoletto* at the Teatro La Fenice in Venice, March 11, with enormous success.	d'Indy born, March 27; Lortzing (48) dies, Jan. 21; Spontini (77) dies, Jan. 14.
1852	39	Composition of *Il Trovatore* to a libretto by Cammarano based on *El Trovador* by Antonio Garcia Guttiérrez, and of *La Traviata*, drawn by Piave from *La Dame aux camélias* by Dumas, jun. (28). Letter to his father-in-law, Barezzi, defending his union	Stanford born, Sept. 30.

Year	Age	Life	Contemporary Musicians
		with Giuseppina Strepponi (37), which has aroused hostile comment at Busseto.	
1853	40	*Il Trovatore* produced at the Teatro Apollo in Rome, Jan. 19, with an unparalleled success. *La Traviata* produced at the Teatro La Fenice in Venice, March 6. It is an utter failure. V. commissions a libretto on Shakespeare's *King Lear* from Antonio Somma, but does not progress far with the composition. *La Traviata* again produced later in the year at the Teatro San Benedetto in Venice, this time with success.	Raimondi (67) dies, Oct. 30.
1854	41	The Paris Opéra having commissioned a work for the Exhibition of 1855, V. goes to Paris, early summer, to discuss the libretto of *Les Vêpres siciliennes* with Scribe (63) and Duveyrier. The opera is finished, autumn, but the rehearsals are delayed at the Opéra. Sophie Cruvelli (28), cast for the principal female part, disappears mysteriously, early Oct. Cruvelli returns, Nov., and rehearsals are resumed.	Catalani born, June 19; Humperdinck born, Sept. 1; Janáček born, July 4; Smareglia born, May 5.
1855	42	*Les Vêpres siciliennes* produced at the Paris Opéra, June 13. Visit to England and return to Italy, summer.	Chausson born, Jan 21; Liadov born, April 29/ May 11.

Year	Age	Life	Contemporary Musicians
		Composition of *King Lear*, to which V. feels he is not doing justice, abandoned.	
1856	43	Production of the Italian version of *Les Vêpres siciliennes*, entitled *Giovanna di Guzman*, at the Teatro alla Scala in Milan. The libretto is recast in deference to the censor. Opera, *Simon Boccanegra*, composed for the Teatro La Fenice in Venice.	Martucci born, Jan. 6; Schumann (46) dies, July 29; Taneiev born, Nov. 13/25.
1857	44	Production of *Simon Boccanegra* in Venice, March 12. *Aroldo*, a revised version of *Stiffelio* (see 1850), at the Nuovo Teatro, Rimini, without success. Composition of *Un ballo in maschera*, to a libretto imitated from Scribe's (66) *Gustave III*, composed by Auber (75) in 1833. It is commissioned by the Teatro San Carlo in Naples.	Bruneau born, March 1; Elgar born, June 2; Glinka (54) dies, Feb. 15.
1858	45	The censor in Naples requires important alterations in *Un ballo in maschera*. V. refuses to comply and the Teatro San Carlo threatens an action against him; but the whole populace takes his part and he is released from his contract for fear of a revolution. The Teatro Apollo in Rome then secures the opera, and when the	Leoncavallo born, March 8; Puccini born, June 22.

Year	Age	*Life*	*Contemporary Musicians*
		pontifical censor there has obtained a change of scene to Boston, it is put into rehearsal.	
1859	46	Production of *Un ballo in maschera* in Rome, Feb. 17. Return to Busseto. V. legalizes his union with Giuseppina Strepponi (44) by marriage.	Ricci (L.) (54) dies, Dec. 31; Spohr (75) dies, Oct. 22.
1860	47	The Duchy of Parma decides by plebiscite to join the newly formed kingdom of Italy. V. appointed to represent Busseto in announcing the result to the king. Cavour (50) urges V. to become a member of the Chamber of Deputies, and he accepts from personal admiration of Cavour, who is anxious to have all the most prominent Italians of the day in the Chamber.	Albeniz born, May 29; Charpentier born, June 25; Franchetti born, Sept. 18; Mahler born, July 7; Wolf born, March 13.
1861	48	The Imperial Theatre at St Petersburg commissions an opera, and Piave constructs the libretto of *La forza del destino* on a drama by Angel de Saavedra, Duke of Rivas (69), *Don Alvaro o La fuerza del sino*. Visit to St Petersburg for the rehearsals of *La forza del destino*.	Bossi born, April 25; MacDowell born, Dec. 18; Marschner (66) dies, Dec. 14.
1862	49	Appointed to represent Italy at the International Exhibition in London, for which he composes an *Inno delle*	Debussy born, Aug. 22; Delius born, Jan. 29; Halévy (63) dies, March 17.

Year	Age	Life	Contemporary Musicians
		Nazioni. Visit to London, May, and performance of the Hymn at Her Majesty's Theatre, May 24, the production at the Crystal Palace in Hyde Park having been frustrated by the intrigues of Costa (54). Meeting with Auber (80), Meyerbeer (71) and Sterndale Bennett (46), who represent France, Germany and Great Britain respectively. Return to Italy and second visit to St Petersburg, where *La forza del destino* is produced, Nov. 10. Return to Busseto.	
1863	50	Visit to Paris for the revival of *Les Vêpres siciliennes.* At the rehearsal the orchestra is very recalcitrant and is supported by the conductor, Dietsch (55). V. refuses to have anything more to do with the production and Dietsch is placed on the retired list.	Mascagni born, Dec. 7.
1864	51	Elected member of the French Académie des Beaux-Arts in the place of Meyerbeer, June.	Meyerbeer (73) dies, May 2; Strauss (R.) born, June 11.
1865	52	*Macbeth* produced at the Theatre Lyrique there in a revised French version, April 21. Resignation from the Chamber of Deputies. During a visit to Paris in November the Opéra com-	Dukas born, Oct. 1; Glazunov born, July 29/Aug. 10; Orefice born, Aug. 27; Sibelius born, Dec. 8.

335

Year	Age	Life	Contemporary Musicians
		missions a French stage work, and V. obtains the libretto of *Don Carlo*, based on Schiller's drama, by Joseph Méry (67) and Camille du Locle. After his return home he begins the composition.	
1866	53	Visit to Paris with the finished composition of *Don Carlo*, Aug. The rehearsals are much delayed.	Busoni born, April 1; Cilea born, July 26.
1867	54	Receives news of his father's death, Jan., and his visit to Italy for the funeral again delays the opera. On his return Dantan (67) makes a bust of him for the foyer of the Opéra. Production of *Don Carlo* there, March 11. Napoleon III (59) and the Empress Eugénie (41) are present. Return to Italy in poor health, March. First Italian performance of *Don Carlo*, at the Teatro Communale, Bologna, Oct.	Giordano born, Aug. 27; Granados born, July 29; Pacini (71) dies, Dec. 6.
1868	55	Is approached by the Khedive of Egypt, Ismail Pasha (38), to write an opera for the Italian theatre to be built in Cairo. V. suggests that a *Requiem* should be composed in memory of Rossini by a number of Italian composers, end of year.	Bantock born, Aug. 7; Rossini (76) dies, Nov. 13; Sinigalia born, Aug. 14.
1869	56	Revised version of *La forza del destino* produced at the	Berlioz (66) dies, March 8; Dargomizhsky (56) dies,

Year	Age	Life	Contemporary Musicians
		Teatro alla Scala in Milan, Feb. 20. Negotiations with Cairo proceed. The subject of *Aida*, invented by the French Egyptologist, Auguste Mariette (48), is suggested. 'Libera me' for the *Requiem* for Rossini composed. Bazzini (51), Cagnoni (41), Coccia (87), Mabellini (52), Pedrotti (52), Petrella (56) and Ricci (60) contribute other portions. Mercadante (74) is unable to do so on account of blindness and infirmity. The performance never takes place, and they all withdraw their contributions. V. composes a *Stornello* for voice and piano.	Jan.; Pfitzner born, May 5; Roussel born, April 5.
1870	57	Libretto of *Aida* drawn up in French prose by Camille du Locle, who comes to Busseto, and turned into Italian verse by Antonio Ghislanzoni. V. refuses an invitation to Cairo to supervise the production in person. It is delayed by the elaborate preparations required, and the Franco-Prussian war keeps the scenery and dresses locked up in Paris.	Balfe (62) dies, Oct. 20; Mercadante (75) dies, Dec. 17; Novák born, Dec. 5; Schmitt born, Sept. 28.
1871	58	Is invited to become director of the Conservatorio in Naples in succession to Mercadante, but refuses, Jan.	Auber (89) dies, May 12; Scriabin born, Dec. 25 (O.S.); Serov (51) dies, Jan. 20/Feb. 1.

Year	Age	Life	Contemporary Musicians
		Production of *Aida* in Cairo, Dec. 24, in V.'s absence.	
1872	59	Production of *Aida,* for the first time in Italy, at the Teatro alla Scala in Milan, Feb. 7. An overture written to replace the short prelude was withdrawn by V. after the first rehearsal.	Carafa (85) dies, July 26; Perosi born, Dec. 20; Tadolini (*c.* 87) dies, Nov. 29; Vaughan Williams born, Oct. 12.
1873	60	String Quartet composed in Naples, where the rehearsals of *Aida* are delayed by the illness of Teresa Stolz (37). Offer to compose a *Requiem* in memory of Manzoni, who had died May 22, aged 88, accepted by the city council of Milan. Most of the work composed during a visit to France, autumn. He incorporates some of the 'Libera me' contributed to the *Requiem* for Rossini (*see* 1869).	Coccia (91) dies, April 13; Rachmaninov born, March 20/April 1; Reger born, March 19.
1874	61	On the first anniversary of Manzoni's death, May 22, the *Requiem* is performed at the church of San Marco in Milan under V.'s direction. Three performances at the Scala follow, the last two conducted by Faccio (34).	Cornelius (50) dies, Oct. 26; Holst born, Sept. 21; Schœnberg born, Sept. 13; Suk born, Jan. 4.
1875	62	Visits to Paris, London, and Vienna for performances of the *Requiem*. At Cologne he sees a performance of Schiller's *Fiesco,* and although he does not understand German	Bizet (37) dies, June 3; Montemezzi born, May 31; Ravel born, March 7.

Year	Age	Life	Contemporary Musicians
		he realizes that Piave's libretto of *Simon Boccanegra*, which was loosely based on it, was badly done, and plans a revised version. Victor Emmanuel II (55) creates V. a senator. V. takes his oath as senator, but still averse to politics, does not avail him-self of his seat.	
1876	63	Visit to Paris for the per-formance of *Aida* at the Théâtre Italien, April 22.	Alfano born, March 8; Falla born, Nov. 23; Götz (36) dies, Dec. 3; Wolf-Ferrari born, Jan. 12.
1877	64		Coppola (84) dies, Nov. 13; Dohnányi born, July 27; Petrella (64) dies, April 7; Ricci (F.) (68) dies, Dec. 10.
1878	65		
1879	66	Vaucorbeil (58), the new director of the Paris Opéra, visits V. at Busseto to obtain permission to produce *Aida* in French. V., who had been much offended by the be-haviour of the Opéra or-chestra in 1863, relents and even promises a new French work, provided that a good libretto can be found.	Bridge (Frank) born, Feb. 26; Ireland born, Aug. 13; Medtner born, Dec. 4; Respighi born, July 7; Scott (Cyril) born, Sept. 27.
1880	67	Boito (38) revises the libretto of *Simon Boccanegra*. Visit to Paris to conduct the first performance of *Aida* in French, March 22. Dinner given in V.'s honour by President Grévy (67). He is promoted to the rank of	Bloch born, July 24; Offenbach (61) dies, Oct. 4; Pizzetti born, Sept. 20; Pratella born, Feb. 1; Tom-masini born, Sept. 17.

Year	Age	Life	Contemporary Musicians
		Grand Officer in the Legion of Honour. *Ave Maria* for soprano and strings and *Pater Noster* for five voices produced at a concert in the Scala, Milan, April 18.	
1881	68	Production of the revised version of *Simon Boccanegra* at the Teatro alla Scala in Milan, March 24.	Alaleona born, Nov. 16; Bartók born, March 25; Miaskovsky born, April 8/20; Moussorgsky (42) dies, March 16/28; Vieuxtemps (61) dies, June 6.
1882	69	Begins to lead a very retired life.	Kodály born, Dec. 16; Malipiero born, March 18; Pick-Mangiagalli born, July 10; Raff (60) dies, June 24–5; Stravinsky born, June 5/17.
1883	70	Continues to live in retirement, occupied only with the management of his estate at Sant' Agata. He employs his great wealth in charitable gifts and the endowment of philanthropic institutions.	Bax born, Nov. 6; Casella born, July 25; Santoliquido born, Aug. 6; Szymanowski born, Sept. 21; Wagner (70) dies, Feb. 13; Webern born, Dec. 3; Zandonai born, May 28.
1884	71	Is invited to go and open the new theatre at Padua named after him, June, but, never anxious to show himself to the public, he declines.	Smetana (60) dies, May 12.
1885	72	Plans an opera on the subject of Shakespeare's *Othello* with a libretto by Boito (43), who frequently visits him in great secrecy, V. still declaring in public that he will not write another work for the stage. Composition of	Berg born, Feb. 7; Gui born, Sept. 14; Rossi (75) dies, May 5.

Year	Age	Life	Contemporary Musicians
		Otello begun, end of year. Sketches previously made at different times are used.	
1886	73	Composition of *Otello* finished. The work is still kept secret, and when the principal artists are engaged for it, they are made to promise to divulge no details of it or of its production. Death of V.'s friend and correspondent, Count Opprandino Arrivabene.	Liszt (75) dies, July 31; Ponchielli (52) dies, Jan. 16.
1887	74	Production of *Otello* at the Teatro alla Scala, Milan, Feb. 5. Faccio (47) conducts. V. having produced no new opera for fifteen years, is given an ovation unprecedented even in his career.	Borodin (53) dies, Feb. 16/28; Lualdi born, March 22.
1888	75	Rumours are spread that V. is engaged on another Shakespearian opera, on the subject of either *King Lear* or *Romeo and Juliet*.	
1889	76	Another rumour is that V. is to write a comic opera on one of Goldoni's comedies.	
1890	77	Composition of the opera, *Falstaff*, begun. The libretto is based by Boito (48) on Shakespeare's *Merry Wives of Windsor*.	Franck (68) dies, Nov. 8; Gade (73) dies, Dec. 21.
1891	78	Composition of *Falstaff* proceeds slowly.	Bliss born, Aug. 2; Delibes (55) dies, Jan. 16; Faccio (51) dies, July 23; Prokofiev born, April 11/23.

Verdi

Year	Age	Life	Contemporary Musicians
1892	79	*Falstaff* finished.	Franz (77) dies, Oct. 24; Honegger born, March 10; Lalo (69) dies, April 22; Milhaud born, Sept. 4.
1893	80	Production of *Falstaff* at the Teatro alla Scala, Milan, Feb. 9. A great demonstration of love and veneration for the veteran composer follows.	Catalani (39) dies, Aug. 7; Gounod (75) dies, Oct. 18; Pedrotti (76) dies, Oct. 16; Tchaikovsky (53) dies, Oct. 25/Nov. 6.
1894	81	In retirement at Sant' Agata.	Chabrier (53) dies, Sept. 13; Rubinstein (64) dies, Nov. 8/20.
1895	82		Castelnuovo-Tedesco born, April 3; Hindemith born, Nov. 16.
1896	83		Bruckner (72) dies, Oct. 11; Cagnoni (68) dies, April 30; Labroca born, Nov. 22.
1897	84	Death of V.'s second wife, *née* Giuseppina Strepponi (82).	Bazzini (79) dies, Feb. 10; Brahms (64) dies, April 3; Mabellini (80) dies, March 10.
1898	85	Publication of *Ave Maria* (on an 'enigmatic scale'), *Stabat Mater, Te Deum* and *Laudi alla Vergine Maria*.	Rieti born, Jan. 28.
1899	86	Three of these works, except the *Ave Maria*, performed at Turin under Arturo Toscanini (32).	Poulenc born, Jan. 7; Strauss (J. ii) (74) dies, June 3.
1900	87	After the assassination of King Humbert (56), Queen Margherita (45) writes a prayer, the composition of which V. sketches, but does not complete. He is becoming very weak.	Křenek born; Sullivan (58) dies, Nov. 22.

Appendix A—Calendar

		Life	Contemporary Musicians

Year Age — Life — Contemporary Musicians

1901 88 V. has a stroke, Jan. 21, and remains unconscious. He is given extreme unction, Jan. 24.
Verdi dies at the Hotel di Milano in Milan, Jan. 27.

Marchetti (70) dies, Jan. 18. Alaleona aged 20; Albeniz 41; Alfano 25; Arensky 40; Balakirev 65; Bantock 33; Bartók 20; Bax 18; Berg 16; Bliss 10; Bloch 21; Boito 59; Bossi 40; Bruch 63; Bruneau 44; Busoni 35; Casella 18; Castelnuovo-Tedesco 6; Charpentier 41; Cilea 35; Cui 66; Debussy 39; Delius 39; Dohnányi 24; Dukas 36; Duparc 53; Dvořák 60; Elgar 44; Falla 25; Fauré 56; Franchetti 41; Giordano 34; Glazunov 36; Goldmark 71; Granados 34; Grieg 57; Gui 16; Hindemith 6; Holst 27; Honegger 9; Humperdinck 47; d'Indy 50; Ireland 22; Janáček 47; Kodály 19; Labroca 5; Leoncavallo 43; Liadov 46; Lualdi 14; Mackenzie 54; Mahler 41; Malipiero 19; Mancinelli 53; Martucci 45; Mascagni 38; Massenet 59; Medtner 22; Miaskovsky 20; Milhaud 9; Montemezzi 26; Novák 31; Orefice 36; Parry 53; Pedrell 60; Perosi 29; Pfitzner 32; Pick-Mangiagalli 19; Pizzetti 21; Poulenc 2; Pratella 21; Prokofiev 10; Puccini 43; Rachmaninov 28; Ravel 26; Reger 28; Respighi 21; Reyer 78;

Verdi

Year	Age	Life	Contemporary Musicians
			Rieti 3; Rimsky-Korsakov 57; Roussel 32; Sabata 9; Saint-Saëns 67; Santoliquido 18; Schmitt 31; Schœnberg 27; Scontrino 51; Scott (Cyril) 22; Scriabin 30; Sgambati 58; Sibelius 36; Sinigaglia 33; Smareglia (47); Smyth (Ethel) 43; Stanford 49; Strauss (R.) 37; Stravinsky 19; Suk 27; Svendsen 61; Szymanowski 18; Taneiev 45; Tommasini 21; Vaughan Williams 29; Webern 18; Wolf 41; Wolf-Ferrari 25; Zandonai 18.

APPENDIX B

CATALOGUE OF WORKS

OPERAS

Title	Librettist	First Performance
Oberto, Conte di S. Bonifacio	Piazza and Solera	Milan, Nov. 17, 1839
Un giorno di regno (Il finto Stanislao)	Romani	Milan, Sept. 5, 1840
Nabucodonosor (Nabucco)	Solera	Milan, March 9, 1842
I Lombardi alla prima crociata	Solera	Milan, Feb. 11, 1843
Ernani	Piave	Venice, March 9, 1844
I due Foscari	Piave	Rome, Nov. 3, 1844
Giovanna d'Arco	Solera	Milan, Feb. 15, 1845
Alzira	Cammarano	Naples, Aug. 12, 1845
Attila	Solera	Venice, March 17, 1846
Macbeth	Piave	Florence, March 14, 1847
I masnadieri	Maffei	London, July 22, 1847
Jérusalem (I Lombardi revised)	Royer and Vaëz (French)	Paris, Nov. 26, 1847
Il corsaro	Piave	Trieste, Oct. 25, 1848
La battaglia di Legnano	Cammarano	Rome, Jan. 27, 1849
Luisa Miller	Cammarano	Naples, Dec. 8, 1849
Stiffelio	Piave	Trieste, Nov. 16, 1850
Rigoletto	Piave	Venice, March 11, 1851
Il Trovatore	Cammarano	Rome, Jan. 19, 1853
La Traviata	Piave	Venice, March 6, 1853
Les Vêpres siciliennes	Scribe and Duveyrier (French)	Paris, June 13, 1855
Simon Boccanegra	Piave	Venice, March 12, 1857
Aroldo (Stiffelio revised)	Piave	Rimini, Aug. 16, 1857
Un ballo in maschera	Somma	Rome, Feb. 17, 1859
La forza del destino	Piave	St Petersburg, Nov. 10, 1862

Verdi

Title	Librettist	First Performance
Macbeth (revised)	Nuitter and Beaumont (French)	Paris, April 21, 1865
Don Carlos	Méry and du Locle (French)	Paris, March 11, 1867
Aida	Ghislanzoni	Cairo, Dec. 24, 1871
Simon Boccanegra (revised)	Boito	Milan, March 24, 1881
Otello	Boito	Milan, Feb. 5, 1887
Falstaff	Boito	Milan, Feb. 9, 1893

CHORAL WORKS

Suona la tromba (Mameli), 1848.
Inno delle nazioni (Boito), for the London Exhibition, 1862.
Messa da Requiem, Milan, May 22, 1874.
Pater noster (Dante) *a 5 voci*, Milan, April 18, 1880.
Ave Maria, scala enigmatica armonizzata a 4 voci (S.A.T.B.), composed about 1889.
Satbat Mater, chorus and orchestra, Paris, April 7, 1898.
Laudi alla Vergine Maria (Dante) *a 4 voci bianche* (S.A.), Paris, April 7, 1898.
Te Deum, double chorus and orchestra, Paris, April 7, 1898.

SONGS

Sei romanze, published 1838.
L'esule, song for bass, 1839.
La seduzione, song for bass, 1839.
Notturno a 3 voci, 'Guarda che bianca luna' (S.T.B.), 1839.
Album di sei romanze, 1845.
Il poveretto, romanza, 1847.
Tu dici che non m' ami, 1869, for the album in honour of Piave.
Ave Maria (Dante), for soprano and strings, 1880.

CHAMBER MUSIC

String Quartet in E minor, composed at Naples, March 1873.

APPENDIX C

PERSONALIA

Andrade, Francisco d' (1859–1921), Portuguese baritone, who made his first appearance in 1882 and sang in opera all over Europe.

Auber, Daniel François Esprit (1782–1871), French operatic composer. Director of the Paris Conservatoire from 1842 to his death. His most famous works are *La Muette de Portici* and *Fra Diavolo*.

Barezzi, Margherita (1814–40), daughter of Antonio Barezzi, merchant of Busseto and Verdi's patron. Verdi's first wife.

Basily (or *Basili*), *Francesco* (1767–1850), Italian singer and composer, became director of the Milan Conservatorio in 1827. *Maestro di cappella* at St Peter's in Rome from 1837.

Bellaigue, Camille (1858–1930), French critic and pianist, attached to the *Revue des Deux Mondes* from 1885. One of Verdi's early biographers.

Boito, Arrigo (1842–1918), Italian poet and composer, studied at the Milan Conservatorio and produced his opera, *Mefistofele*, at the Scala there in 1868. He was Verdi's librettist for *Otello* and *Falstaff*, and revised *Simon Boccanegra* for him.

Bottesini, Giovanni (1821–89), Italian double bass player, conductor and composer. Was engaged successively in Havana, Paris, Palermo, Barcelona and Cairo, and composed some operas as well as many works for his instrument. Conducted première of *Aida*.

Bülow, Hans von (1830–94), German pianist and conductor, first husband of Cosima Wagner.

Cammarano, Salvatore (1801–51), Neapolitan theatre poet, librettist of Donizetti's *Lucia di Lammermoor*; from 1845 collaborated with Verdi and, among others, wrote the libretto of *Il Trovatore*.

Catalani, Alfredo (1854–93), Italian opera composer. *La Wally*, produced in 1892, is his best-known work.

Chorley, Henry Fothergill (1808–72), English journalist, novelist and music critic in London.

Cimarosa, Domenico (1749–1801), Italian opera composer, studied at

Naples and produced his first opera there in 1772. Went to the court of Catherine II of Russia in 1787.

Costa, Michael (Michele) (1808–84), English conductor and composer of Italian birth. He settled in England in 1829.

Cruvelli (Crüwell), Johanne Sophie Charlotte (1826–1907), German operatic soprano, made her first appearance in 1847, at Venice, first sang in Paris in 1851 and was engaged by the Opéra in 1854.

Davison, James William (1813–85), music critic in London, attached to *The Times*, 1846–79.

Delacroix, Eugène (1799–1863), eminent French painter of the romantic school.

Delfico, Melchiorre. See Appendix D.

Dumas, Alexandre, (1824–95) son of A. Dumas the novelist; author of the famous romantic drama, *La Dame aux camélias,* on which *La Traviata* was based. Dumas disapproved of this operatic version of his play.

Faccio, Franco (1840–91), Italian conductor and composer, studied at the Milan Conservatorio and produced his first opera there in 1863. Boito (q.v.) wrote a libretto based on *Hamlet* for him.

Ghislanzoni, Antonio (1824–93), Italian operatic baritone, novelist, musical editor and librettist of *Aida*, edited the *Gazzetta musicale* of Milan.

Grisi, Giulia (1811–69), Italian soprano singer, first appeared at the age of seventeen in Rossini's *Zelmira*, and was engaged for Milan in 1829. She was leading soprano at the Théâtre des Italiens in Paris, 1832–49, and frequently visited London. She married Mario (q.v.) in 1844.

Gutiérrez, Antonio Garcia (1812–84), Spanish dramatist, studied medicine, but began a literary career by translating French plays and produced his first play, *El Trovador,* in 1836.

Halévy, Jacques François Fromental Élie (1799–1862), French operatic composer, whose most famous work is *La Juive,* produced in Paris in 1835.

Ingres, Jean Auguste Dominique (1780–1867), famous French painter.

Ivogün, Maria (born 1891), Hungarian soprano, studied in Vienna and made her first appearance in 1813, at Munich. She excels in coloratura parts.

Joachim, Joseph (1831–1907), Hungarian violinist and composer living

successively at Leipzig, Weimar, Hanover and Berlin, frequent
visitor to England, founder of the Joachim Quartet in 1869, and head
of one of the music departments of the Royal Academy of Arts in
Berlin.

Lind, Jenny (1820–87), Swedish soprano singer settled in England, made
her first appearance in 1838, at Stockholm.

Loewe, Johanna Sophie (1816–66), German soprano singer who began
her career in Vienna and Berlin.

Lumley, Benjamin (1811–75), English operatic manager, in charge of
Her Majesty's Theatre in London intermittently from 1841 to 1859.

Manzoni, Alessandro (1785–1873), Italian poet and novelist, one of the
classics of Italian literature, whose most famous work is the novel
I promessi sposi.

Marcello, Benedetto (1686–1739), Italian composer, pupil of Lotti and
Gasparini in Venice. Of noble birth, he held no musical posts,
but some important government appointments.

Mariani, Angelo (1822–73), Italian conductor, made his first performance
in opera at Messina in 1844. He introduced Wagner's *Lohengrin*
to Italy, at Bologna in 1871.

Mariette, Auguste Édouard (*Mariette Bey*, 1821–81), French Egyptologist,
founder of the museum at Cairo.

Mario, Giovanni Matteo (1810–83), Italian operatic tenor, trained as a
soldier at first, but was persuaded to take to singing in spite of his
noble birth. He made his first appearance in 1838, in Paris. Married
Grisi (q.v.) in 1844.

Maurel, Victor (1848–1923), French baritone singer, went to the school
of music at Marseilles, his native town, after first studying archi-
tecture, and later to the Paris Conservatoire. Made his first appearance in 1867, at the Paris Opéra, but later became as much at home
in Italian as in French opera.

Mercadante, Giuseppe Saverio Raffaello (1795–1870), Italian composer,
pupil of Zingarelli at Naples, prolific writer of operas, church music
and various vocal and instrumental works.

Moriani, Napoleone (1808–78), Italian operatic tenor who made his
first appearance in 1833, at Pavia.

Muzio, Emmanuele (1821–90), the son of a shoemaker of Genoese extraction, was born in the province of Parma. From 1826 he lived at Busseto, where he studied with Verdi's music-master, Provesi, and later with Verdi himself. He became a close friend of Verdi, accompanied him as secretary during his early visits to Paris and London, and looked after his interests there. He settled late in life in Paris, where he acted as Verdi's agent. As a conductor he achieved considerable distinction.

Paisiello, Giovanni (1741–1816), Italian opera composer, student at the Conservatorio di San Onofrio at Naples, had a great success all over Italy, went to the court of Catherine II of Russia, 1776–84, then made his reputation in Vienna and London, and returned to Naples.

Patti, Adelina (1843–1919), Italian operatic soprano born in Spain, made her first appearance at the age of seven, in New York, and after a period of study reappeared there in 1859. She came to London in 1861 and sang at Covent Garden for the first time, and in Paris in 1862. She sang for the last time in 1914.

Piave, Francesco (1811–76), a Venetian, originally trained for the law but attracted to the theatre; resident poet and stage manager at the Fenice Theatre, Venice, in 1843, when he met Verdi, for whom he wrote the libretto of *Ernani*; from that time his constant friend and collaborator; a poet of little distinction but great willingness.

Piccolomini, Marietta (1834–99), Italian operatic soprano, made her first appearance in 1852, at Florence, and first visited England in 1856.

Porpora, Niccola Antonio (1686–1767), Italian composer, theorist and teacher of singing.

Reszke, Édouard de (1853–1917), Polish operatic bass, made his first appearance in Verdi's *Aida* at the Théâtre des Italiens in Paris in 1876.

Reszke, Jean de (1850–1925), Polish operatic tenor, sang at Warsaw Cathedral as a child, studied there and in Italy and made his first appearance in 1874, at the Teatro Fenice in Venice.

Ricordi, Giulio (1840–1912), Italian music publisher, son of the following, became head of the Milan firm on his father's death in 1888. He was also a composer under the name of Burgmein.

Ricordi, Tito (1811–88), Italian music publisher, father of the preceding, succeeded his father, Giovanni Ricordi, in 1853.

Rivas, Duke of (*Angel de Saavedra*, 1791–1865), Spanish poet, dramatist and liberal politician, whose drama, *Don Alvaro ó La fuerza del sino*, was written during exile in France and produced in 1835.

Appendix C—Personalia

Ronconi, Giorgio (1810–90), Italian operatic baritone, made his first appearance in 1831, at Pavia.

Scribe, Augustin Eugène (1791–1861), French dramatist and librettist, wrote innumerable librettos for most of the famous French composers of his time, as well as some others.

Stolz, Teresa (1836–1902), Italian soprano singer of German birth, studied under Lamperti in Milan and made her first stage appearance in 1860. See also Appendix D, *Waldmann.*

Strepponi, Giuseppina (1815–97), Italian operatic soprano, studied at the Milan Conservatorio and made her first appearance in 1835, at Trieste. Verdi's second wife.

Tadolini, Eugenia (*née Savorini*) (born 1809), Italian operatic singer, wife of Giovanni Tadolini (1793–1872), singer and composer.

Tamagno, Francesco (1851–1905), Italian operatic tenor, at first a baker's apprentice and a locksmith. He studied at the Turin Conservatorio, sang in the opera chorus there, studied further with Pedrotti at Palermo and made his first appearance there in 1873.

Tamberlik, Enrico (1820–89), Italian operatic tenor, at first intended for a lawyer, made his first stage appearance in 1840 or 1841, at the Teatro Fondo in Naples.

Thomas, Charles Louis Ambroise (1811–96), French composer, student at the Paris Conservatoire, where he took the Prix de Rome in 1832. His greatest success in opera was *Mignon*, produced in Paris in 1866.

Tietjens, Therese Cathline Johanna Alexandra (1831–77), Hungarian operatic soprano born in Germany, where she made her first appearance in 1849, at Hamburg, her birthplace. She paid the first of her many visits to England in 1858.

Viardot-Garcia, Michelle Fernande Pauline (1821–1910), Franco-Spanish mezzo-soprano singer, studied under her father, Manuel Garcia, and made her first appearance at Brussels in 1837.

Waldmann, Maria. See Appendix D.

APPENDIX D

DELFICO (WITH A NOTE ON THE ILLUSTRATIONS) AND
WALDMANN

Delfico, Melchiorre, caricaturist, drew a series of caricatures of Verdi
and his friends during the rehearsals of *Simon Boccanegra* at Naples in
1858–9. These display Verdi, always very thin with a big head and
abundant hair, at work and play—often in an amusing situation and
sometimes in a rage. Thirty years later Delfico drew a new series of
caricatures of the first production of *Otello*. In these the composer's
hair is white and his figure stout. There is a delightful blend of
humour, admiration and affection in all these drawings. The two
series are reproduced complete in the first volume of *Carteggi Verdiani*.
Those chosen for reproduction here include the final page of the
Otello series, of which the text runs: 'My best compliments on your
new and most fortunate offspring [Verdi holding a golliwog baby].
Also congratulate Boito [dressed as Mefistofele] for me on his
splendid libretto. Remember sometimes your little servant [Delfico
himself as a footman] . . . and protect . . . your faithful friend
[Delfico as a dog]. Melchiorre D. L. Fico [fig].' Delfico visited
England and did some work for *Punch*. He might have settled here
permanently but for his dislike of the climate.

Waldmann, Maria, mezzo-soprano, was from 1872, when she appeared
in the first Italian performance of *Aida,* one of the most intimate
friends of Verdi and his wife. With Teresa Stolz (q.v.) she sang in
the first performances of the *Requiem Mass*, and it is at least probable
that the important mezzo-soprano part was composed with her remarkable voice in mind. An account of a performance in Paris
by the correspondent of the *Chicago Times* draws a valuable contemporary portrait of these two great artists, whose partnership in
so many of Verdi's works may be compared with that of Emmy
Destinn and Kirkby Lunn, which still remains fresh in the memory
of the opera-goers of twenty years ago:

   '. . . Mme Stolz's voice is a pure soprano, with immense compass
and of the most perfectly beautiful quality one ever listened to, from the

lowest note to the highest. Her phrasing is the most superb I ever heard, and her intonation something faultless. She takes a note and sustains it until it seems that her respiration is quite exhausted and then she has only commenced to hold it. The notes are as fine and clearly cut as a diamond, and as sweet as a silver bell [which is precisely how critics described Destinn's voice]; but the power she gives a high C is something amazing. . . . She is a fine appearing woman . . . and has more grace and dignity than is usually seen in one of her years and her manners are charming.

'But Mme Maria Waldmann, if possible, has a grander voice for a contralto than Mme Stolz has for a soprano. It certainly is rare to hear such quality of tone in any female voice. Many times one would think it the tenor, and only when one would look at her and see some slight quiver of the otherwise motionless form, could he realize it was a woman singing. . . . She is a very lovely person, with golden hair and a sweet oval face. She was also dressed in white, with great elegance and taste; but the dress didn't amount to anything—it was the singing. Both Stolz and Waldmann could stand up muffled in Indian blankets and after a few notes have the world at their feet.'

Waldmann retired in 1876 on her marriage to Conte (afterwards Duca) Galeazzo Massari. Her correspondence with Verdi and his wife, which continued until the end of his life, is published in *Carteggi Verdiani*.

APPENDIX E

BIBLIOGRAPHY

Abbiati, Franco, 'La vita e le opere di Giuseppe Verdi'. 4 vols. (Milan, 1959.)

Alberti, A., 'Verdi intimo, 1861–86.' (Milan, 1931.)

Bellaigue, Camille, 'Verdi.' (Paris, 1911.)

Bonaventura, M., 'Verdi.' (Paris, 1923.)

Bonavia, F., 'Verdi.' (Oxford and London, 1930.)

Budden, Julian, 'The Operas of Verdi.' Vol. I, *Oberto* to *Rigoletto.* (London, 1973.)

Cernezzi, L., 'Trent' anni dalla morte di Giuseppe Verdi.' (Milan, 1931.)

Cesari, G., and Luzio, A., 'I copialettere di G. Verdi.' (Milan, 1913.)

Checchi, E., 'Verdi, 1813–1901.' (Florence, 1926.)

Chop, Max, 'Giuseppe Verdi.' (Leipzig, 1938.)

Corte, Andrea della, 'Le sei più belle opere di Giuseppe Verdi.' (Milan, 1946.)

Garibaldi, L. A., 'Giuseppe Verdi nelle lettere di E. Muzio ad Antonio Barezzi.' (Milan, 1931.)

Gatti, Carlo, 'Verdi.' 2 vols. (Milan, 1931, revised 1951.)

Gerigk, H., 'Giuseppe Verdi.' (Potsdam, 1932.)

Luzio, Alessandro, 'Carteggi Verdiani.' 4 vols. (Rome, 1935–47.)

Mackenzie, Alexander C., 'Verdi.' (London, 1913.)

Mancinelli, Luisa, 'Giuseppe Verdi.' (Genoa, 1936.)

Manganella, Renato, 'Giuseppe Verdi.' (Milan, 1936.)

Menghini, G., 'Giuseppe Verdi e il melodrama italiano: saggio di storia e di critica musicale.' (Rimini, 1931.)

Mila, Massimo, 'Il melodramma di Verdi.' (Bari, 1933.)

Monaldi, G., 'Verdi, la vita, le opere.' (Milan, 1951.)

Morazzoni, G., and Ciampelli, G. M., 'Lettere inedite: le opere Verdiane al Teatro alla Scala, 1839–1929.' (Milan, 1929.)

Osborne, Charles, 'The Complete Operas of Verdi.' (London, 1961.) 'Letters of Giuseppe Verdi.' (London, 1971.)

Perenello, C., 'G. Verdi.' (Berlin, 1900.)

Appendix E—Bibliography

Pizzi, Italo, 'Ricordi Verdiani inediti.' (Turin, 1901.)

Pougin, Arthur, 'Verdi: an Anecdotic History of his Life and Works.' Translated from the French by James E. Matthew. (London, 1887.)

Prime-Stevenson, Edward, 'Long-haired Iopas.' (Privately printed; Florence, 1927.)

Rensis, Rafaello de, 'Franco Faccio e Verdi.' (Milan, 1934.)

Ridella, F., 'Giuseppe Verdi: impressioni e ricordi.' (Genoa, 1928.)

Toye, Francis, 'Giuseppe Verdi: his Life and Works.' (London, 1931.)

Unterholzner, Ludwig, 'Giuseppe Verdis Opern-Typus.' (Hanover, 1933.)

Visetti, Albert, 'Verdi.' (London, 1905.)

Walker, Frank, 'The Man Verdi.' (London, 1962.)

Weissman, Adolf, 'Verdi.' (Stuttgart and Berlin, 1922.)

INDEX

INDEX

359

Index

360

Index

Index

Index

364

Index